was £30

£8.50

David Knowles (1896–1974), monk of Downside and Regius Professor of Modern History at Cambridge, was a great historian and a master of prose, and a professor and teacher of wide influence. He was also an austere and solitary monk, and a devout priest ministering to his household and his friends – a very remarkable character who made a deep impression on a wide variety of friends and colleagues, pupils and disciples.

This book is designed to refresh Father David's memory while those who knew him well are still alive. Its authors were all his friends, and in some sense his disciples and pupils. Dom Aelred Sillem, Abbot of Quarr, was a disciple when he was a junior monk at Downside under Father David's direction in the early 1930s; Christopher Brooke was his pupil in the 1940s and 1950s; David Luscombe and Roger Lovatt in the 1950s and 1960s. Dom Aelred Sillem describes his monastic life and spirituality, especially the crisis of the 1930s which led to a breach with his community at Downside; Christopher Brooke sketches his life and studies his major historical writings; Roger Lovatt looks at his career as a Fellow of Peterhouse, Cambridge; David Luscombe surveys his work as a teacher in the University at large. Together they portray a man of many qualities, deeply spiritual, often reserved, yet human, urbane and humorous too, a man of exceptionally interesting character and academic achievement.

David Knowles Remembered

DOM DAVID KNOWLES

From a photograph by Walter Bird

DAVID KNOWLES REMEMBERED

CHRISTOPHER BROOKE
ROGER LOVATT
DAVID LUSCOMBE
and AELRED SILLEM

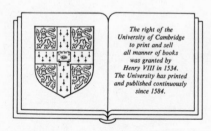

The right of the
University of Cambridge
to print and sell
all manner of books
was granted by
Henry VIII in 1534.
The University has printed
and published continuously
since 1584.

CAMBRIDGE UNIVERSITY PRESS

CAMBRIDGE

NEW YORK   PORT CHESTER

MELBOURNE   SYDNEY

Published by the Press Syndicate of the University of Cambridge
The Pitt Building, Trumpington Street, Cambridge CB2 1RP
40 West 20th Street, New York, NY 10011, USA
10 Stamford Road, Oakleigh, Melbourne 3166, Australia

First published 1991

Printed in Great Britain at the University Press, Cambridge

British Library cataloguing in publication data

David Knowles remembered.
1. Benedictines. Knowles, David
I. Brooke, Christopher *1927–*
271.102

Library of Congress cataloguing in publication data

David Knowles remembered/Christopher Brooke . . . [*et al.*].
p. cm.
Includes bibliographical references and index.
ISBN 0 521 37233 X
1. Knowles, David, 1896–1974. 2. Monks – England – Biography.
3. Historians – England – Biography. I. Knowles, David, 1896–1974.
II. Brooke, Christopher Nugent Lawrence.
BX4705.K58D38 1991
271'.102–dc20 90–2543 CIP
[B]

ISBN 0 521 37233 X hardback

CONTENTS

PREFACE

Our aim in this book is to preserve and refresh the memory of a very notable monk and scholar who was our friend and who deeply influenced us; we have sought to provide a revised version of the memoir which Christopher Brooke wrote for the British Academy and to supplement the book, *David Knowles, a Memoir*, by the late Dom Adrian Morey (1979). Dom Adrian gave an admirable account of Father David's family, early life and the first fifteen years or so of his vocation as a monk; and the whole book is infused with respect and affection. But he was one of those who thought Father David's attempts to lead a new foundation away from Downside – and then, when that failed, to depart himself[1] – were wholly mistaken; and he found it difficult to enter Father David's purposes with full sympathy, though he strove throughout to be open and fairminded in his judgement. At the end of Father David's life they met again and renewed their friendship, but from most of Father David's career outside the community – in London and Linch, and in Cambridge and as a university professor – Father Adrian was relatively remote. In this book Dom Aelred Sillem, Abbot of Quarr, who was a novice and junior at Downside with Father David, and three of his Cambridge friends – pupils, disciples and colleagues – have tried to compose a more intimate picture of the inwardness of his monastic life and the character and achievements of his career as an eminent historian and Cambridge professor.

In preparing the book we have all read each other's drafts and profited by each other's help, and CB – who has acted as editor – would

---

[1] See chapter 2, below.

particularly like to thank his colleagues for their generous collaboration and timely aid. We have all had invaluable help from a number of his pupils and friends; and Rosalind Brooke both recorded the impressions of his first research student and helped to revise our earlier drafts. CB also thanks the Secretary of the British Academy for permission to use his Academy memoir of Father David, originally published in *The Proceedings of the British Academy*, 61 (1975), 439–77, which forms the core of chapters 1 and 3–5, which are here, however, revised and greatly enlarged; and Graeme Rennie for help in checking Father David's university career. We are particularly indebted to the Syndics and staff of the Cambridge University Press, especially William Davies, Lyn Chatterton and Andrea Smith.

By the generous provision of David Knowles's will, Christopher Brooke inherited his copyrights, and so found himself responsible for Father David's own 'Autobiography'. After careful thought and consultation, it was decided not to publish it nor to open it for inspection for a number of years, since it might cause misunderstanding and embarrassment: no use has been made of it in this book. He has encouraged Father David's friends to deposit any letters which they have of Father David's – or copies of them – in the archives of Downside Abbey, and we gratefully acknowledge the kind co-operation of the Abbot and Archivist of Downside in forming this archive and making the letters accessible to us.

Towards the end of his life Father David renewed his friendship with the eminent art historian, Kenneth Clark, whom he had known from his visits in the 1920s to the chalet of 'Sligger' Urquhart, the Catholic Balliol tutor. They were men of very different temperament, yet with many values and interests in common; Clark had an exceptional gift for friendship and Father David was the ideal companion for a talkative man. However it may have come about, Father David went often from his retirement home in Linch to Saltwood Castle – where, as he used to recall, Becket's murderers stayed before they rode to Canterbury on 29 December 1170[2] – and these visits are recorded in a striking passage in the second volume of Lord Clark's autobiography, *The Other Half: a Self-Portrait*.[3]

---

[2] See Knowles 1970a, pp. 140 and 148. This is his life of Becket, for which he chose a photograph of Saltwood Castle in winter as frontispiece.

[3] Clark 1977, pp. 196–7.

As I come to the end of the visitors' book, one name appears more frequently than almost any other, that of David Knowles. Many historians would agree that his history of the Religious Orders in England is one of the historical masterpieces of this century. I had met him when still at Oxford, but had lost sight of him, and as usual I cannot remember when we became such close friends. [From conversations with Father David, it seems probable that their paths crossed again in the British Academy.] There are lots of good people in the world who are simple, or even stupid. David was that rare phenomenon, a very good man who was complex and highly intelligent. He had a sweet smile, but also a penetrating glance which saw through any form of pretence. I knew it was an undeserved privilege to me to be in his company, but he was so easy to talk to that I forgot my sinful state. We talked about history, poetry and nature. David Knowles loved nature as much as Mr Berenson had done and, on our walks in the valleys behind the Castle, he would pause before a tree or a turn in the valley and say "This is good!" He meant more than "I am enjoying it." "Good" meant to him that it was the work of God. We sometimes talked about God, and he showed that width of reasonable understanding which had led him to the brink of excommunic- ation. He once confided in Jane [Lady Clark] that the two happiest people he knew were a monk and a nun who were married. But he was so great a scholar that the Church could not afford to lose him, any more than it could Lord Acton. Although he knew that the thought of the Catholic Church played a great part in my mind, he never once attempted to influence me, still less to "convert" me. He only went as far as to say that he knew I was looking for something. So I was, and still am.

This is characteristically perceptive and penetrating: Father David was a great scholar and his best books are masterpieces; he was a good man, yet a very complex one, and he has sometimes been misjudged by those who looked for simplicity in him. There is an element of paradox in the comparison with Acton – and he was censured not for doctrine but for leaving his community[4] – for he was known in his last years as a conservative in theology, especially in the years of ferment following

[4] See below, p. 40.

Vatican II. Yet the charity of mind which the Clarks observed was also a genuine part of him, and was observed by others not of his communion. We do not aspire to penetrate every depth of a rich and varied mind; but we hope we have opened windows into a number of its rooms, and brought forth things new and old concerning one of the most remarkable personalities, and most eminent historians, whom it has been our privilege to know – and a dear friend to whom we owed much kindness.

Christopher Brooke
Roger Lovatt
David Luscombe
Aelred Sillem

ABBREVIATIONS

For full references, see pp. 159–65.

CUL	Cambridge University Library
GHE	Knowles, *Great Historical Enterprises*
HC	Knowles, *The Historian and Character and Other Essays*
Heads	Knowles, Brooke and London, *Heads of Religious Houses*
MO	Knowles, *The Monastic Order in England*
NMT	Nelson's Medieval Texts
OMT	Oxford Medieval Texts
PL	*Patrologiae Cursus Completus, series Latina*
RO	Knowles, *The Religious Orders in England*
VCH Middlesex	*Victoria History of the County of Middlesex*

I

1896–1974

CHRISTOPHER BROOKE

Many a violinist, as he tunes his strings and tightens his bow, must have reflected how inadequate are his skill, his tone, the subtleties of his expression, to reflect the mind and genius of the composer he is trying to interpret. Yet if he brings to his task a deep knowledge of the music he is playing, and of how it has been interpreted, and an intuitive sympathy with the mind of the composer, he may yet add something worth while to the interpretation of a great work of music. Anyone who seeks to interpret David Knowles as monk, friend, teacher and scholar, must prepare for the task by re-reading his lectures on the Maurists and Mabillon, and 'The Historian and Character';[1] and by pondering *The Monastic Order in England*, his masterpiece.[2] It is a preparation at once disheartening and inspiring. For he was a magician with words, who had reflected on the ways of the human mind with subtlety and depth and humour, and was peculiarly fitted to describe what he had found. He was a shrewd judge of men, whose appraisals – occasionally severe – were tempered with a warmth of sympathy and charitable understanding. He was a man of prayer in whose presence many of quite different temperament felt the touch of his faith and ideals. He was a historian and a scholar who transformed the study of monastic history and in the process made his own approach to and interpretation of the medieval Church an indispensable part of the apparatus of a whole generation of medievalists. Like all rich personalities, his was complex, not easily

---

[1] The lecture on the *Maurists* is in *GHE*, pp. 33–62; the other two in *HC*, pp. 1–15 and 213–39.

[2] For bibliography and full references to Knowles's work, see pp. 159–65, esp. pp. 161–3. Unless otherwise stated the letters used in chap. 1 are in my possession.

caught in the simple phrase or thumb-nail sketch; not caught at all in a cliché. Let it be said at once that to a wide circle he conveyed an inspiration which seemed to lift the subjects and the personalities on which he laid his mark to a higher plane; and from a smaller group, which crossed the frontiers of age and communion, he won friendship and devotion of unusual warmth and depth.

BACKGROUND[3]

David Knowles was born in 1896 at Michaelmas, and baptised Michael Clive – in a technical sense the first of his family to join the Catholic Church, since his father was a recent convert still preparing for reception and his mother was not received till some years later. He was an only child, brought up in Studley in Warwickshire, not far from Birmingham, and in Birmingham itself. He was devoted to his parents, H.H. and Carrie Knowles, and looked back with pleasure to his childhood.

> My father was a very lovable and admirable man [he wrote in later life].[4] Although he was a successful man of business he was by tastes and interests a countryman and a lover of literature and art. He was also an excellent manager of men and things – gardens, poultry, animals – and did a great many acts of help and advice in the village society of Studley, where I suppose half the population were employed (someone in the family) by him. But I remember him chiefly for his goodness and love – and . . . for his mind. In my judgements and tastes I owe more than I can say to him. He was always sane and central, with no bees or whimsies. As a person, he reminded me more of Sir Thomas More (in his personal relations) than any other.
>
> My mother was quite a different character – a very sweet, affectionate nature, simple in her tastes, happy in the common things of life such as the changing seasons and flowers. She had not my father's mental power, but many gifts – she was musical, and played the piano and sang, enjoyed games, had unusually good taste in clothes and decorations, was an excellent hostess. In all my life at home I never heard a single harsh or even impatient word between my father and mother, nor an unjust word of any kind about a third person.

[3] For his early life, see esp. Morey 1979, pp. 11–46.   [4] Letter of 14 Nov. 1961.

Both my mother and father had a fund of affection and care for others, especially young people. Quite recently I thought of this, and added up all those who had been received into our house almost as children of it – and I counted up eighteen without having to think . . . At the basis of it all was their strong and pervading faith, which gave a kind of peace to our home in its happiest days . . .

And in a letter to Z.N. Brooke in 1944[5] just after his father's death, he spoke of his debt

including an example from childhood of deep reverence for the things of God, and a love of English history, literature and churches. We visited together all the old cathedrals of England (save two) and many in Wales and Scotland, and many a ruin from Melrose to Cleeve (Somerset) and from Strata Florida to Byland and Fountains.

The roots of the Knowles family lay not far away from Studley, near Bromsgrove; and the father of H.H. Knowles had been a timber merchant in Birmingham. H.H. himself went into partnership with a friend called John Morgan who had inherited a factory making needles and pins at Studley; Carrie was his partner's sister. Their son was brought up in circumstances of modest prosperity, a prosperity which was later to make the publication of *The Monastic Order* possible, for to both the first edition and the first reprint his father made vital subsidies.

From 1906 to 1910 Michael Clive was at West House School at Edgbaston, a preparatory school where he laid the first foundations of his classical knowledge; and made friends, among others, with a member of one of the patrician families of Birmingham, 'because we were excluded from school prayers (he as a Quaker, myself as RC) and walked about like the forsaken merman while others murmured prayers'.[6] In 1910 he went on to Downside. Although he seems to have had little idea of his own academic prowess while he was a schoolboy it is clear that the school and the abbey made a deep impression on him; and in particular that he greatly admired the Headmaster, later Abbot, Dom Leander Ramsay. When the time came to leave he was already determined to enter the noviciate, and looked forward confidently to spending the rest of his days as a monk at Downside. In the event, it was

[5] Letter of 13 Apr. 1944. [6] Letter of 17 July 1972.

to be divided between a period spent within the cloister, first at Downside (1914–33) then at Ealing (1933–9), and nearly twenty years in academic posts at Cambridge (1944–63), with an interlude (1939–44) and a coda (1963–74).

DOWNSIDE

In October 1914 he was clothed in the habit, and took the name in religion of David. Contrary to what is sometimes supposed, long life in a monastic community tends to enhance the individual traits of a man's character, and there were many remarkable personalities at Downside in Brother – later Father – David's time. Of these, the two most significant for an understanding of his life were Dom Leander Ramsay and Dom Cuthbert Butler, Abbot from 1906 to 1922. 'Dom Leander's high seriousness and inflexible determination contrasted with Abbot Butler's more emotional and flexible nature';[7] but both greatly influenced Father David, and both were members of the remarkable circle of scholars among whom he came to maturity at Downside. Perhaps the most distinguished of the circle was Edmund Bishop, not a monk but a frequent visitor in Father David's early years, down to his death in 1917;[8] and the circle included Dom Hugh Connolly, a patristic scholar of exceptional finesse, and several historians and theologians of Father David's age and younger.

Edmund Bishop was a West Country innkeeper's son who had little formal education – and none at university – and earned his keep in early life as a third-class clerk in the Education Office, yet found his own way into the Roman Catholic Church and the study of medieval liturgy – and became in due course a liturgical scholar of international fame. He had been for many years the friend and collaborator of Downside's former prior, Dom Aidan Gasquet, promoted cardinal in the same year, 1914, in which David Knowles was clothed a novice. Gasquet was to be the subject of one of Father David's most searching and hilarious lectures, at once critical and sympathetic. He was a scholar whose 'capacity for carelessness amounted almost to genius',[9] and the friendship between Gasquet and Bishop, 'highly strung, fastidious, sensitive and lonely', one of the most meticulous of all English medievalists, has a

---

[7] From D.K.'s memoir of Abbot Butler, *HC*, pp. 306–7.
[8] On Bishop see especially Abercrombie 1959, with foreword by David Knowles, pp. xi–xv.   [9] *HC*, p. 254; for what follows, *HC*, p. 243.

paradoxical air. Bishop indeed was more than meticulous; he was a scholar of the finest sensibility, one of the immortals; and no one who dwells on the formation of the young scholars at Downside in his lifetime can fail to wonder how he influenced them. Direct contact between Bishop and Father David was evidently slight; there is a charming account by the latter of one long conversation;[10] and it is characteristic of Father David's early bent that its theme was English literature, not history. Yet in some ways the influence of Edmund Bishop must have been important to him. The memory of Bishop, and the presence of his remarkable library in the Abbey, could not but affect him when he came to the studies from which *The Monastic Order* grew. At a fairly superficial level, one can see that the constant urge in that great book to curb a natural romanticism may be a reaction against one of Bishop's noted weaknesses;[11] and Father David (perhaps revealing in this more his generation than any particular influence) followed Bishop in his strange faith in national characteristics as a key (for example) to liturgical eccentricity. At a deeper level *The Monastic Order* reveals an exceptional sensitivity to the language and intellectual quality of scholarship. Two characteristics are manifest in almost every page Bishop wrote: precise accuracy, and a fine, almost philosophical, precision in the use of scholarly language. Father David never quite captured Bishop's minute sense of accuracy; and his style was of a different *timbre*. But he shared to the full Bishop's dedication to the use of correct and appropriate language; and it is not perhaps fanciful to see some direct influence here. In any event Father David can hardly have failed to reflect on the quality of the eminent, eccentric scholar he had met in earlier days.

Far more substantial is the evidence of Abbot Cuthbert Butler's influence upon him. In his early days Butler had been active in the struggle for the reorganisation of the English Benedictine Congregation along lines more in accord with the historical tradition of Benedictine Monachism – to use the words which were later the title of one of Butler's best known books.[12] He had also laid the foundations of great

---

[10] See pp. 52–3.
[11] See below, p. 65. Bishop's weakness is rarely apparent in his best work, e.g. in *Liturgica Historica* (Oxford, 1918); but his favourable view of medieval monks was (so Father David himself told me more than once) readily apparent to those who knew him.
[12] *Benedictine Monachism* (London, 1919; 2nd edn, London, 1924). On the *Lausiac History*, see *HC*, pp. 344ff.

learning in monastic history, of which the edition of the *Lausiac History* of Palladius (1906) was to be the main fruit. When Butler first came to Downside, it was a priory with only a limited autonomy; lacking its own noviciate, fostering a community most of whose members were destined to go out on 'the mission', that is to say to become parish priests. The monks' destiny lay wholly in the hands of the Abbot President and the rulers of the Congregation; and the consequence of this was illustrated by Father David himself in his account of how the young Gasquet, bent on scholarship, found the threat of the chaplaincy at Acton Burnell hang over him.[13] When the reforms were complete, Downside was an autonomous Abbey with its own noviciate, its commitment to the mission, though still substantial, had been pruned, and the full and regular observance of choir and cloister established. Thus it came to pass that within the cloister, from 1906 on, the reform was represented and symbolised by Dom Cuthbert Butler, now Abbot. In the world at large Downside came increasingly to be noted as a centre of scholarship, a place almost in the Maurist tradition.

Cuthbert Butler now lives for many who never met him in the remarkable memoir which Father David composed for the *Downside Review* in 1934.[14] It was a 'memorial of words', a work of piety; but yet much more than that, for it is his most substantial essay in contemporary biography, and incorporates a brilliant character sketch and portrait, and a history of the movement in which the young Butler had been involved. It has a warm and generous appreciation of the Abbot's kindly qualities and positive achievement, and an affectionate enumeration of his eccentricities: of his tactlessness, of such proportions that it was suggested of him that 'laying the first stone' of a new building be changed to 'dropping the first brick'; of his untidiness of dress, and practice of gardening in 'ancient trousers and tail coat green with age, with a shapeless green cap on his head, worn back to front . . .' 'Even when so clad he would never have passed for an ordinary man.'[15] All this gives us an insight into Father David's lively humour and perceptiveness which those of us who only knew him after he had left Downside can still readily recognise and imagine. More surprising in a man who shows himself so just and charitable in this as in many of his writings is the stern note of criticism which enters from time to time. Above all, he observes how the reforms fell short of expectation: the mission parishes were not

[13] *HC*, p. 244; cf. pp. 245 and 255.
[14] Reprinted in *HC*, pp. 264–362.   [15] *HC*, pp. 333–6.

curtailed to the extent that had been hoped, the involvement with the school grew greater, both, in Father David's view, hindrances to the full and proper monastic observance.

Thus he wrote in retrospect in 1934. But he would readily have admitted that his idea of the Benedictine life, and the place in it of both communal and private prayer, and of spiritual reading and scholarly work, owed much to the Abbot's inspiration. There is some evidence of a more direct influence. The Abbot was given to encouraging the young monks to have a task in hand, 'a pot on the boil', as he put it, and he recommended Father David to the study of Cluny.[16] A reading of Sackur's *Die Cluniacenser* not surprisingly failed to inspire; and in the circle of Butler and Bishop, Cluny, though greatly respected, invited a certain reserve, since it had been one of the first major houses to break down the Benedictine tradition of autonomy. Yet there is no reason to suppose that Father David acquired at this time the dispraise which marked his later references to Cluny, especially in his papers on Peter the Venerable. Indeed, in his little book *The Benedictines*, published in 1929, he linked Peter the Venerable with Mabillon: 'No better expositions of Benedictine ideals and aims have ever been framed than the defences of Peter the Venerable and Jean Mabillon against the attacks of Saint Bernard and de Rancé.'[17]

The Benedictines, published shortly before the last phase of Father David's life at Downside began, and just before he started work for *The Monastic Order*, is a beautifully composed, succinct exposition of the doctrine of Benedictine Monachism. The true monastic community is inward looking; its *raison d'être* lies in its own work and worship, not in any exterior influence, vital and valuable though that may be. Yet the vocation is not a special nor a narrow one; variety, sobriety, moderation have been its keynotes as well as utter dedication and obedience. 'As a member of a family he [the Benedictine] comes to realise that charity is often better than zeal and sacrifice; that it is ill quarrelling in a small boat on a long voyage; that he must take from others what they have, and not demand from them what they lack; that many things are healed by time.' There is already a personal note in his emphasis on the total dedication and inner life of a monk. 'Neither habit nor choir nor community life are essential to sanctity and a life of prayer. If the end of all monastic observance, the monasticism of the soul, be once attained, it

[16] Stacpoole 1975, p. 79.   [17] Knowles 1929, p. 85.

7

may be retained *ubique terrarum*.'[18] From Abbot Butler Father David derived much fundamental instruction on the nature of the monastic life; though not the personal impress of a close friend and pastor, which Abbot Ramsay gave him in more abundant measure; nor the direct teaching in scholarly technique, for which too he probably owed more to Ramsay.

The Benedictines laid stress on the variety of the monastic life, and Father David's growth between 1914 and 1929 had several branches.[19] No one who knew him in later life, or read his monastic writings, could fail to realise the deep foundations laid in his early monastic years. Some elements in his idea of the monastic life deepened, or changed direction, in the late 1920s; doubtless it was the deepening of an experience moulded by reflection over his first fifteen years as a monk. Still, in *The Benedictines*, he does not speak of contemplation or the mystical life as enjoying the central place in the monastic scheme or in his own interests which one might have expected from his later writings; and his references to St John of the Cross are somewhat critical. Yet it is clear that he had long before formed – from his own experience and inclination, no doubt, as well as from the teaching of Abbot Butler and others – the notion that the monk's life was dedicated wholly to the cloister; and with this went a growing concern for contemplative prayer which issued in the first edition of *The English Mystics* in 1927.

For the rest, we must be content to observe the externals of his life, leaving with pleasure his inner life to Aelred Sillem (see below, chap. 2). He was clothed as a novice on 4 October 1914, took simple vows on 9 October 1915, minor orders in 17 October 1915, solemn profession on 18 October 1918.[20] Thus he passed the years of the First World War, in which many of his boyhood friends were killed; and in 1919 he set off for Cambridge, to spend three years at Benet House, the Downside house of studies then in Park Terrace, as an undergraduate of Christ's College. In 1920 he was awarded a College scholarship, and in October he characteristically followed this up with the Skeat Prize for English Literature; he went on to take a first in both parts of the Classical Tripos with a Distinction in philosophy in part II.[21] From these years came two significant elements in his equipment, his knowledge of classical

---

[18] Knowles 1929, pp. 87, 78.
[19] For this period, see esp. Morey 1979, pp. 28–60; and for what follows, A. Sillem, below, chap. 2.
[20] These details were kindly furnished from records at Downside for use in *HC*.
[21] Morey 1979, pp. 40–2.

literature and Greek philosophy. He had a knowledge wide and deep of classical literature which was greatly enlarged and fostered by reading classics at Cambridge. His love of Thucydides sprang from this experience; and his study of Greek philosophy gave him a deep knowledge of Plato's *Republic* and an extensive first-hand acquaintance with Aristotle – which was to bear fruit in his later work on medieval thought. As he progressed through the tripos, *pari passu* he was advancing in the orders of the Church: sub-deacon on 12 December 1920, deacon on 25 September 1921, and priest on 9 July 1922. The jubilee of his priesthood in 1972 was the central event of his last years.

Throughout his life Father David was a voracious reader, but everyone who has tried to follow the course of his early years must wonder how so much came to be fitted into the dedicated life of full monastic observance. In part this may be attributed to the exceptional power of his memory. To a scholar memory is a two-edged sword: it provides him with a weapon which he must have, his most basic equipment; but if it is too good, and he learns to trust it, it will let him down. In later years he was inclined to trust to it too much; but those of us who say this say it in part out of envy, for his marvellous memory was even more the key to many of his most notable successes. His literary skill owed much to his power to produce the apt quotation, the lapidary phrase, from every corner of his extensive reading; and this gave the impression that he had spent one lifetime scouring English literature, and another in the Greek and Latin classics. In his later years a Swedish medical student, a nephew of Elizabeth Kornerup, came to stay at their Sussex home; and he has described to me how walks in the woods listening to Father David reciting classical poetry inspired him to read a degree in classics before he returned to the medical fold. Great and constant as was his delight in such literature, it was in later years fed mainly from his memory, for perhaps by an act of deliberate renunciation he spent little time in such reading. He would himself have laid equal stress on the time he spent on philosophy and theology. The groundwork for these was laid at Downside in his earliest years, and developed side by side with his studies in classical philosophy, culminating in a rapid programme filling the summer of 1922. Later he spent the best part of a year, from October 1922 to the summer of 1923, at Sant'Anselmo at Rome, completing his theological studies.[22]

Philosophy and theology were to enter many areas of his later life and

[22] Morey 1979, pp. 43–6.

writings, and three especially: into his work on mysticism, into his study and teaching of medieval thought at Cambridge and into the articles and leaflets of his last years. To the study of mystical theology he made a significant contribution; and many of his most distinguished pupils were to be inspired by his lectures on medieval thought.[23] Yet it is hard to think that theology brought out what was most gifted or original in his mind. He developed and sustained a carefully founded, but essentially simple, respect for St Thomas, and showed no profound sympathy for any more recent philosopher. From the early 1930s on mysticism came increasingly to be judged in his eyes by the single standard of John of the Cross. His success in these studies witnesses first to the general power of his mind, and second to his skill and influence as a teacher, but it is as a historian that he will be remembered and honoured. Meanwhile, at Sant'Anselmo, he studied theology, talked German – as he later said, learned hastily out of Goethe and Schiller and spoken with a fine disregard to grammar – in the mainly German community, and saw Rome.

Among the many renunciations of his later life, he very rarely travelled. He never toured the congresses, but in the twenties he had travelled as extensively as an observant monk reasonably could. First there was the year in Rome; then, in the mid- and late twenties, there was an almost annual visit to the Chalet of F.F. Urquhart on the borders of France and Switzerland. Urquhart was a Fellow of Balliol: 'he was a cultivated, gentle, and tolerant man who never said or did anything especially remarkable, but he had a great talent for subtle social catalysis, and he was the hub of Balliol life for many years'.[24] Urquhart invited a number of the brightest and most remarkable Oxford undergraduates of the twenties to his legendary Alpine retreat, where they read and walked and talked. He was a Catholic and a native of the Mendips; hence a not infrequent visitor to Downside where he met Father David and served his mass. By these visits David Knowles came to meet men of such varied talent as R.H.S. Crossman and Cyril Connolly, and to form friendships which later matured with future colleagues in the British Academy, Kenneth (Lord) Clark and Sir Roger Mynors.[25] Once, breaking his sequence of Alpine visits, there was a tour of Greece in 1927. In his last years he looked back to his visit to Greece as 'one of my real

---

[23] Which were published as Knowles 1962a/1988. For his mystical theology, see pp. 31–3.

[24] Jones 1988, p. 235; on Urquhart see Bailey 1936; Morey 1979, pp. 40, 41, 44, 51, etc.

[25] For a very interesting passage on Father David by Kenneth Clark, see above, p. xi.

infidelities',[26] believing that a devotion to its beauty and the haunting remnants of the pagan classical world were ill fare for a monk. Yet his broad culture was an essential element in his greatness. It was the range of vision and reading which he could bring to bear, with intense concentration, on a single way of life in a particular epoch, which accounted for much of the stature of *The Monastic Order*, and of his influence as a professor at Cambridge.

His first article, 'A preface of Mabillon' (*Downside Review* 1919), comprised the last and most mellow version of the great Maurist's defences of monastic studies; and Father David's vision of the monastic life never excluded scholarly work. But it was a long while before he found his own *métier*. For a time in 1918–19 he served as assistant to Leander Ramsay as he worked, in convalescence from a major illness, on an edition of the works of St Cyprian;[27] this was no doubt a useful introduction to textual study. Most of Father David's writings in the 1920s reflect the broad interests of a man of culture, especially deeply read in English literature. If 'The religion of the Pastons' (1924) shows already a medieval bent, and 'Italian scenes and scenery' (1924) and 'A Greek August' (1930–1) his wonderful sense of the history behind countryside minutely and devoutly observed, 'The thought and art of Thomas Hardy' (1928) and 'Honest Iago' (1931) hardly suggest an author embarking on a major historical enterprise. Even more surprising is his adventure into modern history, *The American Civil War* (1926). He has himself described the story which lay behind this, and its influence on his growth as a historian, in an address to a gathering of historians in London in 1962.[28]

> May I give you for a moment the story of my own search for Clio, not on account of its personal value or interest, but because I am sure it reflects our common experience. What did I love in the Muse and how did I approach her?
>
> At school I was never, either in fact or in desire, an historian. I was a classic, and in my school days the only spell that bound me was that of great literature. The classics were supreme, and apart from Greek and Latin I read all I could find of English poetry. I took Roman history as an examination subject, and as an exercise

[26] Stacpoole 1975, p. 81.
[27] Stacpoole 1975, pp. 79–80; also *ex inf.* D. K. For what follows see Bibliography in *HC*.   [28] Knowles 1962b.

in memory. Thucydides stood out for me among all writers of prose, but almost entirely as recording the splendour and tragedy of Athens, and as an analyst of the motives of men. On leaving school there was an interval of some years before going up to Cambridge, and in those years I read widely in English, French and some German literature. History formed a part of this, and by the pure accident of their presence on a bookshelf I read Macaulay's *Essays* with avidity and went on to the *History*, or part of it, and the *Life*. I read Gibbon through in ten weeks, the last six or so volumes of Grote, Clarendon's *History of the Great Rebellion*, Robertson's *Charles V*, Prescott and Hallam, Creighton and Pastor, Acton's *Lectures*, Holland Rose's *Life of Napoleon* and Thiers's account of the Moscow campaign. All these I read simply as literature. When I went up to Cambridge it was to read classics, and I took the minimum then possible of history. I re-read Thucydides, but still as literature rather than history, and I would have echoed Macaulay's judgement upon him as the *ne plus ultra* of human genius while still regarding history, as perhaps Macaulay himself always regarded it, as essentially a literary discipline, almost as a kind of drama that had been lived. Yet in Roman history I saw for the first time the growth, development and dissolution of a great political system, accompanied by the growth and decline of an immense empire, where both processes could be seen as it were *in vacuo*, with cause and effect clearly visible, and without the innumerable cross-currents and off-stage catastrophes that obscure the story of medieval or modern institutions and nations. It is for this reason that Roman history is a text-book without rival for an historian in training, showing as it does the inexorable march of time and the sequence of wisdom and error and their consequences, in which every problem has been isolated and debated by some of the acutest minds of Europe for five centuries.

During these years I had retained a particular interest from childhood in a period remote from all this – the history of the United States before and during the war of North and South, and I wrote for my own amusement a long essay which I later revised in the light of further reading . . . My inspiration came, at an infinite distance, from Thucydides. I did not approach the subject primarily in order to discover the truth, but to share with others what the story had meant for me. Some reviewers of that book were justifiably severe on the lack of depth and technical knowledge, and I realized for the first time that history was a totalitarian business – that one could not produce work of any historical value without exhausting or eliminating all the sources available.

Yet the book has remarkable qualities: it is beautifully written, and the portraits of Robert E. Lee, whom he deeply admired, and of Stonewall Jackson, show already his interest in portraying human character.

As a general Stonewall Jackson must be placed below his great chief [Robert E. Lee] . . . As a man, also, he cannot compare with Robert Lee in all those qualities that go to produce a perfect balance in heart and mind. The two men were, indeed, close friends during the short time they were associated upon earth, and each thought the life of the other more important than his own to the cause which both held so dear, but while Robert Lee attracts all who read of him by the peculiarly exquisite poise of his mind, and the warmth and sincerity of his nature, Jackson's charm – if charm it can be called – lies in the fiery originality of his character. Though he was a leader in the party which has often been called that of the Cavaliers, he himself has been compared, not inaptly, to the Parliamentary generals of the English Civil War. He stands apart alike from the materialistic views and keen alertness of the best Northern leaders, and from the proud traditions and frank geniality of his colleagues in the Army of Northern Virginia. Sprung from a home beyond the mountains in Virginia, and alien in descent and religion from the First Families of his State, an Ulster Calvinist who joined an up-to-date professional knowledge to a view of life recalling that of the Puritans or Covenanters, he brought into the careless armies of the South an element of fanaticism. To him, as to many of Cromwell's generals, the words of the psalm might have been applied in their most literal sense. The high praises of God were in his mouth and a two-edged sword was ever in his hand to purge his country of those who had crossed her borders.

On almost all points he was stiff and narrow in the extreme. His rigid arms, his unseeing gaze, his hand perpetually jerked heavenward, were the outward index of an obstinacy of will which could punish an officer for using the fence-rails of his own land for fuel when once the order had been issued that the farmers' fences were not to be touched. The most innocent form of profanity was requited with his severe displeasure; whatever he was pleased to consider conduct in the least degree insubordinate was visited – often mistakenly and unjustly – with immediate and enduring punishment; for a word a colonel was compelled to march swordless behind his regiment. His grotesquely large feet, his one uniform which grew more and more threadbare, the lemons which he sucked to counteract some supposed disorder – all these early became the talk of his command. Some other traits affected their lives more seriously. His men were marched through every kind of country and weather till they acquired the name of the Foot Cavalry; they were marched farther than they or their officers thought they were capable of marching; they knew neither where they were going nor why they were going, for Jackson's plans and destinations were concealed even from his staff and generals of division, who had often no orders to bear to the exhausted and bewildered colonels of their regiments other than the message, 'General Jackson says, "Press forward".'

Like Lee, Jackson was deeply religious, of stainless purity, and incapable of a dishonourable or knowingly cruel act, but his religion was tinged with a fanaticism which often identified his own views and successes with those of the Almighty, and he lacked the humanity of his chief, who could not view even the most victorious field without a keen sense of sorrow. Yet if Jackson could at times be hard and inflexible he was all tenderness to his wife, and the story of his stopping an army on the march in order that a countrywoman might find her son and give him a pair of socks and a chicken is only one of many such.[29]

Few who have relished the skill with which fine strokes of the brush perfect the portraits of Ailred of Rievaulx or Thomas Becket or Jean Mabillon have realised that the technique had been practised and perfected – in imagination, for he never crossed the Atlantic – in the forests and plantations of Virginia.

Meanwhile, his mind was turning towards monastic history, for many influences in Downside and from without must have combined to set him to work on *The Monastic Order*. Among these must be set the

[29] Knowles 1926, pp. 77–80. On this book see the interesting study Green 1989.

influence of a remark of G.G. Coulton's that the history of medieval English monasticism was still to be written, as Father David hinted in the preface to the book, and stated more fully in a letter to Dr John Moorman.[30] But the origin of his greatest works must be sought in a deeper enquiry in the next chapter. Meanwhile, in the late 1920s he began serious work on monastic history, and at the same time a new phase opened in his religious life.

THE 1930S

At the deepest level, and with the benefit of hindsight, one cannot but think that in his studies during the late 1920s he found at last his vocation as a scholar, and a profound reconciliation between his intellectual and spiritual aspirations. Between 1929 and 1938 *The Monastic Order* was written, and it is the fruit of mature reflection on a major theme, calm, peaceful and full of wisdom. Yet these years in Father David's life were anything but calm. There is a deep and striking contrast between the unruffled surface of his masterpiece and the storms within. From 1923 to 1928 he had taught classics in the school, and in spite of the happy relationships that this brought him, he came in the end to feel that the school, growing rapidly into a large public school mainly for the well-to-do, was capturing a disproportionate amount of the community's attention. In the late 1920s he was coming to a more intense vision of the monastic life as having a contemplative centre. After recovering from a serious motor accident – he was the passenger in a collision in July 1928 – he was in September 1928 made temporary novice master; later, from 1929 to 1933, he was junior master. These positions brought him in closer contact with the younger monks – including Dom Aelred Sillem, who gives a much fuller and deeper study of these events below – and face to face with his responsibility for their formation. In common with a number of the young monks, he feared a retreat from the age of reform: he saw no abatement in the mission, but ever larger involvement in the school – though in truth the mission was being curbed (and was to be much reduced later) and the place of the school in the community's life was less than he allowed.

The anxieties of those years brought into the minds of some of the community that a new start should be made, a new foundation away

[30] *Monastic Order*, p. xvi. The letter is quoted by Dr Moorman in *The Report of the Friends of the Lambeth Palace Library for 1975*, p. 18. Cf. Stacpoole 1975, pp. 88–9.

from Downside, still Benedictine, but unencumbered by any responsibility for school or mission. Of this group Father David became the head, and permission was sought. The Abbot was reluctant to see some of his most talented confrères depart, and the gifted Abbot Chapman, not far from his death, failed to handle a difficult situation with sympathy or tact. In the event, after Chapman's death, Father David led an appeal to Rome on behalf of the new foundation. The appeal failed; his supporters accepted that Rome had spoken and made their submission. In such a community a movement of this kind is bound to cause a trauma, and if it persists it will be viewed as a faction. But to Father David it seemed that his superiors and confrères had forsaken the inner vision of the monastic ideal to which he held, and he never quite entered into an imaginative understanding of their predicament. From then on, the monastic life became for him personally an inner vision, 'the monasticism of the soul . . . retained no matter where one is'. The full story is told by Abbot Sillem, and a clearer light thrown on the way in which Father David reconciled in his own personality the ability to be a delightful, warm, inspiring leader of a group, and the inner firmness, the sharp and individual vision that forbade any compromise, even under obedience.

From 1933 to 1939 he lived at Ealing, then a priory of Downside. He was an exile, and seems to have been already withdrawn into the deeper reserve which still in the early 1940s made him an exile from all but his closest friends. None the less, these years had a positive, creative side, for they witnessed the writing of his greatest book.

They also saw his first meetings with Dr Elizabeth Kornerup, the skilled physician under whose devout and expert care he was nursed back to health and so enabled throughout his last thirty-five years to live a full and active life. When Father David first met Elizabeth Kornerup in 1934, she was a medical student still of Swedish nationality, brought up a Lutheran, but now a Catholic convert. She became a qualified doctor and practised for many years in London and Sussex, specialising in her later years in forensic pathology – helping the police prepare evidence for inquests: to hear this gentle, kindly, sentimental and frail old lady describing the reactions of a shop assistant when she asked for warm winter boots because it was cold in the mortuary, brought home some of the contrasts in a strangely complex personality. It was never easy to understand her; and her flights of fancy sometimes made understanding more difficult still. Father David's monastic confrères naturally saw in her an unwise counsellor who led him away from his community; and it is hard not to accept this judgement in some measure. But their relationship was not a simple one. On his side it was based on a faith in her sanctity and divine inspiration all the more remarkable since he must at once have recognised that her piety was eccentric – even granted that he also knew that in Catholic tradition special privileges in such matters have been permitted to the saints. Her liking for frequent confession – she claimed to have a different confessor for every day of the week – and for extraordinary devotions, was quite outside the normal code of Catholic lay piety. Beside this was a warm human friendship and the growing partnership of many years. For both, it was founded on the vow of chastity: had this given way (as I think was apparent to all who knew them at all intimately) the fabric of their partnership would have been torn beyond repair. He was a man who yearned for friendship; two or three of his pupils – of whom I was one – enjoyed the delight and privilege of being treated like sons. We knew that the closest of his ties was to her. For Elizabeth it went a little further than this: she yearned for the social recognition marriage alone could have brought her – one must recall how extremely precarious her situation was. In their early days together this helps to explain the strange contradictions and shifts in the medical advice she gave and the harsh letters she sometimes made him write to his former confrères.[31] She felt that the authorities of the Church were ranged against her and the ties by which she held him to the course she so powerfully believed to be right were slender and brittle. The story illustrates at every turn her extraordinary tenacity of purpose, and his too – and her deep and genuine devotion. She was extremely possessive and determined beyond the strength of an ordinary mortal; but also, and genuinely, devoted to him, and to what she supposed to be his real needs.

In 1939 the tension in his relations with his monastic community became, in his eyes, finally impossible, and he left Ealing, living at first in a flat adjacent to Elizabeth Kornerup's in London and later partly in Sussex through the central years of the war. His departure from Ealing involved an automatic suspension; but happily as the years passed this was relaxed, and Dom Christopher Butler (later Bishop Butler), when he became Abbot, was able to arrange a formal process of exclaustration, which left Father David's monastic character, restored to him his priestly functions, but set him under no obligation to reside at

---

[31] See esp. Morey 1979, pp. 94–7.

Downside.[32] The Abbot at the time of his departure, Dom Sigebert Trafford, never lost his admiration and affection for Father David; and it is pleasant to record, after the separation of the thirties, that many years later they met in the chambers of the Athenaeum; and there, over a dish of tea, they were reconciled.

Meanwhile, by a strange irony, the fugitive monk had become an eminent historian. His work was already known to a small circle of experts through the important series of 'Essays in Monastic History' published in the *Downside Review* between 1931 and 1934. *The Monastic Order*, after some vicissitudes, was published in 1940, and won immediate acclaim. My father, Z.N. Brooke, read it in 1941, and I still recall his warm approval, the more striking since in later years he was inclined to be over-critical of new books and new authors. It fell to his lot as Chairman of the History Faculty Board at Cambridge to present its author for the degree of Doctor of Letters in November 1941; and I still possess the copy of the book (by now reprinted) which Father David presented to him on that occasion. In the course of that winter or the following spring I read a considerable part of it, and as a brash schoolboy did not hesitate to note a few misprints and minor inconsistencies in the large array of its scholarship. My father passed these on with glee, and the author replied (17 May 1942): 'It is a sobering reflection that I have two generations of Brooke to sift out the chaff. I feel something of Macbeth's dismay at the escape of Fleance.' It was at this time that my father unfolded a project for compiling a who's who of twelfth-century churchmen, and Father David (in a letter of 28 May) suggested collaboration on the monastic part of this. Many years later our work on monastic *fasti* with Father David issued in *Heads of Religious Houses*, vol. I, of which he and Vera London and I were the joint editors.[33]

Meanwhile, this letter led directly to my first meeting with him. On my way back from school in July 1942 I met my father and brothers, and

[32] Morey 1979, pp. 95–6; see below, p. 40.
[33] *The Heads of Religious Houses, England and Wales, 940–1216*, ed. M.D. Knowles, C.N.L. Brooke and Vera C.M. London (Cambridge, 1972). The story is told (mainly in his words, save for the sentence quoted at p. 19, n. 34) in the preface, p. vii. The completion of the book was made possible by the work of Miss London, and its final shape as a mass of indigestible references was mainly of my devising; but both of us felt throughout that the work in inspiration and basis was his, and even in the last stages owed much to his constant interest. At one time or another we sifted several hundred cartularies; and almost at the end of our work he was visiting the British Museum Department of Manuscripts to help me by disposing of some of the remaining cartularies.

we all went to call on Father David in his flat in Pimlico, in Warwick Square. There was little to see of the richness of mind revealed by his book, only a slight touch of the wit shown in his letters. I was greatly impressed by the thought that such learning and accomplishment could be hidden in a frame so small, so silent, so reserved; yet already I felt the touch of his presence which many felt later, however near or far they were from him in faith, the presence of a man of the spirit. From the visit we took away the black note-books of abbatial *fasti* later to be over many years my constant companions, and I 'left them on the top of a bus. Fortunately, a swift pursuit on foot led to their recovery; and the pursuit has continued ever since', as we wrote in the preface to *Heads*, 'though rarely at the original pace or with the same hazard'.[34] Soon after, I received the first of many letters, in which he characteristically and immediately treated me as friend and colleague; I was then fifteen.

In the early forties knowledge of his gifts was spreading, especially in Cambridge, where it was fostered by my father and other medievalists, including Philip Grierson and Munia Postan.[35] The immediate credit for bringing him to Peterhouse must go to Herbert Butterfield, who in 1944 took the initiative in arranging for him to be invited to a Fellowship. In 1946 he became a University Lecturer, and a few months later, following my father's death in October 1946, he was elected to succeed him as Professor of Medieval History (1947–54). He started late on the academic ladder, but few have climbed so rapidly. From his exile a new and very fruitful life was to grow, a reminder, as a friend who knew him over many years has observed, of the exile of Thucydides and Dante.

CAMBRIDGE 1944–63[36]

The passage of time, the devoted care of Dr Elizabeth Kornerup, the widening circle of friends at Cambridge and the growing sense of achievement all doubtless helped to bring Father David out of the deep, withdrawn reserve of the early 1940s. W.A. Pantin summed up the impression of those who knew him well in his middle years, of a personality that

---

[34] *Heads*, p. vii.
[35] The three are linked with Sir Herbert Butterfield in the closing paragraph of the preface to *RO*, III: see below, p. 84 – this phase is more fully studied by Roger Lovatt. The date of his University Lectureship is given as 1945 in *HC*, p. xxiv. It took effect from 1 October 1946 (*Cambridge University Reporter*, 20 August 1946, p. 1180).
[36] For a fuller account, see chapters 6 and 7 by Roger Lovatt and David Luscombe.

is a combination of quietness and strength, and it is a combination which commands instinctive respect. It would be difficult to imagine anyone further removed from the combative, self-assertive, self-important personalities that are sometimes to be found in the academic jungle, or from the dons

> Who shout and bang and roar and bawl
> The Absolute across the hall.

At the same time, no one who has met him could fail to see at once that his quietness is not due to timidity or to lack of conviction or of toughness.[37]

He combined in quite an exceptional degree two characteristics of sensitive academics: an inextinguishable determination never to compromise a principle, with a natural wish to avoid fuss, a hatred of noisy debate. This could give the impression of timidity. His quiet dignity and command of English, coupled with a quick mind and ready humour, made him often a good and effective chairman or committee member; but he was not quick to handle or turn rising temper or opinions fiercely stated, and he sometimes shrank from human difficulties. In his later years he became increasingly deaf, and this made it difficult for him to take part in discussion or mingle socially; but in the late 1940s and 1950s he had no such difficulty, and he mingled freely in combination room and committee; one was always aware of his character as a man of God, of his dignity and austerity. I recall an occasion when Father David was late for a meeting – a very rare occurrence – over which Sir Maurice Powicke was presiding; as he entered Powicke leapt to his feet in instant recognition of his character. More than this, the high seriousness of his writing set an example to his academic colleagues; history became for a time in many people's eyes a less frivolous, less detached field of study than it had sometimes appeared. But he never allowed these qualities to disguise his genial good humour, and sometimes the humour bubbled freely. His sense of pure fun, carefully controlled, sometimes broke through in unexpected situations. At the end of his lecture on Macaulay he noted how his greatness was recognised by contemporaries – and in particular by 'the two young ladies at the Zoo, when they caught sight of him, "Is that Mr Macaulay? Never mind the hippopotamus!" . . . I am not prepared to challenge either their preference or his greatness.'[38]

[37] *HC*, pp. xxiv–xxv.   [38] Knowles 1960, p. 31.

Of Father David as a teacher I have two abiding impressions. First, of his power as a lecturer, which was sometimes quite beyond the effect of the words themselves. He normally wrote his lectures out in full – except for some of his more specialised inquiries into the sources for St Francis's life. He had no training as a teacher, but an instinctive feel for an audience, especially on a set occasion; the contrast of his small figure and slight voice – he impressed one friend as 'a boy whose voice has never quite broken properly' – with the beauty of his language and the depth of his thought made his best lectures memorable and impressive. In nearly all, the care and thought and effort of preparation were apparent. In both his inaugurals many in his audience felt the impress of a feeling and a culture rarely associated with a historian's utterance; and the first inaugural,[39] much the slighter of the two when re-read twenty years later, affected me at the time as much as any lecture I have heard.

The other impression is of the consultation or the class in his room. If one went to ask his advice on work in hand, or if one attended the classes attached to his special subject, he sat quietly in his rooms in Peterhouse, listening carefully, talking little. My wife, who was his first research student, and I both found him rather sparing in advice and instruction. In my case to be sure this was due to my talking too much; he listened in the most friendly and respectful manner to the outpourings of a very young disciple – plying me the while with a sumptuous tea. Perhaps I wasted my opportunities; but I have never regretted the manner of our conferences, for a few words can be savoured more readily than a torrent, and one always learned as much from his silence as from his talk. In his classes he listened with like respect, helping and directing and sowing seeds; and it must have been equally so with his lectures and classes on medieval thought, since his own series of *Cambridge Studies in Medieval Life and Thought*[40] was much enriched by studies in theology and philosophy which he had partly or mainly inspired.

He was elected Professor of Medieval History in 1947, and in 1954 he received a letter from Winston Churchill translating him to the Regius

---

[39] Knowles, 1947.
[40] The 'New Series', between the first, edited by G.G. Coulton, and the third, by Walter Ullmann – two scholars very different from him, and from one another, for whom he had deep respect. His own series is wide in scope, but is most obviously a major contribution to medieval thought, with volumes by Brian Tierney, Gordon Leff, J.A. Robson, M.J. Wilks and D.E. Luscombe, all of whom acknowledged a debt to him, three of them specifically as his former pupils. His tradition is now continued in the fourth series.

Chair; in the late 1940s and 1950s began a long tale of honours – as Fellow of the British Academy (1947), as Ford's and Raleigh Lecturer (1949), and President of the Royal Historical Society (1956–60); and honorary degrees which he piled up, if not with the collector's abandon of some distinguished academics, at least with the steady and sure stroke of a good cricketer; starting in Oxford, going on to Bristol, Leicester, Kent, London, York and Birmingham,[41] where he felt a little like a prophet being accepted among his own people; and the University of Cambridge, having given him a Litt.D. long before, sought to honour him *honoris causa* in Divinity. In Cambridge too he became in due course Honorary Fellow of both Christ's and Peterhouse. The list could be extended to a characteristic conclusion, for he died President-elect of the Classical Association. The last was a singular delight. 'I somehow feel like Newman', he wrote to a friend on 31 March 1974, 'when he received the red hat, that "the cloud is lifted from me for ever" – the cloud with which my early classical masters covered me when they cursed my stupidity in dealing with North and Hillard and similar hurdles . . . There are few gifts of my education that I value as much as the ability which still remains with me, to read the Iliad or the Agamemnon with no more than the occasional failure to know the meaning of a word.'

In the meantime he gave a helping hand to many historical enterprises. He served on the Board of Management of the Institute of Historical Research, and freely and frequently gave help and advice to the Editor of the Victoria History.[42] He attended regularly meetings of the Committee intended to re-edit Wilkins's *Concilia* and gave much needed encouragement to the younger scholars attempting to join that endless adventure.[43] He served on several Committees of the British Academy, and in particular its Medieval Texts Editorial Committee, and he completed a term as Chairman of Section 2 (Medieval History). He was for many years a member of Council of the Canterbury and York Society. His help and encouragement played a crucial part in the successful launching of the Ecclesiastical History Society, of which he was first President. In this the initiative came from C.W. Dugmore,

[41] Stacpoole, 1975, p. 71, gives the most comprehensive list I have found.
[42] The Editor, the late Professor R.B. Pugh, often spoke to me of his work for the *VCH*, which went a good deal beyond the article he wrote on religious houses in *VCH Middlesex*.
[43] From which have sprung *Councils and Synods* I (ed. D. Whitelock, M. Brett and C.N.L. Brooke, Oxford, 1981), and II (ed. F.M. Powicke and C.R. Cheney, 1964).

whose work for the *Journal of Ecclesiastical History* Father David also steadily supported over many years.[44] He gave much encouragement, which was deeply appreciated, to H.P. Morrison, the enlightened Managing Director, later Chairman, of Nelsons of Edinburgh.[45] His name first came to Parkside Works in 1945 in a letter from G.G. Coulton as an author to watch; one of the last books which Peter Morrison commissioned as Chairman was *Great Historical Enterprises: Problems in Monastic History*, reprints of his Royal Historical Society presidentials and his Birkbeck Lectures, delivered at Cambridge in 1962.

In 1963 he retired, and his friends and disciples, with the ready collaboration of the Cambridge University Press, which had already provided so elegant a setting for his greatest books, presented to him a collection of his own papers, *The Historian and Character and other Essays*. Giles Constable and I were the editors; but we consulted with many senior friends and colleagues, and above all with W.A. Pantin, who wrote for it a fine *Curriculum Vitae*. We felt that no 'memorial of words' could compete with his own, and that it was a singularly appropriate opportunity to force him to reprint his best studies; and we tried to make it reflect the range of his mature published work.

1963–74

In 1963 he retired, and the remaining years of his life were spent between a tiny cottage in Sussex, of great age and charm, surrounded by rolling hills and quiet woods of the kind he most appreciated in English scenery, and a small house in Wimbledon. In both he enjoyed the care and companionship and medical skill of Dr Elizabeth Kornerup. At Linch he had peace and quiet, and in a tiny study, like a summer-house, out in the garden, he could read and write, away from traffic and visitors. In London he could see his friends and keep in touch with libraries. He wrote and reviewed to the very end of his life; and in many ways these were years of peaceful content, though not untroubled.

He suffered first from a sense of failing powers; yet his touch never left him, and he was capable of clear and effective prose to the end. His second trouble lay in his health. But again, there was a remarkable

---

[44] His last public appearance was at a lunch of his own arranging to celebrate the jubilee of Professor Dugmore's work as Editor, on 31 October 1974.

[45] As I know from many conversations with the late H.P. Morrison; what follows is in a letter temporarily in my possession.

compensation: Dr Kornerup's care enabled him to live an almost normal life in a manner scarcely otherwise conceivable. He died of a heart attack on 21 November 1974, aged 78 – no bad age for a delicate man; and it was the first discernible sign of serious illness that he had in his last years.

His third affliction was one common among those growing old, a sense of the excessive rapidity of change about him. He was particularly troubled by the changes in his Church. Always humane, always charitable, never a proselytiser, never narrow or rigid in his views of other men's faith, he gave a welcome and a cautious approval to the ecumenical movement. His view of ecumenism and his attitude to Christians of other folds never substantially varied, in my experience. To a Free Churchman, also a distinguished ecclesiastical historian, with whom he felt a clear affinity of mind and spirituality, he wrote in 1963:

> I agree with you in not being a full-blooded ecumenist, at least if ecumenism means agreeing upon an L.C.M. or lists of ἀδιάφορα. I prefer to begin at the other end, so to say, to recognise and rejoice at all real love and faith in God and our Lord Jesus Christ. It is one of the unexpected happinesses of my work that it has brought me into relations of sympathy with yourself and others whom I should not otherwise have known. *Cor ad cor loquitur.*

And in 1974, 'A love of our Lord is the only – and a sufficient – criterion of a fellow-Christian'.[46] His friends included many non-Catholics and agnostics; his influence as historian and man of God was freely shared and widely felt. But in the wake of the Vatican Council he came to the conviction that a search for change for its own sake had seized his fellow Catholics and led to the destruction of much that was valuable and central to Catholic tradition, above all to the total destruction of the traditional Latin Mass and to the denial of authority. He was among those who welcomed *Humanae Vitae* – Paul VI's encyclical on contraception – as an attempt to assert that Rome could still speak, and its widespread rejection must have brought him sorrow.

The two most impressive celebrations of the Latin Mass which I have witnessed were Pontifical High Mass at Downside in the late 1940s, and the private mass in Father David's cottage twenty years later. His slender figure, in simple vestments, served only by Dr Kornerup, stood in wonderful contrast to the majesty and richness of the liturgy beautifully

---

[46] Letters of 18 June 1963 and 13 June 1974 kindly shown me by the Reverend Dr Geoffrey Nuttall.

enunciated in his small, clear voice; so that my Protestant ancestors would have been constrained to say, 'Surely the Lord is in this place – Vero Dominus est in loco isto.' In my visits to Linch I used also to note a pleasant contrast in his dress. All the friends of his mid- and late years saw him most often in a simple suit of clerical black; and might also see him in his habit, worn with a doctor's scarlet at a Cambridge feast, when he ate little and drank nothing, yet was always as grave and cheerful as the occasion and his presence demanded. At Linch I saw him too in ancient gardening clothes, trimming the large hedge beside the cottage with exquisite care and precision. He himself likened Abbot Butler in similar garb to an impoverished nobleman; the monk turned Regius Professor savoured more of a genial dignified upper-class peasant, and this helped one to understand his enjoyment of the novels of Hardy. In all these costumes he looked more frail than one who would pass, or had passed, the three score years and ten; and the slightly awkward step seemed hardly compatible with the former Chalet walker, who still in his sixties daily measured Grantchester meadows or another Cambridge walk, and in his seventies, even a few months before his death, on our last visit to him in Sussex, took a joyous ramble in wood and mud.

After one of the last lectures I heard him give, he became involved in a discussion of how great change appears to those who live with it; and with a rueful smile he observed that of all things in his world he had supposed the Latin Mass and the steam engine the most stable and lasting – and both were gone. It reminded me of a phone call from a Public Orator in search of Father David's minor pleasures, who asked me if it were true that he had a passion for trains and cricket. The second had always been a blind spot with me, and I confessed an ignorance for which Father David – once a dedicated follower of the fortunes of Warwickshire – later rebuked me. The first I confirmed, recalling a long hour spent with him in Bletchley returning from Oxford to Cambridge in the days when British Rail recognised the link between these places: I had expected it to be a pleasure for me, a trial for him; in the event he enjoyed it fully as much as I, hopping from side to side of the platform with boyish glee as the expresses approached. As a boy, I believe, he had driven a steam engine, and the devotion to railways was even to colour his appreciation of the English Carthusians, whose first house was founded near a Great Western main line.[47]

[47] *MO*, p. 391.

Human, urbane and humorous; a great historian and master of prose, a professor and teacher of wide influence; an austere and solitary monk; a devout priest ministering to his household and his friends. He was all these things and none of them by halves. I have tried to show a little of how they all came together in his life and character; but it would be foolish to imagine that even those closest to him saw to the full his richness and his depth. Many of those who met him casually came to see that the world was a larger place than they had realised; when he died it was hard for those who knew him well not to feel the world much poorer for his passing. Yet few men, and very few scholars, live so securely in their books; and for all his austerity, that is a judgement which would have given him pleasure. He was not without failings. But to his friends these served to sharpen their sense of his exceptional endowment. To echo an author whose works he savoured, he

was a good man, and did good things.

2

FATHER DAVID AND THE MONASTIC AND SPIRITUAL LIFE

AELRED SILLEM

My contacts with Father David were relatively short as measured in years. As a schoolboy and an undergraduate, between 1924 and 1929, I stayed often at Downside; walks with Father David were always part of the visit, and he became more than an acquaintance, but the relationship did not become deep. During my two years in the noviciate, from September 1929 to September 1931, under Dom Richard Davey, my contacts with Father David were rare, but became closer. When I passed from the noviciate into the community, in September 1931, he was my junior master, responsible for my spiritual and monastic formation; but in October 1931 I was sent to Munich to do theology, and saw him only during the vacations; on the other hand, I had the benefit of long letters from him while I was at Munich, and during the vacations my relationship with him became very close, until the separation of our ways in September 1934, when I came to Quarr. It is the close relationship between September 1931 and September 1934 – three decisive years for us both – which gives me what title I may have to write of his monastic and spiritual thought.[1]

This is the fruit of the convergence of three factors: a personal spiritual problem which he shared with others at Downside, an evolution in his theological views, and what he saw as a watershed in the monastic policy of the community he loved.

[1] What follows is based principally upon personal knowledge, and upon Father David's letters to me which I have given to the Downside archives. I am very grateful for the comments of the Abbot of Downside and of the Prior of Downside. And I owe a special debt of gratitude to Dom Adrian Morey, not only for his Memoir of Father David, which is presupposed by much that I have written, but also for a friendship which, through vicissitudes and interruptions, endured for more than fifty years.

The constitutional changes in the English Benedictine Congregation at the end of the nineteenth century, by guaranteeing the autonomy of each house, allowed each also to shape its own policy: and at Downside this had taken the form of a gradual reduction in the number of parishes served by monks outside the monastery, and the building-up of the community resident at Downside, with the school as its principal work. But the problems involved in integrating the requirements of a growing public school for the sons of the well-to-do, with the exigencies of the monastic life, were real; and, although the community could in no sense be called a divided community, there were inevitably some who appeared to give priority to the demands of the school, with resultant repercussions upon the monastic observance, while others felt that the logic of the policy of withdrawing from the parishes demanded a strengthening of monastic observance, even if this entailed a check upon the development of the school. No one advocated the abandonment of the school: Father David himself felt the need for greater spiritual austerity, and felt that the policy of the house should move in that direction; but he never questioned the suitability of education as a work for monks until his last years. But, precisely because he dearly loved and deeply enjoyed the work of the school, he felt that it raised spiritual problems for the individual, affective problems and problems of priorities which went deeper than the ingenious dovetailing of timetables.

His problem was one that faces most Benedictines at one time or another, in one form or another. In a famous passage, Cassian defines the monk as

> unum dumtaxat desiderans,
> unum sitiens,
> ad unum non solum actus suos uerum etiam cogitationes
> semper intendens.

> desiring one thing only,
> thirsting for one thing only,
> constantly setting upon one thing only
> > not only his actions,
> > but even his thoughts.[2]

---

[2] Cassian, *Collationes*, vii.6; ed. E. Pichery, *Conférences*, I (Sources Chrétiennes, 42, Paris, 1955), p. 253.

Simplification of mental and affective furniture is a defining element in the monastic vocation – hence 'separation from the world', simplicity and austerity of life: the monk chooses to travel light, *mente et corpore pariter expeditus*, 'disentangled alike in mind and body'. But how reconcile this essential element of the monastic life with the tradition of Christian, and especially of Benedictine, humanism? The problem is as old as monasticism, and St Jerome tells us that he was scourged in a dream for preferring Cicero to the Scriptures.[3]

The tension between renunciation and humanism is particularly strong where a monastery is committed to running a large public school: an educator must widen horizons, and he can only do so if his own reading and experience are wide. And on the practical level, the proximity of the school makes accessible to the monk a range of hobbies and relaxations, some of them expensive. The tension can be a bracing one, and has produced saintly monks and given a peculiar power to their influence. In *The Benedictines* (1929) Father David himself states admirably the spiritual value of this tension:

> The Benedictine would, in part, agree with some modern religious thinkers who urge what they have called a double polarity in the religious life – of other-worldliness and detachment, and of this-worldliness and attachment.[4]

And in an earlier passage he had written of

> the desire among religious thinkers for simplification and renunciation – not of self, for that can never be too thorough, but of material satisfactions and intellectual occupations. We long for a Monism of the spirit. Undoubtedly some souls are thus led by God; but there is a danger lest the uncompromising logic of such renunciation, and the intellectual intolerance and limitations of even the holiest, may canonise such a life, not only as a very high religious state, but as the only high religious state. It is a last infirmity of noble minds.[5]

One wonders how Father David would have judged these two passages a few years later: but they reveal that the spiritual problem was one that already preoccupied him, and very early in his monastic life he felt called to greater simplification and unification. Much later, he told me that

---

[3] Jerome, *Lettres*, I, no. 22.   [4] Knowles 1929, p. 94.   [5] Knowles 1929, p. 85.

Abbot Ramsay had agreed that he should in due course try his vocation with the Carthusians: only Abbot Ramsay's death in March 1929, and other responsibilities, postponed and ultimately excluded the attempt. Meanwhile, no one was obliged to avail himself of all the facilities provided by the proximity of the school, and he gradually pruned away much of which he had at first availed himself. In 1927 he travelled in Greece with two former pupils, in conditions which involved the impossibility of saying Mass: he persuaded himself that this was in the interest of his Sixth Form classical teaching, but subsequently he judged that this had been self-deception and a grave infidelity to grace. It is surprising that as late as 1930–1 he published an entirely delightful account of the journey in the *Downside Review*.[6] But after 1930 there was, with one small exception,[7] no more foreign travel: he either spent his holidays with his father, or he visited contemplative monasteries in England with two like-minded brethren (Quarr in 1930 and Mount Saint Bernard in 1931 and again in 1932). It seems that after 1930 he read no more novels, and he ceased to use the facilities of the school for squash and other recreations.

It is a principle of Benedictine life that 'singularity' should be avoided: a monk should conform himself unostentatiously to the approved practice of his community. But most of what I have described above would pass unnoticed – at least at first, and until Father David's example came to be followed by disciples who were not always discreet. It is clear that he felt the need for an interior austerity which could in fact be practised within the framework of the common Downside observance without attracting attention or implying criticism of others. And this course he came to recommend to those who were responsive to his influence. His standing in the community as a whole had been due, chiefly indeed to his quality, but also to the fact that he was regarded as a 'moderate', as a non-party man free from that cult of picturesque external practices regarded as marks of the 'usque':[8] as his evolution in the direction of austerity came to be noticed, and perhaps to be dis-served by the zeal of some disciples, several who loved and revered him began to be a little anxious.

[6] Knowles 1930–1.

[7] A brief visit to Sweden with Dr Kornerup when she visited her family.

[8] In 1890, Leo XIII had pronounced that the English Benedictine Congregation, far from being primarily a missionary body, was 'usquequaque monastica', wholly monastic. Those who hoped for a fuller monastic life were nicknamed 'usquequa-ques', abbreviated into 'usques', which came to have a slightly ironic connotation.

The second important factor in Father David's development was a doctrinal one. Not only the personal pursuit of the life of prayer, but an interest in the theology of mystical prayer, was an important part of the Downside tradition, especially since the abbacy of Dom Cuthbert Butler, 1906–22, whose influence upon Father David was profound and lasting, although he came later to question some of Abbot Butler's views. Today, interest in the life of prayer is widespread and perhaps more realistic than in the first half of the century, and the problem which loomed large in Father David's thought to the end of his life may seem remote, though in fact its practical consequences are considerable. To simplify the issue ruthlessly, it may be said that all agreed that the goal, not only of the monastic life, but of the Christian life, was personal holiness; and that personal holiness consisted in the perfect love of God and neighbour. But how would this perfect love of God and neighbour express itself in the life of prayer? For one school of thought, to which Cuthbert Butler gave powerful expression in *Western Mysticism* (1922), all, whatever their state of life, are called to a simple form of contemplative prayer, St John of the Cross's 'prayer of loving attention', or 'prayer of simplicity'. This, like all prayer, is the work of grace: but the grace upon which it rests is an 'ordinary' grace. Beyond this, however, are higher degrees of prayer – mystical prayer, and, in turn, its higher degrees as described by St Teresa and St John of the Cross: these are special gifts of God, and perfect holiness can exist without them.

This is the view adopted by Father David in *The English Mystics* (1927), and in *The Benedictines* (1929). It is important to underline that it does not imply any lowering of the ideal of Christian or monastic sanctity, but simply a particular assessment of the link between holiness and mystical contemplative prayer.

However, when Father David stayed at Quarr in 1930, he found in the library a copy of Père Garrigou-Lagrange's *Perfection chrétienne et contemplation* (1922–3), which he had hitherto known only second-hand from Abbot Butler's *Afterthoughts* in the second edition of *Western Mysticism* (1927). Père Garrigou was what was once described as a man-eating Thomist, a systematic theologian lacking in historical sense; but the book, within its limitations, is a great one, and its impact upon Father David was decisive. For one thing, he found the theology of mystical prayer treated as a branch of theology, and in particular of the theology of grace; and this he found intellectually far more satisfying than Abbot Butler's empirical and descriptive approach, with its characteristic distrust of systematic theology. But, more important, he was won by the ruthless simplicity of Père Garrigou's central thesis: there is only one Christian sanctity, which consists simply in the perfect love of God and neighbour. But the perfect love of God and neighbour will be reached only through the purifications of the Night of Sense and the Night of the Spirit, and it culminates in the heights of the mystical life: if these are rare, so also in fact is perfect holiness rare. The fullness of the mystical life is indeed rare, but it is in a strict sense 'normal'. It is not an exceptional vocation.

The corollary is demanding: if all are called to the heights, the call can only be answered by deepening generosity and renunciation; those so called must embark upon the active nights of sense and spirit, if God is to lead them through the passive nights to perfect holiness. The responsibility of the spiritual director is correspondingly great: he must adjust his counsels to the stage of growth of his disciple, but the time will come when his demands must be absolute: he must not be ashamed of the cross of Christ. And the observance and spiritual teaching in a religious community must maintain the same demands. Did Father David come to think that the other view of the relationship between sanctity and mystical prayer, if it did not in principle lower the ideal of perfect holiness in the love of God and neighbour, tended to lead in practice to a lowering of sights and standards, to a more indulgent asceticism, and even to spiritual mediocrity?

To the end of his life, with some nuances, Father David adhered to the Thomist reading of St John of the Cross, though not all students of St John would accept without reservations Père Garrigou-Lagrange's integration of his teaching into the Thomistic synthesis. It is illuminating to compare the opening chapters of *The English Mystics* (1927) with the corresponding chapters of *The English Mystical Tradition* (1961), as well as with *What is Mysticism* (1967). But in the years immediately following his conversion to Père Garrigou's view, he studied the problem in depth, and published some important articles in the *Downside Review* and the *Clergy Review*, which unfortunately passed largely unnoticed, perhaps because English theologians were not interested in the problem, and French theologians did not read English.[9] Henceforth, for Father David, St John of the Cross's analysis of the unfolding of the life of grace from baptism to the Spiritual Marriage became a canon: other spiritual writers

[9] Knowles 1933a, 1934a, 1934b.

are assessed according to the degree in which they approximate to the teaching of St John of the Cross.

Father David had found a theology of the spiritual life which strengthened and justified his own spiritual aspirations. And in these years he was brought into close contact with the Good Shepherd nuns, an 'active' order founded for the care of problem girls, but with a strong tradition of prayer. Here he found, often among simple lay sisters, the teaching of St Teresa and St John of the Cross lived out quite unselfconsciously. He became particularly close to the superior of their house in the suburbs of Bristol, a woman of holiness and wisdom. He became the 'extra' confessor of this house, and would take one or the other of his juniors with him to talk to the superior: for my part I look back on this contact with gratitude, and regret that with Father David's move from Downside to Ealing in September 1933 his contact with her ceased, and he passed under the influence of a woman less wise.

The convergence between Father David's personal need for a life of spiritual austerity, and the development of his theology of the spiritual life, were not things that concerned him alone: they converged with problems of policy which concerned the whole community of Downside. For in these years, the issues of ideal and principle took concrete form in practical decisions which had to be taken. The monastery building was over-crowded and more accommodation was needed: the library was scattered all over the house, which made difficult its utilisation for the intellectual work which it was hoped to develop. On the other hand, the preparatory school at Downside was most inadequately housed. Abbot Ramsay decided to give priority to enlarging the monastery and providing adequate accommodation for the library: this was felt by many, and no doubt by him, to symbolise the desire to strengthen the resident community so that its energies would not be wholly absorbed in the school, and to provide equipment for serious study and research as a normal activity of some of an enlarged community.

Abbot Ramsay's plans met with opposition, partly on aesthetic grounds – Father David being prominent among the active critics – and his relatively sudden death on 14 March 1929 postponed a decision. Abbot Chapman, his successor, was unenthusiastic, and the project of new buildings was allowed to slumber, its place being taken by a 'temporary' building of wood and asbestos, destined to last some fifty years. And at this moment the needs of the preparatory school were put forward, and in a form which won the support of some – including Father David – who would otherwise have distrusted the proposal. It was proposed to purchase Milton Abbey in Dorset, a great eighteenth-century house with the choir and transepts of the medieval abbey church in perfect condition; and the idea of restoring an ancient abbey, and of recovering a pre-Reformation monastic church, captivated some who would later oppose a new foundation to house the preparatory school. The Milton project fell through because the Anglican authorities felt unable to renounce their right to use the church for Anglican worship, but by now the idea of a new foundation had become almost taken for granted, and all idea of new monastic buildings at Downside was abandoned. A period of energetic and sometimes a little comical house-hunting followed. Early in 1933 the choice fell upon Paddockhurst near Worth in Sussex, and in May its purchase was put to the vote of the Chapter. It is ironical to recall that if Abbot Ramsay's building plans had not been postponed in view of opposition in which Father David had played a part, there would have been no funds available for the purchase of Paddockhurst (henceforward to be called Worth Priory) or for any new foundation.

Of what followed immediately I write with hesitation, partly because, not being in solemn vows, I was not a member of the Chapter; partly because I was still in Munich, and did not return to Downside until July 1933, by which time positions had already hardened. On the other hand, much that had passed at the Chapter inevitably became common knowledge; and letters from Father David – who himself was reticent of details – and from others who were less reticent, gave me a fairly full picture of the situation. Opposition to the proposal to purchase Paddockhurst, to move the preparatory school there, and to entrust it to a community enlarged by the Downside juniors – young monks doing their theological studies – was not limited to those who would later form the core of Father David's proposed foundation. There was an underlying distrust of the monastic priorities of those most enthusiastic for the project: it seemed that the foundation of Worth was demanded primarily in the interest of the school, and that thus it was the school, not the monastic life, which was determining policy. The excellent observance, established in fact at Worth from the beginning, would be made possible only by depriving Downside of a large group of young monks: this would inevitably postpone the building-up of a larger community, and consequently of a fuller monastic observance, at

Downside, in order to give a monastic character to what was essentially the provision of an adequate setting for the Downside preparatory school. The majority in favour of the foundation was not a large one, though there would have been differences of emphasis among those who voted against. Father David based his opposition, not primarily upon grounds of monastic policy, but on the ground that, in his judgement, Downside was not spiritually in a condition to take the responsibility of making a foundation. Few others would have based their opposition upon this judgement, and some were dismayed by its expression. But it was an assessment which was to colour his attitude to Downside increasingly in the years to come; it was an expression of a spiritual teaching which was to determine his historical judgements also.

As Dom Adrian points out,[10] it is difficult to reconcile this very severe assessment of Downside in May 1933, with what he had written in a letter to me only a few months before. I can only say that this letter was written to encourage a young monk in his charge, at a period when, with the background of house-hunting, all horizons had become uncertain; and also that in the intervening months the secrets of many hearts had been revealed. As the event was to make poignantly clear, it had been the problem of Father David, and of others in positions of authority, to encourage and indeed to authorise ideals and aspirations for the development of Downside which seemed at the time both legitimate, and, on a long-term view, realistic.

Abbot Chapman reacted vehemently to the opposition, seeing in it nothing but a lack of humility and obedience; he seems even to have demanded the equivalent of a retraction, which was not forthcoming. He and Father David were not made to understand each other, and there had already been clashes with Father David as junior master. Abbot Chapman was a profoundly spiritual man, and a man of prayer, deeply read in the spiritual writers who meant so much to Father David – and reading them very differently – but there was in him a love of paradox, and even a streak of perverseness, wholly uncongenial to Father David's cast of mind. He had a flair for the boutade which could usefully deflate, but which could also dishearten. His comment upon Father David's hope to study the history of medieval English monasticism had been that 'the less we know about that, the better'. It would be unjust to say that the specifically monastic way of life had come to mean little to him, but

[10] Morey 1979, p. 97.

35

certainly he tended more and more to speak as though in the last resort – and perhaps well before the last resort – nothing mattered but charity, prayer and obedience; and this made him unsympathetic to those who seemed to him preoccupied with observance, and whose attitude could be seen as disobedient, and perhaps as tinged with spiritual arrogance and uncharitable judgements upon others. He lived increasingly by the teaching of de Caussade, the early eighteenth-century Jesuit spiritual writer, seeing everything in the fulfilment of God's will in the present moment: this may have had something to do with Father David's increasing view that de Caussade was a great spiritual writer who needed to be read with circumspection.[11] In the introduction which he wrote to a new edition of de Caussade's *Self-Abandonment*,[12] Father David puts de Caussade among 'the ten greatest spiritual guides since St Bernard', but he felt that de Caussade's teaching on Self-Abandonment to Divine Providence could be misinterpreted so as to lead to an abdication of personal responsibility.

Abbot Chapman was the kindest of men, but he did not realise that Father David, and those who, with varying degrees of insight, stood with him, believed themselves faced with a real spiritual problem. They had been encouraged, not only by Father David but by others with responsibility for their formation, to hope for an evolution of the monastic life at Downside which the decision to found Worth appeared to them, rightly or wrongly, at least to postpone indefinitely; and, more gravely, which the Abbot's reaction and language appeared to repudiate. In view of later developments, it should be said clearly that no one had dreamt of, or desired, the abandonment of the school: the development hoped for had been simply a building-up of the resident community so that its energies would not be wholly absorbed by the school, and an evolution of the observance in the direction of a greater simplicity of life, with the primacy of the contemplative elements safeguarded in what must always remain a 'mixed' life. I think most of us would have accepted the ideal depicted in chapter 22 of Cuthbert Butler's *Benedictine Monachism*, 'A Benedictine Abbey in the 20th Century': we were being forced to ask ourselves whether this ideal would in fact be realised at Downside, and even whether it was an ideal accepted by the Abbot whose monastic principles seemed limited to the unconditional appeal to humility and obedience.

[11] Morey 1979, p. 138.   [12] Caussade, de, 1959.

For Father David, the anguish was intensified by his sense of responsibility for others: he had encouraged these aspirations, and therefore felt it his duty to stand by those who had made them their own. This played its part in the decisions which he was to take. The suggestion that those who now felt unable in conscience to abandon their aspirations should be allowed to embody them in a new foundation, was not made first by Father David: I believe it came from Alban Brooks, and Father David was slow to accept it. But he came to see it as the only way out of the deadlock. His first proposal, made early in June 1933, was that he and those with him should take up the offer of a foundation in Australia, which would include a school. This, in view of subsequent developments, comes as a surprise, but it should be remembered that hitherto all had accepted education as a normal Benedictine work: their misgivings had been about the actual impact of the school at Downside upon the life of the monastery. Soon afterwards, however, Father David and those with him came to feel that the new foundation could prove to be the providential opportunity to create a monastery which would at once express the spiritual insights and teaching of the last years, and yet perpetuate the spiritual and monastic tradition of Downside, but with all the accretions laid aside: the inspiration was not a revolt from Downside but on the contrary in continuity with it. That is why it was never suggested that the group should transfer as a group to some pre-existing community such as Quarr. The sketch of the proposed foundation was drawn up and presented to Abbot Chapman: re-reading it after more than fifty years, I still find it on the whole a sober and realistic programme, and in some ways in advance of its time. It expressed admirably the source of the problem:

> A whole series of circumstances has made it possible at Downside in the last twenty years, and particularly since the large novitiates began in 1923, for a novice with a contemplative vocation to be received here, and to enjoy during his years of formation almost all the helps and instructions necessary to develop that vocation. During the same period, on the other hand, Downside has considerably increased its activities. Hence, when all accidentals are brushed aside, the origin of our group and its difficulties.[13]

[13] Morey 1979, pp. 144–53, at p. 145.

37

Abbot Chapman rejected the whole project, and saw in it only a failure in humility and obedience: when I returned from Munich in July, positions had hardened. Abbot Chapman himself was a very sick man, though at the time no one realised that he was a dying man: on the one hand this must have affected his judgement and helps us to understand his failure to show sympathy for what was a sincerely felt spiritual problem; on the other hand, it was tragic that the last months of a deeply spiritual man should have been embittered by problems and tensions which he felt endangered the community entrusted to him by God.

For many of those who had opposed the foundation of Worth, Father David's proposed foundation seemed a tragic mistake: they thought the project wrong in itself, and felt no call to the purely contemplative life it envisaged. But looking back to those long months of stress, I can only admire the great charity and tolerance showed alike by those who welcomed the foundation of Worth, and by those who had opposed it, but felt themselves abandoned by Father David's project.

In September 1933, judging that at Downside Father David's influence could only be divisive, Abbot Chapman sent him to Ealing Priory. Father David was to say later that if he had then been allowed to remain at Downside, he would never have left it. He was only to visit it once more, for the funeral of Cuthbert Butler in April 1934. Downside held him by too many bands. It had been his home since boyhood, he loved its traditions and its memories, deep or trivial, he knew how much he owed to the inspiration and example, spiritual and intellectual, of those who had formed him there, and how much he had given and received there of affection and friendship. On November 7th Abbot Chapman died, and was succeeded by Abbot Bruno Hicks, whose attitude was at first sympathetic, but whose indecisiveness complicated the negotiations of the coming months; these were permitted by him, and aimed at by-passing the authority of the Downside Chapter and making the foundation with the direct permission of the Holy See.

This was refused in July 1934, with kindly words. But in the meantime a new factor had intervened, whose influence upon Father David himself was to be decisive, and, most would judge, disastrous. A Swedish medical student, a convert from Lutheranism, called at Ealing Priory, and asked for a spiritual director: the Prior asked Father David to see her. He rapidly became convinced that she was a saint, a 'perfect soul' to use his own words of her, living profoundly the teaching of St John of the Cross whose writings she knew well. Her instruction in the more central elements of the Catholic faith was imperfect: she had apparently extracted from confessors permission for quite indefensible devotional practices such as carrying the Blessed Sacrament on her, receiving the Anointing of the Sick at frequent intervals, and so forth. But Father David clearly believed that a soul exceptionally gifted by God could claim such privileges. And it seems that rapidly the roles of director and directed became reversed. He told her all about the projected foundation, and she advised him about the spiritual measures to be taken to assure its realisation. It sometimes looked as though Father David and his group were to be animated by her influence rather as St Catherine of Siena inspired her *famiglia*. Those of the group who passed through London were invited to meet her – I was never able to do so – and some felt uneasy at the part she was beginning to play. There can be no doubt that from April 1934, and especially after Rome's refusal of the foundation in July 1934, her influence upon Father David's words and actions was decisive, and unfortunate. To me, Father David's unconditional acceptance of Dr Kornerup as a mystic and saint, and of her guidance, remains a mystery and a stumbling-block. I can only see it as due, partly to the beginning of nervous exhaustion, the effect of the strains since May 1933, which was to end in the breakdown in 1939; and partly to Father David's loneliness at Ealing after the intimate affections of the last years at Downside. He intensely needed someone to whom he could talk of the things nearest to his heart.

This became all too clear, when in July 1934 the Rescript came from Rome, refusing to authorise the foundation. All Father David's group accepted the Roman reply as final, and each had to make his individual decision, either to stay at Downside, or to look elsewhere for the fulfilment of his vocation. For Father David, a battle had been lost, but not the war: we were to obey provisionally, but still hope for the foundation, and in some way or other work for it. And he sent round to the group, with a covering note for each, an instruction to hold firm, which was printed by Dom Adrian.[14] This document I find painful reading: it implied the kind of spiritual tyranny from which St Francis de Sales delivered St Jane Frances de Chantal, and is contrary to all principles of spiritual direction. It is impossible not to see in it the hand of Dr Kornerup.

When this document was sent out, I had taken my individual decision,

[14] Morey 1979, p. 86.

39

without consulting Father David, and was already at Quarr: it seemed necessary to make my position clear, so I returned the document to Father David unread, explaining that the problems of the group, who remained most dear to me, no longer concerned me directly. The document itself I read for the first time in Dom Adrian's book. I had no further contact with Father David until he allowed me to visit him at Peterhouse in 1958: we talked for a couple of hours on monastic and spiritual things, as in the old days at Downside; and from then onwards there was an occasional exchange of letters, with the old expressions of affection on his side as well as on mine. But I never saw him again.

From September 1934 until September 1939 Father David lived on at Ealing, following the observance faithfully, but otherwise isolating himself completely from the community, working on *The Monastic Order* in the London Library, and constantly visiting Dr Kornerup in her flat in Pimlico. In December 1938 Abbot Hicks was succeeded by Abbot Trafford, who had always thought Father David's exile to Ealing to have been a mistake: now, relying upon their old friendship, he recalled him to Downside. Instead, without permission of any kind, he left Ealing in September 1939, and went to live in a flat rented by Dr Kornerup above her own. By this he automatically incurred the penalties of Canon Law: suspension from saying Mass and excommunication.

Dom Adrian has given an account of the complicated attempts made to regularise Father David's position – made wearisome by his reluctance to co-operate.[15] The patient efforts of the Downside authorities were blocked by Father David's refusal to act in any way which could be taken to admit the justice or the validity of the sanctions which it was hoped to lift. They were lifted only in 1952 in the form of 'exclaustration', by which, while remaining a monk, he was withdrawn from the authority of the Abbot of Downside, and placed directly under that of the Holy See. This solution, because it seemed to him to imply the justice and validity of the sanctions incurred, he accepted only in 1957. This is for me the period of his life for which I feel the least sympathy.

It is clear that by 1939 Father David was in some sense mentally ill, and had undergone a breakdown: the mystery is that it is precisely in these years that he wrote *The Monastic Order*, a tremendous mental and psychological achievement. In July 1928 he had been involved in a car accident: he suffered head damage and a dangerous haemorrhage. Some

[15] Morey 1979, pp. 94–6.

have seen in this accident the source of a personality change which would explain not only his breakdown after 1939, but also a flawing of his judgement considered to have underlain already his whole reaction to the foundation of Worth, and his project of a contemplative foundation. This view is perhaps the fruit of hindsight – when was the personality change first noticed? – but it provided for some who loved Father David a compassionate explanation of actions of his which seemed to them indefensible and inconsistent with his past. The breakdown is surely sufficiently explained by the strain of working for the foundation, with all the heart-searchings which this must have involved for him; by the shock of its refusal by Rome; by what seemed to him his desertion by his followers; and by the self-imposed isolation from brethren and friends in which he had lived for five years at Ealing.[16] But his leaving the monastery without permission in 1939, and his putting himself in the hands of Dr Kornerup, had about it an ambivalence which played its part in his attitude to the canonical sanctions. On the canonical level, he justified his equivocal position by claiming that he was simply a very sick man in the hands of his medical advisor: it was a purely professional relationship. And undoubtedly we owe Dr Kornerup gratitude for her skill in bringing him safely through the coming years. But on the spiritual level he saw the relationship quite differently: he was the monk fulfilling his monastic vocation by caring for a perfect soul entrusted to him by God. Outwardly, the price for fulfilling this lofty vocation might be canonical suspension and disgrace, but inwardly he was living out in a unique way that 'monasticism of the soul' of which he had written many years before.

But how would he justify his position to himself, faced with the classical doctrine of monastic obedience? To put this simply: short of an order to commit sin, God's will is made known to the monk through the decisions of those we have vowed to obey, and, however disconcerting this may sometimes seem to us, that is the way to a more perfect love of God by giving up our own way, and therefore the road to true holiness, outside which there is only self-will and illusion. The motive of obedience lies not in any greater spiritual wisdom in the superior, but in his office; it does not mean that his decision is necessarily the best in the abstract, but God's will for us here and now. But what when the order given seems to us contrary to our deepest spiritual interest – as Father David judged the recall to Downside to be? The classical answer would

[16] Morey 1979, pp. 87–88.

be that it is the monk's duty to explain his misgivings to the abbot, and the abbot's duty to listen, but if the abbot then maintains his decision, the monk must obey, and what his obedience commits him to, will in fact bring him closer to God.[17]

In the last of his Sarum Lectures, 1965, Father David expressed a view of obedience which underlay his actions since 1939, and was already hinted at in a letter of 1934: mature, as opposed to infantile obedience, demands that an order or decision be scrutinised before God; and if it be judged contrary to the Rule or to the spiritual good of the subject, exterior obedience must be withheld in the name of a deeper, more spiritual obedience.[18] The obedience taught by St Benedict, he thought, envisaged simply obedience in the practical organisation of the house and its work: he had not faced the problem of obedience where deeper spiritual issues were involved. This came to be faced by St Bernard, and still more by St Francis, who taught that 'if the superior commands something contrary to what his [the brother's] heart knows to be right, he is to refuse obedience and abide by the consequences'.[19] This is not the place to discuss Father David's reading of St Bernard and St Francis, but the quotation exactly expresses the way in which he would have justified his own actions from September 1939, and perhaps, less explicitly, from May 1933. Already in a letter of 1935, he had written that 'true, spiritual obedience . . . can only be given to one more enlightened than oneself'.[20]

Naturally, the standards set by the spiritual teaching which he had made his own, and which he put before those who accepted his spiritual direction, also determine his judgements in monastic history. These are first stated in the last pages of *The Monastic Order*:

> Unless it give to those who enter it an invitation to the highest perfection, together with the doctrine and discipline without which . . . that invitation cannot be followed, a religious institute must be pronounced a failure, and unless a monk . . . live in spirit apart from the world, with all his powers dedicated to the love of God, he must be pronounced unfaithful, in greater or less degree, to his profession.[21]

---

[17] St Benedict's teaching on obedience is found in chaps. 5 and 71 of the Rule, though it recurs frequently in other contexts. Father David will have been familiar from his noviciate with the sober and careful statement of the common teaching on religious obedience, in Augustine Baker's *Holy Wisdom* I.ii.9., and II.ii.14. (ed. Gerard Sitwell, London, 1964).   [18] Knowles 1966, pp. 76–85.   [19] Knowles 1966, p. 83.
[20] Quoted Morey 1979, p. 142.   [21] *MO*, p. 693.

It is instructive to compare Father David's application of these principles to the Benedictines and to the Carthusians. From the beginning, he underlined that the Benedictine vocation is open to all:

> St Benedict nowhere suggests that he is legislating . . . for any uncommon type or temperament. His monks are ordinary men, and he will lead them in a way accessible to ordinary men.
> St Benedict intended the preceptive portions of the Rule to be . . . the minimum standard of an evangelical life, which could be demanded of all, but which proficients could transcend while yet fulfilling.[22]

Later, he was to express this judgement less gently: the Rule, 'while it is spiritually uncompromising',

> supposes an excellent abbot governing a very mediocre community, or, in spiritual terms a perfect abbot instructing a mixed group of many beginners and a few proficients.

Hence a besetting danger for Benedictines:

> St Benedict's humanity and gentleness . . . have often been degraded into something merely human and commonplace by leaving out of the reckoning the complete self-sacrifice without which they cannot be attained . . . St Benedict never confuses charity with mere good nature, filial respect and obedience with human affection, peace and order with comfort and ease, measure and discretion with faintheartedness and mediocrity.[23]

In contrast with the Benedictine way, open to all, with a moderation which can easily degenerate into mediocrity, we have the Carthusian way of life, absolute and unconditional in its demands, accessible not to 'ordinary men' but only to those possessed of 'a very rare combination of spiritual, psychological, and physical qualities'.[24] The expression 'âmes d'élite', linked especially with the Carthusians and with the Carmelite nuns, recurs often,[25] and it is difficult to resist the impression that Father David, who in a letter of 1972 declared himself to be in all areas 'an unrepentant élitist',[26] judged that his standards had been realised more consistently by the Carthusians, who had been an early though not a first

---

[22] Knowles 1929, p. 32; *MO*, p. 10.
[23] Knowles 1969, p. 34; Knowles 1966, p. 73; *MO*, p. 15.
[24] Knowles 1969, p. 199.
[25] For instance *MO*, pp. 224 and 379; *RO* III, p. 224.   [26] Morey 1979, p. 114.

love, than by the Benedictines, who seemed to him to have fallen away often from the 'spiritually uncompromising' demands of their Rule.

The final paragraph of *The Religious Orders*, III, must be quoted here, because, coming at the conclusion of what is in a sense his life's work, it is the most weighty statement of the principles by which, in the main part of the Epilogue, he had assessed six hundred years of monastic history; but it is also a statement of the principles by which he himself had striven to live:

> At the end of this long review of monastic history, with its splendours and its miseries, and with its rhythm of recurring rise and fall, a monk cannot but ask himself what message for himself and for his brethren the long story may carry. It is the old and simple one; only in fidelity to the Rule can a monk or a monastery find security. A Rule, given by a founder with an acknowledged fullness of spiritual wisdom, approved by the Church and tested by the experience of saints, is a safe path, and it is for the religious the only safe path. It comes to him not as a rigid, mechanical code of works, but as a sure guide to one who seeks God, and who seeks that he may indeed find. If he truly seeks and truly loves, the way will not be hard, but if he would love and find the unseen God he must pass beyond things seen and walk in faith and hope, leaving all human ways and means and trusting the Father to whom all things are possible. When once a religious house or a religious order ceases to direct its sons to the abandonment of all that is not God, and ceases to show them the rigours of the narrow way that leads to the imitation of Christ in His Love, it sinks to the level of a purely human institution, and whatever its works may be, they are the works of time and not of eternity. The true monk, in whatever century he is found, looks not to the changing ways around him or to his own mean condition, but to the unchanging everlasting God, and his trust is in the everlasting arms that hold him. Christ's words are true: He who doth not renounce all that he possesseth cannot be my disciple. His promise also is true: He that followeth me walketh not in darkness, but shall have the light of life.[27]

It would be easy to dismiss these words with a reference to the ambiguity of the monastic status of their writer, but surely no monk, and no abbot, can read them without searchings of heart. Yet it would be wise to

[27] *RO* III, p. 468.

44

complement them by the words of Cuthbert Butler: he too had a profound knowledge of monastic history, though he was less at home with its medieval phase than Father David, and indeed was unsympathetic to it. His characteristically expressed judgement is worth quoting here:

> I think monastic history written from the standpoint of reforms will be a picture out of perspective. At all times there has been some monastery, some congregation, some reformer, in the limelight, the salt of the earth: my knowledge of monastic history leads me to the belief that at all times there has been a background of old-fashioned houses in which a very respectable religious life, with good, if not showy, observance and real spiritual religion, was being lived in a quiet way outside of the reform-circle of the hour.[28]

I have said that the principles by which Father David assessed the past were the principles by which he strove to live. That is why it would be wrong to regard his writings on the theology of mysticism, from the articles written in 1931-4, to *The English Mystical Tradition* (1961), and to *What is Mysticism* (1967), as representing simply another department of his interests. On the contrary, these were the issues which were central in his mind and life, and which gave to them their pattern, as well as determining his judgements of the monastic past. *What is Mysticism* is a short, lucid and persuasive statement of his theology of the spiritual life, but it is cold and impersonal. In the *New Foreword* which he wrote to the third edition of *Western Mysticism* (1967), in an assessment of Abbot Butler which jars a little, he puts among the 'three essential qualifications' for writing upon mystical theology, which he judged Abbot Butler to have lacked, 'wide and intimate knowledge of the experience of others'. But from 1934 onwards, this is precisely what Father David himself lacked. He will no doubt have judged that the experience of guiding a 'perfect soul' in Elizabeth Kornerup outweighed in its depth a wider range of experience. Father David could have encouraged and guided many on the road of holiness and prayer. But the loss was in a sense his as well as ours. *What is Mysticism* was written many years after he had ceased to give and receive from others as he had once given and received in his own monastery, and in the retreats which he gave outside, as in his relations with the Good Shepherd nuns. There must have been

---

[28] Butler 1919, pp. 359-60.

in his spiritual life in those later years an element of loneliness which the sympathy of Dr Kornerup could have only partially relieved. And the problems which had loomed so large in the 1930s now interested only a few: *What is Mysticism* set out to answer questions which few were asking. For a monk who had shared the monastic life with him at Downside, there must always be about Father David's subsequent life an element of tragedy, human or spiritual or both: a break with a much-loved past, a parting of the ways, which his own sense of continuity of spiritual purpose could never bring into complete unity.

Father David had a rare gift of inspiring and influencing others. And his influence was always ultimately a spiritual one. This was felt by his pupils in the History Faculty: it was exercised there, not deliberately, but by the evident primacy of spiritual values in his own life, and by the recognition of them which he evoked by his teaching. His power to influence came partly from the attractiveness of his personality, the range of his perceptiveness and interests, his combination of deep seriousness with lightness of touch, with a puckish and boyish humour. Much of this comes out in the footnotes to *The Monastic Order* and *The Religious Orders*. On the purely spiritual level, his influence came from the fact that he never asked of others what he did not carry out in his own life; it came, too, from the fact that there was nothing forbidding or insensitive about his inner austerity: no one had deeper insight than he into the value of things which he left aside in order to pursue unhampered the one thing necessary.

His position after 1934 made virtually impossible his role as a spiritual guide of others, except through his writings. And the witness of his writings is still, for some, disqualified by the ambiguity of his own history. A pure historian may feel that his leaving the monastery was a *felix culpa* which has given us a distinguished historian, and leave it at that; a monk might be inclined, by the logic of his vocation, to judge simply that, in St Augustine's phrase, his achievements as a historian were *magni passus sed extra viam*, 'great strides, but aside from the right road', bought at too high a spiritual price. One who accepts that some psychological flaw or illness diminished responsibility for words and actions objectively indefensible, may still respect Father David's spiritual integrity and indeed his personal holiness, and regard the witness of his monastic and spiritual teaching as having an objective weight which can be assessed quite apart from the paradoxes of his personal monastic life. For my part, I can only express unashamedly the love and gratitude I feel towards him for all that he gave me in those few decisive years.

3

'THE MONASTIC ORDER IN ENGLAND'

CHRISTOPHER BROOKE

The register preserved in the Library at Downside records that on 20 May 1929 Father David borrowed the Surtees Society's 107th volume, which is the *Rites of Durham*, that nostalgic vision of the monastic round written after the Dissolution by a man who recalled the happy past. Sterner stuff was to follow: on 2 June, Domesday Book.

> When . . . I began to study English monastic history [Father David said in his lecture of 1962] the first task I set myself was to go through *Domesday Book* . . . copying out every entry relating to a monastic house, with Maitland and Vinogradoff as constant companions. I seemed to leave all subsequent history behind me and to sink into the England of the eleventh century with its ploughlands and meadows, woodland and waste, crofts and tofts, sheep and swine, mills and churches . . . For almost ten years I read little but contemporary documents – chronicles, charters, letters and lives. I can well remember the purely mental satisfaction of unravelling a complicated story, such as a disputed episcopal election, and finding that in some details at least the documents had yielded something new, and that the truth had been to that extent attained. I remember also the intellectual satisfaction of discovering for oneself the movements of institutions and ideas. The subject was a remote one, the exemption of certain religious houses from the jurisdiction of the bishop. The documents showed two completely different situations, separated sometimes by more than a century; the earlier group of charters were grants by Anglo-Saxon kings or the Conqueror of fiscal and other immunities, together with a prohibition addressed to all the bishops forbidding

their interference with the monks; the later group were papal bulls of the twelfth century, giving, with increasing definition and amplitude, exemption from episcopal jurisdiction and immediate subjection to the Apostolic See. Suddenly I saw a whole climate of ideas changing before my eyes. The purely secular, quasi-feudal protection of the king, standing wholly outside any Roman or canonical tradition, was suddenly replaced by the hand of the centralising Gregorian papacy and the machinery of canon law. The monks of Chertsey or Battle cared nothing for this; they were concerned solely in making sure of what the kings had given them. The popes, without a thought of the past, were concerned solely in defining the categories of their client churches. Yet one world had slipped into another; the *Eigenkloster* had become an abbey subject to the Apostolic See *nullo mediante* . . .[1]

The Monastic Order is commonly reckoned his masterpiece; beyond doubt it laid the foundations of his fame. It gave him a Litt.D. in 1941; it led to his Fellowship at Peterhouse in 1944 and to his Chairs. Only once did he produce a book comparable in scale and structure; and that is *The Religious Orders*, III. Between these two volumes there is a marked difference: *The Monastic Order* is more restrained in style, more elaborately structured; *The Religious Orders*, III tells a great and moving story with all the varied colours, now tragic now comic, of Tudor drama.

The structure of *The Monastic Order* is all the more striking since it was not sustained in *The Religious Orders*, I and II. They are not shapeless, but all his works depended on the sources he could use and these did not provide the framework or the unity he enjoyed in *The Monastic Order*. He set to work to tell in ample detail – both in narrative and in themes – the story of English monasticism in one of its golden eras, from the Conquest to the early thirteenth century. Since his formation had been literary and he deeply appreciated the best literature in his sources, one might have expected a book flowing with extravagant quotations from Eadmer and William of Malmesbury and Walter Daniel on St Ailred. They are there all right, but carefully restrained; they do not provide the structure for the book. As he set out on his Odyssey he prepared two remarkable tools for use in his travels: a catalogue of the religious houses of England and full lists of abbots and priors.[2] He was later to accuse

---

[1] Knowles 1962b, pp. 230–1. On the theme of chaps. 3–4, see also Stacpoole 1975 and below, pp. 103–9.　　[2] See above, pp. 18–19.

himself of being an amateur;[3] and there were some grounds for the charge – for his work was mostly done out of printed books and he first spent long hours in the Public Record Office when he came at long last to write *Religious Orders*, III.

Yet the approach to *The Monastic Order* was in the highest degree professional. That is to say, he saw from the outset the need to provide a complete framework for his study – and to work from original materials only. No doubt he exaggerated when he said that he read 'little but contemporary documents', for he also freely acknowledged the help and inspiration of other scholars; he even said that 'in no department of English history, perhaps, do students owe so much' to so many;[4] and it was his peculiarly vivid insight into other scholarly minds which seems to have enabled him to become, almost untaught in any obvious formal sense, one of the great scholars of his day. It is clear from his own account that the reviews of his *American Civil War* opened his eyes to the difference between the literary history in which he had been engaged and 'totalitarian' history as it must be if lasting scholarly work is to emerge. Doubtless he felt the need, as he embarked on monastic history in the cloister at Downside, of proving to the world that he was not another Gasquet. In the preface to *The Monastic Order* he acknowledges very particularly the help of a group of scholars, Joseph Armitage Robinson, Sir Maurice Powicke, R.R. Darlington and André Wilmart.[5] It is a very revealing list, but it does not help us to solve the fundamental problem: how did he come to the idea of rewriting in this comprehensive fashion English monastic history from the roots? Of the four, he had long known Armitage Robinson, Dean of Wells, personally – they may not often have met, but Armitage Robinson was well known as a personality at Downside.[6] His eager searching out of the by-ways of monastic history, and of the early history of Glastonbury in particular, provided Father David with a model of acute scholarly enquiry; but the ceaseless meandering of the Dean's accounts of the world of St Dunstan could provide no help in forming a coherent narrative – save a negative one.[7] Father David hints at the inconsequence

---

[3] See below, p. 108.   [4] *MO*, p. xx.   [5] *MO*, p. xx.

[6] Cf. Morey 1979, pp. 49–50, 118–19; the relevant books are Robinson 1919, 1921, 1923 (and cf. *MO*, p. 740). Morey (p. 118) emphasises the influence of Dom Lucius Graham who taught Father David in the School.

[7] In this region he was doubtless indebted to the work of Dom Thomas Symons, later titular abbot of Glastonbury, even though Symons 1941 and 1953 appeared too late to be directly useful for *MO* (see now also Symons 1962, 1975). The quotation on Armitage Robinson which follows is in *MO* (1940), p. 31n. (omitted in edn of 1963).

of some of the Dean's studies and the difficulty of using his work, while paying tribute to 'his clear mind and sober judgment'. It is very instructive to see the way in which the pages on Dunstan and his contemporaries bring order out of chaos.

It is surprising that he failed to pay tribute – as we must do – to his Downside mentors before he turned to Armitage Robinson; it is only too likely that his estrangement from Downside when he wrote the preface held him back. But if we ask, where did he learn that the true approach to monastic history is by the systematic study of materials and of texts? – The answer lies immediately to hand: from Dom Cuthbert Butler, the abbot who had received him at Downside, and whose memoir he wrote while *The Monastic Order* was in the making.[8]

Abbot Butler, wrote Father David,

> was . . . by inclination and capability a scholar; he moved more easily in the world of books and of ideas than of men and events; he enjoyed above all the society and conversation of scholars. He himself habitually wrote of the Venerable Bede and Mabillon as the 'type for all time' of the Benedictine student and scholar; he may be allowed to speak on in words which many would have applied to the writer [Abbot Butler] himself:
>
> 'Benedictine history has not produced many Bedes . . . who . . . "amidst the observance of regular discipline and the daily care of singing in the church, always took delight in learning, teaching and writing" . . . At no time have the general mass of Benedictines been learned. But they have tended to produce at all times individuals reincarnating the type of Ven. Bede. And when monks of this type do appear they are recognised as no chance product, no extraneous growth or grafting; but the natural fruits of certain elements of Benedictine life and the character and temper of mind it fosters.'

> The period of his early manhood at Downside was in many ways favourable to him. It is true that the level of teaching and achievement in the school could not for a moment bear comparison with the standards of contemporary public schools, and the ecclesiastical prohibition against Catholics attending the universities was still in force. But there was the presence of Edmund Bishop, who at that time was a stimulating and helping force of great power, and whose own tastes had led him along the lines of

[8] Reprinted in *HC*, pp. 264–362.

ecclesiastical and monastic history – indeed, in the latter field, and in that of liturgy, he probably had a sweep of accurate knowledge, based on a wide reading of the sources, unsurpassed by any contemporary Englishman . . . It was possible, under the inspiration of Bishop, for the most gifted of the young monks to suppose that the chief work of Downside for the Church in England – apart from the mission – might well be in the realm of letters, thus reviving some of the Maurist glories.[9]

The realisation of this dream was not without its ironies, for it was Dom Aidan Gasquet who first made a notable career in this field, and was indeed Edmund Bishop's closest associate among the community – in a strange alliance between Bishop, an immortal scholar, profound, refined and sensitive, and Gasquet, a student of monastic history who was no scholar at all, but gathered material with a pitchfork. If Gasquet inspired Father David in any degree, it was with a determination to be as little like him as possible. More positively, Gasquet had offered the world a complete list of English religious houses in the Middle Ages so useless for any critical purpose that it helped to determine Father David that he must make one for himself. More positively still, he inspired him to compose his hilarious Creighton lecture on 'Cardinal Gasquet as an historian'.[10] Meanwhile, Cuthbert Butler was a scholar much more after the pattern of Mabillon – or Father David himself; and there were others at Downside with him: Dom Leander Ramsay, who worked on an edition of Cyprian's works never completed, but in whose preparation Father David shared, learning the arts of patristic scholarship and textual criticism as he worked; and Dom Hugh Connolly, a scholar almost as learned and refined, though hardly so creative, as Bishop himself.[11]

Edmund Bishop was born in 1846, and became a Catholic in the 1860s.[12] He was never at university, and taught himself to be a scholar at a time when Oxford and Cambridge were alien to the Catholic community: the formal disabilities were only finally removed in 1871, and the Catholic hierarchy, led by that pillar of the Oxford Movement, Cardinal Manning, so strenuously disapproved of the ancient universities, that there was a long delay before a substantial Catholic presence could be felt there. Bishop indeed shared all Manning's prejudices

[9] *HC*, pp. 341–2, quoting Butler 1919, 1924, pp. 336–7.

[10] Reprinted in *HC*, pp. 240–63.

[11] See p. 11; for his memoir of Connolly, Knowles 1948.

[12] For what follows, see Abercrombie 1959, with foreword by David Knowles.

against Oxford, and it was largely due to his influence that Downside's Benet House came at last to be set up in Cambridge – and that Father David was bred a Cambridge man. Meanwhile, Bishop had established contacts with scholars in many European countries save his own; and he and his Downside disciples knew full well that the centre of medieval scholarship of their day – that is, of the last third of the nineteenth century – lay in Germany. But Bishop's scholarship was truly international, and, in Father David's words, 'he had been regarded as an equal by such men as Felix Liebermann, Léopold Delisle, Franz Ehrle, Armitage Robinson [his only close contact among Cambridge professors] and the two Mercati brothers'.[13] One of the finest portraits in *The Monastic Order* is that of Henry of Blois, the twelfth-century prince bishop of Winchester (1129–71);[14] and the geniality of the portrait, and many of its individual traits, can be traced back to a paper by Edmund Bishop first published in the *Downside Review* in 1884.[15] Thus the roots of Father David's scholarship may be discerned in an apostolic succession in which the Maurists of the seventeenth century – the founders of historical method as we know it in the age of the scientific revolution – and the leading medievalists of the nineteenth century in Germany, France and Italy played their part; but which owed very little to Oxford or Cambridge.[16]

Edmund Bishop remained throughout his life a bachelor, and even for a time tried his vocation as a postulant at Downside. But he remained a layman, often visiting the abbey; and he lives there now for ever in his library. He and Cuthbert Butler were perhaps the most important influences on Father David. Here is Father David's description of an encounter with Bishop:

> I well remember the only conversation of any length that I had with him, in August 1916, the last summer of his life, when I was nineteen and still technically 'in the novitiate' at Downside. He sent for me, ostensibly at least, because he had noticed that I had moved too rapidly about the sanctuary at some ceremony. He wished to tell me that all appearances of haste ruined the dignity of the occasion. He then went on to ask what I was reading in the summer vacation. I happened to be finishing Boswell's *Life of*

---

[13] Knowles, in Abercrombie 1959, p. xi.   [14] *MO*, pp. 286–93.

[15] Reprinted in Bishop 1918, pp. 392–401: 'Gifts of Bishop Henry of Blois, abbat of Glastonbury, to Winchester Cathedral'.

[16] For Father David on the Maurists, see *GHE*, pp. 33–62 and *HC*, pp. 213–39; cf. E. Bishop on their foundation in Bishop 1918, pp. 462–74.

Johnson for the first time, and he told me that as a child he had known an old lady who, when a girl, had 'knocked at Mrs Thrale's [must it not have been then Mrs Piozzi's?] door'. I mentioned Macaulay, and he told me to read Trevelyan's Life. I had recently been through 'In Memoriam'; he said that many years ago he had analysed the sequence of thought throughout the poem, 'and then,' he said, 'I came across a book [no doubt that of A.C. Bradley] in which the author had done the same thing, and we differed all the way through.' As he talked, one great name after another came up. He had seen Swinburne only once 'in a hansom cab – but there was no mistaking him. He made English musical, and you can't ask more than one thing of a man.' Matthew Arnold was blamed for beginning the downward curve (which I remember to have thought a strange one) that led through Walter Pater to Oscar Wilde. Kipling's name occurred, and he surprised me with the warmth of his admiration for the 1897 'Recessional'; *John Inglesant*, another old love of his, was commended to me – I fear, in vain, though the historical novel that won unbounded admiration from Lord Acton and Edmund Bishop was no ordinary book. That this chance conversation should have remained so clearly in the memory after more than forty years is perhaps a measure of the personality and distinction of mind – as also of the sympathetic approach to young people – of the man whose casual words bit so deep.[17]

It is a strange reflection that this formed the theme for the only prolonged conversation between two of the greatest of English medievalists; if they had studied literature alone they would now be forgotten. But Father David noted that Bishop's 'casual words bit so deep', and there is more of the grandeur and the marvellous detail of Bishop's *Liturgica Historica* in *The Monastic Order* than quite appears on the surface. Perhaps it is most clear in Father David's highly professional approach to the study of liturgy and church music – and in his portrait of

[17] Knowles in Abercrombie 1959, pp. xiv–xv. Morey 1979, p. 118, says that Bishop's influence 'came at second hand, from the scholarly tradition which he had done so much to encourage among an older generation in the Downside community, and from the specialist library which he had bequeathed to the Abbey'. Strictly this is true, save that it discounts the effect of a close reading of *Liturgica Historica*, one of the most exciting collections of scholarly studies in the English language – and other works besides. But in any case it puts Bishop at too great a remove from Father David: their meeting helped him in imagination to know Bishop much better than 'second hand' suggests.

Henry of Blois.[18] Father David always showed a certain indulgence to
this lordly Cluniac, in spite of his aversion to worldly monks and to
Cluniacs in particular. It is partly to be explained by Henry's later
support for Thomas Becket when most of the bishops shunned him. But
in this and all points his defence followed Bishop's article closely. I recall
a conversation between Father David and Sir Frank Stenton, in which
Stenton, with a twinkle in his eye, took him to task for this indulgence –
observing (as Father David did not attempt to deny) that it was 'a bit
much to burn down your episcopal city'. Most of all, Father David
inherited from Bishop the notion that a very precise use of language is
part of a scholar's equipment: there was little in common between their
styles, not much in common in their taste for literature; but they are both
scholars in whose works every medievalist should study and admire the
genius of the English language as a scholar's tool.

No doubt Father David was more aware of what he owed to
Cuthbert Butler. Much positively: for the idea of solid, systematic work
on the sources as the basis for sound and lasting work – and the deep
admiration of, and sense of kinship with, the Maurists – he owed to
Butler. The Maurists were doubly important; for as Father David's
monastic vocation developed in the late 1920s and early 1930s he
renounced the reading of imaginative literature; he rejected foreign
travel and blamed himself for his visit to Greece; he withdrew from
every human relaxation.[19] But he never renounced the study of history.
For this he had a mentor of unique authority in Jean Mabillon.[20]

The plain fact is that Downside in the early twentieth century was a
place more conducive to the scholarly study of monastic history than
any university town in Britain. It contained a galaxy of scholars and it
had and has (for this specific purpose) a marvellous library. As well as
Bishop, Butler, Ramsay and Connolly, there were several of Father
David's contemporaries who became notable scholars, including Dom
Thomas Symons, editor of the *Regularis Concordia* and a leading expert
on the tenth century, and Dom Adrian Morey, later a distinguished
exponent of the twelfth century – and author of *David Knowles, a
Memoir*.[21] But none of this quite explains the remarkably systematic way

[18] See above, n. 15. On liturgy, see *MO*, chap. xxxi.   [19] See pp. 10–11, 30, 119.
[20] His first article (Knowles 1919) was a reprint of one of Mabillon's crucial prefaces on
monastic studies.
[21] For Thomas Symons, see n. 7; for Adrian Morey's scholarly work, see esp. Morey
1938; Morey and Brooke 1965, 1967; Morey 1979.

in which Father David set about his task. He planned to begin at the Norman Conquest, and he set to work to copy out all the relevant extracts from Domesday Book. The results play a modest role in the finished book, but they are important: he had studied the figures quoted in a famous chapter by W.J. Corbett in *Cambridge Medieval History*, V, published in the very year in which he embarked on his work; and he laid out in an appendix to *The Monastic Order* the result of his own much more thorough study of the Domesday figures for monastic houses.[22] Thus he started with a concrete notion of the number, size and substance of the early Anglo-Norman monasteries. He also set out to make a list of English Religious Houses between 1066 and 1216. This was subsequently extended to the Dissolution, and published in the wake of *The Monastic Order* as *The Religious Houses of Medieval England*.[23] The list was a great improvement on Gasquet's − or on anything which could be culled from the *Monasticon Anglicanum* − though it naturally owed much to Dugdale and the *VCH*. But it had been composed as a working tool and was intended to be an aid to other scholars, not a definitive catalogue. Meanwhile Neville Hadcock had been preparing his own list in connection with his splendid work for the Ordnance Survey Maps of Monastic Britain, and was irritated to find the footprints of Man Friday. Father David responded to his rather severe criticism by suggesting collaboration;[24] and out of this approach came a long friendship − for Neville Hadcock was a generous man and quickly won − and the two editions of Knowles and Hadcock, which have totally altered our knowledge of the whole range of medieval houses, have been admirably imitated for Scotland and Ireland, and are the envy of our continental colleagues.

Father David had also, in the course of composing *The Monastic Order*, prepared the black notebooks containing lists of abbots and priors, based on original sources, not on the *Monasticon* nor on the early volumes of the *VCH*. Once again, they comprised simply a working tool, needing fundamental reshaping by Vera London and myself before they issued in *Heads of Religious Houses*, I (1972), above all, because, they began only in 1066.[25]

This underlines the original intention, to span the years 1066–1216. But as he worked he realised the need for a prologue describing the

---

[22] *MO*, pp. 702–3.   [23] Knowles 1940; Knowles and Hadcock 1953, 1971.
[24] The criticism began in a review in *The Tablet*.
[25] Unlike *Heads*, which begins in 940.

inheritance of Anglo-Saxon monasticism. And this no doubt explains his reference in his preface to Joseph Armitage Robinson, Dean of Wells. For the Dean had illuminated, in a fitful but learned manner, 'the dark places of the tenth century'.[26] To him, Father David owed in particular the perception that the tenth-century monastic reformation marked an entirely new beginning, and thus the arrival of Dunstan in Glastonbury about 943 – or, as was subsequently proved, in 940 – made a perfect opening for his book.[27] Doubtless the Dean and Father David exaggerated the break; and there has been much sniping, and much serious discussion of the origins and nature of tenth-century monasticism since 1940.[28] Meanwhile, the book was greatly enriched by two prologues, the first on St Benedict, the second on the tenth century. For the last phase of the Old English Church Father David spoke of his debt to R.R. Darlington, who, by editing the life of St Wulfstan, and by reconstructing in remarkable detail the career in church and state of Æthelwig abbot of Evesham, revealed how much can be known of the English monastic world on the eve of the Norman settlement.[29] He also acknowledged the influence of Dom André Wilmart, 'ce Mauriste de nos jours', the natural successor to Edmund Bishop, 'whose vast erudition, borne so lightly and displayed so gracefully, alternately stimulates and shames those who profit by its achievements'.[30] In Wilmart he especially admired that mixture of delicacy, refinement and precision which enabled him to place securely in their context of time and place many notable prayers and poems and works of spirituality. He found in Wilmart the kind of sensibility which he was peculiarly fitted by nature to grasp and to make his own. This influence fructifies many passages on monastic spirituality and literature, though the only reference to Wilmart in the text, and so in the index, is appropriately to his attribution of 'the beautiful and solemn prayers in preparation for Mass, familiar throughout the Church for many centuries owing to their inclusion in the Roman Missal, where they pass under the name of St Ambrose' to Abbot John of Fécamp.[31] This was one of Wilmart's most remarkable *tours de force*, and it enabled Father David to set the tone of Norman monasticism which grew under the inspiration of St William of Volpiano and Dijon, Abbot John's master, as never before or since.[32]

[26] *MO*, p. xx. [27] See *MO*, p. xvi.
[28] See esp. papers of Eric John listed in *MO* (edn of 1963), p. 747; Parsons 1975.
[29] Darlington 1928, 1933. [30] *MO*, p. xx.
[31] *MO*, p. 86, citing Wilmart 1932, pp. 101–25.
[32] *MO*, pp. 84–8; the fullest account is now Bulst 1973; cf. France 1989.

The main body of the book describes the history of English monasticism in the twelfth century. The whole is underpinned by a unique knowledge of the sources and the monks – one cannot pretend that the nuns have their share of attention, and the canons, originally represented by St Gilbert, hardly impinge on the book as finally published.[33] It combines to a remarkable degree a powerful grasp of every detail of monastic history with imaginative and spiritual insight rarely brought to the historian's task. The black notebooks performed something of the role in *The Monastic Order* that similar lists, of kings and bishops, arduously gathered, had played in the *Ecclesiastical History* of Bede.[34] In both cases a wonderful capacity for converting often unpromising materials into a flowing and coherent story has hidden the structure from the eyes of a casual reader.

The Monastic Order is a work of literature. Father David had first approached history through literature, and retained to the end of his life a special admiration for great narrative history. In this he had been inspired above all by Thucydides and Macaulay – and his lecture on Macaulay was one of the most characteristic products of his later life.[35] Narrative history, in the grand manner, has been out of fashion with the leading masters of our profession since the passing of G.M. Trevelyan, and there is a strange irony that the finest expressions of it in this century composed by men with the letters patent of a regius professor in their knapsacks should include the military epic by Trevelyan on Garibaldi and an account of the progress of *The Monastic Order in England*. The irony was fully revealed when Father David was elected to the Regius Chair which Trevelyan had formerly adorned. G.M. Trevelyan was a Victorian liberal in every sense of the term, and a devout agnostic who in early life had shared the passionate anti-clericalism of his Italian secular friends. When the Faculty of History at Cambridge gave him a dinner to celebrate his eightieth birthday he gave us some account of the men who had succeeded him – and Father David himself used later to recount his anxiety when his own turn approached. 'David Knowles comes from another tradition' – yet the old man gave us a warm encomium of one in whom he had found surprising common ground – in their romanticism and their devotion to Macaulay, and to the notion of history as literature. Their common interests are well represented in the copy of the first volume of *William Wordsworth: a Biography*, by Trevelyan's

---

[33] See below, pp. 137–8.
[34] See Wallace-Hadrill 1988, *passim*; Kirby 1965–6.   [35] Knowles 1960.

daughter, Mary Moorman, which is in my possession: a gift to 'David Knowles, with much gratitude, from G.M. Trevelyan, Feb. 1957'.

Perhaps the deepest quality revealed in *The Monastic Order* – a quality found in all his best work – is a deep intuitive understanding of how other scholars' minds worked. It is this, coupled with his determination to be objective, which help most to explain the maturity and shrewdness of his judgements. The matching of scholarly minds is especially apparent in his acknowledgement to 'Professor F.M. Powicke, who has made Ailred of Rievaulx and his contemporaries live and move again before our eyes'.[36]

It is extremely instructive to compare the earlier version of Powicke's study of the Life of Ailred (1922) – first with Father David's pages on the St Bernard of the North in *The Monastic Order* (1940), then with Powicke's mature version in his edition of 1950.[37] It could be thought that Powicke's *Ailred* will prove the most lasting of his works; and I am not the only lover of *The Monastic Order* who, if urged to point to his favourite passage, would choose the chapters on the early Cistercians, and most specifically the pages on Ailred.[38]

> Ailred's biographer, in a vivid phrase, describes the crowded church on feast days, when the majority of the *conversi* would be back from the granges, as packed with monks as closely as a hive with bees; so close that they cannot stir, and resembling crowded choirs of angels as pictured by devout fancy. The coming of such large numbers to Rievaulx was not merely the response of the north to the call of Cîteaux, still less was it due to a good-natured *laissez-faire* on the part of the abbot; it was Ailred's explicit desire and invitation. He never tired of repeating that the supreme and singular glory of Rievaulx was that it had learnt, beyond all other houses, to bear with the weak and to have compassion on those in need:
>
> 'All (he said), strong and weak alike, should find in Rievaulx a haven of peace, a spacious and calm home . . . of it should be said: Thither the tribes go up, the tribes of the Lord, unto the testimony of Israel, to give thanks unto the name of the Lord. Yea, the tribes

[36] *MO*, p. xx.   [37] Cf. Powicke 1922, 1950.
[38] *MO*, pp. 257–66; what follows is from pp. 258–62, citing Walter Daniel, now in Powicke 1950, pp. 36–8; and Ailred's *De spiritali amicitia*, PL 195, 672, 691–2, 698–702 [now in *Opera Omnia* I, ed. A. Hoste and C.H. Talbot (Turnhout, 1971), pp. 305, 335–6, 345–50].

of the strong and of the weak. For that cannot be called a house of religion which spurns the weak, since: Thine eyes have seen mine imperfection and in thy book are all written.'

And so there flocked to Ailred men of every type from near and far:

'Was there ever (asks Walter Daniel) anyone weak in body or character expelled from that house unless his evil ways gave offence to the whole community or ruined his own hope of salvation? Hence there came to Rievaulx from foreign nations and distant lands a stream of monks who needed brotherly mercy and true compassion, and there they found the peace and sanctity without which no man can see God. Yea, those who were restless in the world and to whom no religious house gave entry, coming to Rievaulx the mother of mercy and finding the gates wide open, freely entered therein.'

Clearly for Ailred the Cistercian way of life was no garden enclosed, in which only rare and pure souls could find green pasture, but rather something in its way as catholic as the Church, a home for souls of every kind who should find each the help most suited to him. And it must not be forgotten that three out of every four who came were simple, unlettered, stolid labourers, come to swell the ranks of an army of *conversi*. The dangers accompanying such a policy as Ailred's are obvious, and must have been so to his own clear mind. But the influence of such a man as he was can scarcely be over-estimated, and all the evidence that exists points to the maintenance at Rievaulx of a sustained fervour for many decades after his death. Ailred's condescension was not weakness or compromise; the strict rule of Cîteaux was honoured, and the latter years of the abbot's life, when his physical suffering was all but unceasing, must have made it abundantly clear that the way of mercy was not the way of delicate living.

More than two-thirds of the family of Rievaulx were made up of the *conversi*, and it is certain that of the choir monks many, no doubt the majority, were men of no refinement or intellectual gifts. Yet all the sources reveal the existence, alike at Rievaulx and the other houses of Ailred's family, of a numerous class of monks who had passed through the new humanist discipline of the schools and retained, even within the framework of the Cistercian life of labour, silence and simplicity, a warm eagerness of mind and heart which few who visit the ruins of Rievaulx would associate with its walls. It was with these that Ailred's relations were at once most characteristic and most individual. Hard though it be to fill in the details of the picture, the main outlines are given us, clear beyond the possibility of misconception, by Gilbert of Holland, Walter Daniel and Ailred himself. We see him, the Cistercian abbot, the centre of a group of listeners and interlocutors, engaged in one of those discussions, half Platonic, half scholastic in character, which in one form or another absorbed for more than two centuries the interests and energies of many in Western Europe. With Ailred, especially in his later years, the aim was primarily spiritual, not intellectual, but the young monks who surrounded him had, like himself, steeped themselves in Cicero and followed the young Augustine; they had even given themselves to a newer spirit, that of the Arthurian romance; they had much to learn and to leave before they could follow Ailred with the fourth gospel to the Cross. We can watch him treating with one such, the young monk Gratian, to whom two of the three dialogues *De Spirituali Amicitia* are principally addressed, and who is introduced to us in words put by Ailred in the mouth of no other than Walter Daniel as:

'One whom I might fitly call friendship's child; for his whole occupation is to love and to be loved.'

Ailred had learnt much since the days at [King] David's court. He now defines friendship with his eyes upon the later chapters of St John's gospel: All things which I have heard of my Father, I make known unto you; and: You are my friends if you do what I command you.

'"By these words (he continues), as St Ambrose says, he gave us a way of friendship to follow, that we should do the will of our friend, that we should lay bare the secrets of our hearts to our friend, and know his in return . . . A friend hides nothing. If he be a true friend, he pours out his soul, as the Lord Jesus poured forth the mysteries of the Father." Thus Ambrose. But how many do we not love, to whom it is unwise to open our soul and pour forth all that is within! Either their age or their understanding is unable to bear it.'

To this Walter Daniel replies:

'This friendship is so sublime and perfect that I dare not aspire to it. Gratian here and I are content with that described by your favourite Augustine [*Confessions* iv. 4, 7, 5] – to talk together, to laugh together, to do each other services, to read together, to study together, to share things trifling and serious; sometimes to disagree, but without passion, as a man may do with himself, and by such disagreement to season the numberless judgements which we share together; to teach and learn the one from the other, to feel the want of our friends when absent, and welcome their coming with joy. Such signs of heartfelt affection as these, translating themselves upon the countenance, or in the speech and eyes of those who love each other, and in a thousand affectionate gestures, are like tinder to set hearts on fire, and to make of many one mind and heart [cf. Acts 4:32]. This it is that we think to be lovable in our friends, so that our conscience seems guilty, if we do not return another's love, whether he or we first gave it.'

To which Ailred:

'This is the friendship of the flesh and above all of the young, as were once the writer of these words and the friend of whom he spoke. Yet, saving trifles and deceits, if nothing evil enters in, it may be tolerated in hopes of more abundant grace to come, and as the foundation of a more holy friendship. As one grows in the religious life, and in spiritual discipline, together with the gravity of maturer years and the enlightenment of spiritual understanding, such friendships pass easily into higher regions, as the affections become purified. For we said yesterday that it was easy to pass from man's friendship to God's, by reason of the resemblance between them.'

This passage has been quoted at length, as showing Ailred at his most characteristic. In its outspoken humanism and serene optimism it recalls the atmosphere of the Academy or of Tusculum, and indeed the two chief treatises of Ailred are documents not yet perhaps sufficiently familiar to historians of the culture and religious sentiment of the times . . .

Father David went on to quote Ailred's account of two of his closest friendships, which comes to this conclusion:

'Thus rising from that holy love which reaches the friend to that which reaches Christ, he will joyfully pluck the rich spiritual fruit of friendship . . . and this friendship, to which few are admitted, will be poured out upon all and returned by all to God, when God shall be all in all.'

The writer of these lines was not a philosopher, writing at ease on his terrace, untroubled by the hard realities of life, nor even an Augustine among his pupils in peaceful, sunny Cassiciacum, but an infirm, tireless abbot, the ruler of a vast household, the counsellor of bishops and kings, who snatched time, between his solitary prayer and the visits of those who needed his help, to add a few sentences to the roll in his bare and comfortless cell . . .

The Monastic Order has all the marks of immortality upon it. But, large as it is, it is not complete. Father David wrote chapters on monastic building and on St Gilbert of Sempringham, both of which were omitted. The Syndics of the Cambridge University Press, acting on the advice of Professor A. Hamilton Thompson, recognised the value of the book but blenched at the cost. They insisted that part of the expense of publication be borne by the author; as he was nearly destitute at the time this might have prevented the enterprise altogether, save for the generous intervention of his father. It appeared in the year of doom 1940, and few readers were expected: 500 copies were printed and the type was allowed to disperse.[39] It was rapidly reassembled – again at his father's cost – and it has sold steadily ever since, although it was many years before the author's royalties overtook the original mulct.

The Press also insisted on the omission of the two chapters and more. 'Monastic buildings' later found a home in *The Historian and Character*;[40] the chapter on St Gilbert has never been published until now: we have included it as Appendix I below (pp. 141–55). It may readily be confessed that it would have sat uneasily in a book in which canons and nuns are virtually ignored, since Gilbert founded an order which combined the two. It seems evident that Father David had taken the trouble to study the canonisation dossier in its manuscripts – some years before Raymonde Foreville began its full publication[41] – and wished to give a place to a document for the religious life of exceptional value.

Yet even if the book had been complete as originally planned, there are notable omissions. Why should the nuns have so little place in the book, and the canons none at all? Father David had written a book about monks. But when he turned to the future these questions became ever

---

[39] This is based on personal information: some of the correspondence preserved in Cambridge University Press archives, now in Cambridge University Library, has been used in McKitterick 1984, p. 154.

[40] Chap. 9 is the revised version of it intended for *RO* III.

[41] Partially in Foreville 1943, fully in Foreville and Keir 1987.

more insistent. Not till the Bridgettines did the nuns enter much into his scheme, but the canons have a modest place in the later volumes, and the friars are of its essence. Hence the later volumes are *The Religious Orders in England*, I–III.

Meanwhile *The Monastic Order* was the work of a monk, writing from a monastic viewpoint, inward looking, little concerned with the relations of the monastic communities and their patrons. To him a monastic church was a place where monks worshipped, and he never gathered or seriously meditated on the evidence for the lay use of monastic naves for worship. To monastic involvement in pastoral work he was naturally unsympathetic, and has seemed to many who know the eleventh century in particular to underestimate the evidence and significance of the monastic 'mission' in that age.[42] His reserve towards Cluny was mainly due to his powerful sense of the inspiration of St Bernard and Cîteaux; but it perhaps owed something too to his acceptance from early youth of Abbot Butler's view of autonomy as of the essence of Benedictine monachism.[43] Yet it would be a mistake to read too much of the influence of his own circumstances into the rare lapses into prejudice or subjectivity in his major works. No one can fail to be influenced by his own experience; and contrariwise few can read *The Monastic Order* without being impressed by his steady, firm judgement. Integrity lay at the heart of his scholarship. He was never a man to be blown by every wind, and in later years he showed many signs of intellectual conservatism; yet there are few more impressive *retractations* in medieval scholarship than those implicit in his Birkbeck Lectures on the *Rule* of St Benedict and its relation to the *Regula Magistri*, and on the early Cistercian documents.[44] To a devout monk who never relinquished his deep faith in the *Rule* of St Benedict it must have seemed at first peculiarly perverse to suggest that Benedict had simply copied large sections of his *Rule* from the rambling *Regula*

---

[42] The central evidence lies in the controversies on tithes: the sources which show that it was widely assumed that monks did or should or could engage in pastoral work – whatever precisely that meant – are very fully discussed in Constable 1964, esp. pp. 165–85; for other literature Brooke and Swaan 1974, p. 253, n. 10 to chap. 6, including the note of caution in Chibnall 1967; for England, see also Kemp 1980.

[43] Cf. his own note on the reserve with which Benedict of Aniane had been treated (*MO*, p. 27n.).

[44] Knowles *GHE*, pp. 135–95 ('The *Regula Magistri* and the *Rule* of St Benedict') and 197–222 ('The primitive Cistercian documents'). On the *Regula Magistri* see now Dunn 1990.

Magistri. Yet in his Birkbeck Lectures, Father David with wit and candour accepts the virtual *bouleversement* of the fundamental assumption of Benedict's originality. Similarly, the assumption of the authenticity of the known texts of early Cîteaux – and especially of the *Carta Caritatis* – lay near the heart of his vision of the Cistercian reform; and although his acceptance of the notable revisions coming to light in the 1940s and 50s was – with good reason[45] – full of safeguards and nuances, he wholeheartedly accepted that the landscape had altered. In the addenda to the *The Monastic Order* published in 1963 he quoted the 1951 edition of a standard work on Cistercian history: 'Few religious orders possess a history of their origins as clear and simple as the Cistercian Order.'[46] To which Father David commented drily: 'Today those words can serve only as a warning to historians that their general judgements, even when apparently based upon solid rock, may be washed away overnight.'[47] It is interesting to observe how like and unlike have been two of the immortal Benedictine scholars who have adorned our world, Father David and Dom Jean Leclercq. Father David, by nature cautious and conservative, but with a mind open to serious conviction when the weight of the evidence bore in upon him; Dom Jean, serenely open to every new idea; both possessed of a shrewdness of judgement which often brought them close together in the end. I recall Father David describing with a wry smile a meeting with Dom Jean in which his visitor had tried to convince him that St Benedict never existed. Years later, in a gathering of Benedictine abbots, Dom Jean said to me that he had changed his mind – had undergone a kind of conversion: he now believed that St Benedict existed – though we cannot prove it. Yet both were deeply devout disciples of Benedict and his *Rule*.

In my early twenties I presumed to castigate some points in Father David's Ford Lectures. He wrote to me from Peterhouse (the letter is dated 21 November 1949, 'written during College Audit Meeting'), 'There is nothing I value more than your criticism, because it helps me to learn.' I quote this, not in vanity – for the sentiment, though sincerely and affectionately meant, is absurd – but because it shows his deep and genuine humility as a scholar.

[45] Since some of the writing he was analysing represented extreme positions, and on a number of points agreement has not yet been reached. On the early legislation, see the admirable interim report by C. Holdsworth in Norton and Park 1986, pp. 40–55.
[46] Quoted in French in *MO* (1963), p. 752 from Mahn 1951, p. 41.
[47] *MO*, p. 752.

Yet the power of *The Monastic Order* owed much to his involvement in the story. If there is an austere restraint in many passages, and a general absence of the humour which gives an edge to many pages of *The Religious Orders*, III, yet there are moments when his literary flair is given full rein. I have quoted his evocation of St Ailred, and there are many similar passages in the chapters on the Cistercians. At the outset, in the chapter on 'The new model of Cîteaux', the marks of Cîteaux are listed almost in note form; the account is formal and strictly economical. But on St Bernard's entry the author changed to a new key, and in the section on 'The Cistercian vocation' there is a fervour and inspiration which has carried many a reader in imagination inexorably into the Cistercian fold. At the end of the book comes a note of sombre warning, that the historian may judge the external works of the monks by their contribution to contemporary life, but

> the inward, spiritual, individual achievement of their lives . . . by the abiding standards of Christian perfection . . . He must . . . resist with all his power the siren voice of romanticism. Few indeed who have written with sympathy of the monks of medieval England have wholly escaped the spells of that old enchantress, who has known so well how by her magic of word and brush to scatter the golden mist of the unreal over the generations of the past . . . By the prescriptions of [the Rule of St Benedict], understood not indeed with antiquarian literalness, but in full spiritual strength, must the monasticism of every age be judged.[48]

In his warning against romanticism he speaks with the fervour of the convert, for there was a deep romantic streak in his nature, and he first knew medieval monastic life through its most romantic ruins. But the stern call to obey the Rule lies at the heart of the whole project, and explains why many a reader has felt – for all the balance of the picture, for all the charity that he brings to so many erring monks and human errors – that his judgement, at heart, was sterner than Coulton's.

[48] *MO*, pp. 692–3.

4

'THE RELIGIOUS ORDERS IN ENGLAND'

CHRISTOPHER BROOKE

It was already indicated in the preface to *The Monastic Order* that a sequel was planned to carry the story to the Dissolution. Like many great projects, it grew as it developed, both in scale and scope. The next volume was simply entitled *The Religious Orders in England*, and nearly half of it allows the intrusion of the Friars into a scheme originally monastic in the narrow, English sense of the word. A discreet star on the cover again indicated that a sequel would follow, though author and publisher refused to tempt providence by displaying it on the title-page; the next two items in the great work were called volumes II and III. But he saw them himself, and every attentive reader has seen them, as the conclusion of four consecutive volumes.

The entry of the Friars, and in their wake a major study of scholastic thought in England, still did not render the work as comprehensive as its title. The canons were only represented by the Augustinian Order: save for a brief summary, St Gilbert had been banished by the publisher from *The Monastic Order*, and the Premonstratensians had effectively to wait for volume III. The Military Orders never aroused his interest, and the orders of women are only slightly represented anywhere in the scheme. To the encouragement and advice of Eileen Power he owed some of his understanding of economic history; and she had lived long enough to write one of the first reviews of *The Monastic Order*. The excellence of her early book *Medieval English Nunneries*[1] may have made him less inclined to intrude among them. In any case whatever omissions may be

---

[1] Cambridge, 1922. For a new study of religious women in medieval England see Thompson 1991.

found, few will regret that he was selective, for it made possible the ample nature of his text, and its completion during the years of his full power.

Many readers have noticed the changes of plan in successive volumes.[2] First of all, *Religious Orders*, I and II contain no flowing narrative such as provides the core of *The Monastic Order*. This is in part due to the nature of the sources: the basic evidence for *The Monastic Order* lies in monastic narratives and lives and literature which, with all its ups and downs, can command the lively and continuous interest of a historian looking for excellence. Further, he never carried on the notebooks of monastic *Fasti* which provided the other foundation for his studies down to 1216. This may have been partly the effect of time and of other concerns and preoccupations; but it was also due to a sense that it could not bear fruit for his own work in the same degree. The twelfth-century *Fasti* contained many names which live and move in his narrative; relatively speaking, later volumes of *Heads* will contain more who are ciphers.[3]

The monastic chapters at the outset of *Religious Orders*, I, take shape round major sources – Pantin's Benedictine Chapters and Salter's Augustinian at the start,[4] the visitation records at the end – and substantial themes. Some readers have been surprised by the large part economics and administration play in these themes; and no doubt his moving tribute in the preface to a young friend recently dead when it was published, R.A.L. Smith, helps to explain this. 'Without his handful of papers and his enthusiastic companionship the chapters on those subjects could never have been written.'[5] Nor could any historian working in Cambridge and Peterhouse in the 1940s or 1950s fail to feel the inspiration and importance of M.M. Postan's work. Perhaps there was also in his mind a feeling, not only that these topics were strongly represented in the surviving sources, but that the interior life of the monasteries in these centuries was largely humdrum and ordinary, scarcely penetrable, indeed, and so not his chosen theme. In 1953 I

[2] See especially the penetrating reviews by R.W. Southern of *RO* II and III, in *Journal of Theological Studies*, New Series, VIII (1957), 190–4; XIII (1962), 469–75.

[3] *Heads* II, *1216–1377*, ed. V.C.M. London and D.M. Smith, is nearing completion; David Smith will carry it on to the Dissolution. David Knowles was not able to use the fundamental prosopographical studies of A.B. Emden; nor Dr Moorman's still unpublished dictionary of British Franciscans. The substantial nucleus in Moorman 1952 was already available to him when *RO* II and III were published.

[4] Pantin 1931–7; Salter 1922. [5] P. xiii; cf. his memoir in R.A.L. Smith 1947.

submitted to him a draft introduction to an account book of a fifteenth-century almoner[6] in which I tried some general reflections on the life of a fifteenth-century monk. In his letter to me on the draft, he commented on the difficulty: first 'all that remains is, as you say, "getting and spending". But was this all the almoner's real life? Giving lectures and writing books is, I hope, not all my real life . . . And . . . how bad (or good) were these places? There is the standing difficulty of the two standards, the two planes – are we to judge, so to say, with our eyes on the Last Supper and the Crucifixion, or looking simply for standards that would be passable for a hospital or a regiment?' The letter itself was written on two planes. On the one hand it was dated (approximately) on the eighth centenary of St Bernard's death,[7] and the monk's true function was more than ever in his mind; on the other he was delivering a mild and kindly rebuke to me for passing judgement on monastic success where the sources did not permit any fair judgement. I suppressed the passage and learned from him the lesson he was by some critics supposed not to have mastered himself. Yet it is true that there are great gaps in volumes I and II, and it is to be regretted that he did not make more use of liturgies and custumals and monastic remains to reveal the normal round of monastic life in the late Middle Ages.

In the chapters on the Friars he set the English material firmly in the context of a great continental movement, as he had done so often in the earlier book. It is an admirable introduction to the history of the friars in general. It is not impeccable. His Francis touches as many of the deepest and subtlest chords as any account in English; yet the chapter is a little too slight, and here and elsewhere he was not able to take full note of work in progress which he had himself inspired;[8] thus too the section on Matthew Paris later in the book would have gained much from Richard Vaughan's work carried out under his direction in the fifties.[9] His Dominic, it must be admitted, has little of the quality of his Francis. For once, his reading in the sources let him down: he seems to have relied wholly on the anodyne narrative of the origins of the Order by Jordan of Saxony, which reveals (deliberately as I would think) little of the personality of the saint, and to have ignored the canonisation process

---

[6] *The Book of William Morton . . .*, ed. W.T. Mellows, P.I. King and C.N.L. Brooke (Northants. Rec. Soc., 1954). [7] 'In festo S. Bernardi 1953', i.e. 20 Aug.

[8] E.g. my wife's work on Brother Elias, later published in his own series, R.B. Brooke 1959.

[9] Vaughan, 1958. For what follows see Brooke 1971, ch. 11; Tugwell 1981.

which shows a much more impulsive, complex and interesting human character. Perhaps the most original sections of the book are those on the friars in the universities. Above all he put scholasticism on the map as an academic discipline for historians in this country, and put England on the map in a world which had been mainly German and French territory.

Even more than its predecessor, volume II, 'The End of the Middle Ages' (1955), is a collection of essays. The lack of a clear framework and sense of direction have been sufficiently remarked by his reviewers; and it is easy to forget that some of the finest of his essays are here. The sheaves of monastic portraits include unforgettable studies of Thomas de la Mare, William Clown – in whom he rashly saw a possible model for Chaucer's monk, and who seems indeed to have ruled canons and hounds with equal tact and skill – John Whethamstede, and the mirror of monastic life in Margery Kempe's Book. On the spiritual life of the fourteenth and fifteenth centuries he gave admirable distillations of his work on the mystics, and much more. His chapter on Fitzralph, Wyclif, Langland and Chaucer, as critics of the religious, is justly famous both for the brilliance of his Wyclif and the delightful insight of his Langland.

> Of a truth he had a kind of nostalgia for the cloister, or for a golden phantasm of the cloister that had never wholly faded from his imagination . . . But these traits, while they soften the picture the poet paints, render his stern judgement on the religious and especially on the friars all the more impressive. They were to him corrupting what had been of the best; they had taken Love out of the cloister:

> For there that Loue is leder. ne lacked neuere grace.[10]

In volume III we are presented once again with a great story greatly told. As literature, it is perhaps the finest of his books; and though errors may be found both in the minutiae and in his broader understanding of the Tudor world, it is hardly likely that an account of the Dissolution deeper, fairer or more moving will see the light for many a decade. It is also of great importance to the understanding of how history can be written; for there is no error more common than to suppose that style is unimportant to scholarship. Medievalists have long recognised that the influence and effect of F.W. Maitland's writings were greatly enhanced by the lucidity and wit of a distinguished master of style; and we have

[10] P. 111.

observed the significance of correct and appropriate English in making
Edmund Bishop's best essays immortal. Here, it is not the effect of
language only, but of the structure of the book. It opens by setting the
scene in the fifty years or so before the Dissolution; positive signs of
monastic activity, in music and the chant for instance, and new
movements such as that of the Franciscan Observants, have their part, as
well as intimations of mediocrity or decay. There are some more
monastic personalities, and the splendid full-length portrait of that early
Tudor squire, Prior More of Worcester. The author of the *Rites of Durham*,
looking back in sorrow from Elizabeth's reign, is allowed his say.

William More, prior of Worcester from 1518 to 1536 – that is, to the
eve of the Dissolution – plays a very significant role. His account book is
a rare and illuminating source: some of the chapter is taken up with
careful appraisal of what one can and cannot learn from such a book and
its relation to other accounting evidence. The picture of More's life is
built up with a host of minor details from the accounts – including
payments for church ales and amateur theatricals, carol singers and
modest exceedings of every kind. The portrait which emerges is of a
substantial country squire with very little of a religious character about
him – though Father David frequently warns us that account books hide
as much as they reveal. Especially significant are the prior's services to his
family: in 1519 he rebuilt one of his manor houses, at Grimley, as a
retirement home for his father, Richard Peers, though the old man 'did
not live to see the house-warming. He must in any case have been well
stricken in years and he died suddenly towards the end of February 1520.
When he was buried on the 20th at Grimley the little place could seldom
have seen a costlier funeral [a characteristic echo of one of Tennyson's
least felicitous lines]: what with candles and Masses and breakfast for the
monks at Worcester and sundry other provisions the obsequies brought
a bill of more than £9. This, however, was exceeded when Mrs Peers
died.'[11] By such deft strokes, and by a combination of a great pile of
fascinating detail and a scatter of literary allusions – 'we might think
ourselves to be in Justice Shallow's orchard or by the table dormant in
the hall of Chaucer's Franklin'[12] – he built up an immortal portrait of a
bucolic Tudor squire. He is studiously fair – he allows the evidence to
speak for itself without venturing a judgement beyond what the
evidence will bear as to how worldly More truly was or how widespread
his kind of worldliness may have been. We are given a deep insight into

[11] *RO* III, 118.   [12] *RO* III, 119.

one type of monastic character before the Dissolution. 'His life, though it may have had little of the monastic in it, was morally blameless . . . In all respects he was the child of his age. When the moment came, he and his community duly subscribed to the Oath of Succession and to the series of declarations repudiating the pope. He followed, in fact, both for good and for evil, the way of the world.'[13] It is most soberly performed: we are almost lulled into forgetting that it was not the life monks had been called to follow – nor that the various subscriptions of the 1530s could be viewed as the ultimate betrayal. Father David deploys a great range of scholarly and literary techniques, but little rhetoric save that of understatement.

From Prior More he passes presently to Erasmus, handling him with a rare subtlety and edge and insight. Father David was not a deeply learned Erasmian, but he had a great deal more of the intellectual and spiritual armoury of the great humanist than most of his modern interpreters. Then the storm gathers. By the time it breaks the whole stage has been set, without hurry or fuss, but also without longueurs; we feel ourselves at home in the England of the early 1530s. A severe judgement on a great number of religious has been passed – but with great restraint – for failing to resist the breach with Rome. All that is explicitly said is put in another's mouth: 'In the words of More's trenchant apologue, they were first deflowered that they might afterwards be devoured.'[14]

The effect of this restraint, coupled with the implication of doom, is to make the cautious, searching, charitable appraisal of the evidence of the notorious *comperta* of the Visitors far more telling. Similarly with the king and his minister. If Henry and Cromwell had been treated at length as was Prior More, it would have been impossible to avoid the sense that the author was a partisan; for it is hard for anyone of strong sensibility to ponder Henry's treatment of his queens, his servants and the religious without feeling nausea and repulsion. No doubt Father David felt this in good measure, and he made no attempt to disguise it. But Henry is revealed by deft and often surprisingly urbane touches of his brush.[15] After the first trial suppression, 'Henry's mind . . . continued to brood over the matter, and in the course of time the voice of conscience began to make itself heard' – that is to say, he began to ponder that it might be incompatible with his coronation oath to leave monastic property in monkish hands. And after it was all over, and Cromwell has followed

---

[13] *RO* III, 126.   [14] P. 179.
[15] The quotations which follow are from pp. 201, 204 and 205.

the monks into oblivion, he advised his nephew the king of Scotland to follow his own 'example and realize the monastic wealth of his kingdom, thus putting to far better use what was at present spent on "untruth and beastly living"'. Father David goes on, it is true, to probe the puzzle of how Henry, 'self-willed, obstinate and able as he was' could allow two such ministers as Wolsey and Cromwell apparently almost unbridled power; and to mark the contrast (which perhaps Father David exaggerated) between 'the essentially traditional, orthodox, unbloody rule of the cardinal, and the revolutionary, secular and ruthlessly bloodstained decade of his successor'. Yet Henry and Cromwell remain background figures, and he restrained his rhetoric – in a book notable among all his writings for its range of literary effects – as he had not in his handling of Wyclif.

The consequence is twofold. First, monks, friars, king and minister are exposed to our inspection and our judgement in a manner which is wholly fair. He was perfectly aware that this was a drama still capable of arousing deep passions on one side and the other. Nor did he attempt to hide where his own feelings lay. For my eighteenth birthday he had given me a copy of Roper's *Life of More*, accompanied by a letter in which he already showed that insight into the slow groping which occupied much of More's life: 'his was such a keen, subtle, ironic mind, used for so many years to the most agile funambulism in the courts, at the Court, and in controversy . . . that I, for one, find it extremely hard at more than one crucial moment to be certain whether he is speaking with absolute frankness . . . More, I think, is seen at his deepest and best in the letters he wrote in the Tower . . . I don't think I am used to the melting mood, but they are one of the few things in any literature that I can scarcely read without getting near tears – they and the account of More's last meeting with Margaret [here he returns to Roper's *Life*], which Wordsworth, I think, said was one of the three most pathetic passages in English.'[16] His feeling for More, and for the great cause in which he suffered, underscores the restrained passion of *Religious Orders*, III; and the restraint had its reward, for it has been, I fancy, the most widely read and acclaimed of his books among men of quite different background and persuasion; still more, it is inherent in its success as a model of the historian's craft.

The other effect of his treatment of the high political figures of the age

[16] Letter dated 25 June 1945; cf. *HC*, pp. 3–9, esp. 7.

is to make clear sense of his principle of selection. The Dissolution is an enormous subject, on which many interesting books have been written, but not yet the tithe of what is to come. It provides a mass of evidence, and a hundred mirrors, in which the political, social, economic, religious and intellectual life of sixteenth-century England and Europe are illuminated. Excellent books have been written on the Dissolution since 1959 which only modestly overlap the territory he explored in depth.[17] He was fully aware that this must be so, even though he had set out to write a large volume of 500 pages. He was also aware that if the book was too selective, historical perspective, and much of the point of the story, would be lost. So he sketched in the background of an ample canvas, and in the centre of the picture told the story of the religious who had been his theme from the first pages of *The Monastic Order*.[18]

Study of the Reformation can conduce to sectarian strife or ecumenical understanding, and it is sometimes quite a fine line which marks off one from the other. But his book is never marred by sectarian prejudice. His account of the Visitation of 1535–6 by Cromwell's stooges is a delicious mingling of sober fact and delicately hinted farce. It opens with a rare moment of rhetoric.

> From the grey turrets and lichened gables, set among the red roofs of a town or framed by the ricks and elms of the open country, bells still rang to Mattins and Mass, and the habits, white or black, still crossed the great courtyard or passed down the village street. When, five years later, their work was done, nettles and the fire-weed were springing from the dust, and the ruins of Hailes and Roche and Jervaulx were already beginning to wear the mantle of silence that covers them today.[19]

Gradually the character of the visitors and the details of their missions unfold.

> The visitation did not pass without an occasional contretemps . . . Layton was first off the mark with a roving commission, whereas Legh and Ap Rice had their objectives fixed for them by Cromwell. Consequently, the abbot of Bruton who, after some initial unpleasantness, had succeeded in giving a fairly favourable

---

[17] E.g. Youings 1971.

[18] Including, of course, the story of the few, especially in the London Charterhouse, who resisted the Dissolution.   [19] *RO* III, 274.

impression to Layton, had a disagreeable shock a few days later when Legh arrived at the gate with a written commission. Some plain speaking followed, for the abbot, having already parted with a substantial fee and a venerable relic, in addition to hearing the comments of his canons on his regime, had no desire for a repetition of the experience within a fortnight. Nevertheless, he was only in part successful in avoiding it, for Legh, though refraining from a formal visitation, demanded to see Layton's *comperta* and proceeded to stiffen up his injunctions.[20]

No one who reads *The Religious Orders*, III, will doubt that great issues were at stake, and that the author was a devout Roman Catholic. But perhaps an Anglican who has known and savoured the book for thirty years may note that there is not a phrase in it which – on any religious ground – he would wish had been differently worded.

At the end he looked briefly forward to the destiny of the monastic life in Britain, and of the crumbling buildings.[21] 'In a still more powerful way the ghost of medieval monasticism remained and remains to haunt this island. The grey walls and broken cloisters, the

bare ruin'd choirs,[22] where late the sweet birds sang,

speak more eloquently for the past than any historian would dare, and pose for every beholder questions that words cannot answer.

'At the end of this long review of monastic history, with its splendours and its miseries, and with its rhythm of recurring rise and fall, a monk cannot but ask what message for himself and for his brethren the long story may carry. It is the old and simple one; only in fidelity to the Rule can a monk or a monastery find security . . .' The passage implies a judgement on the humdrum and mediocre more fearful even than that on Henry and Cromwell, though a judgement tempered by his sense that there were good men and good lives hidden by the absence of record, and that many whom he condemned by Benedict's standard had never realised what was expected of them. As at the end of Thackeray's novel, the puppets were put away and the box closed. But the Rule of St Benedict lived on.

---

[20] *RO* III, 281.
[21] What follows is from *RO* III, 468; it is quoted more fully on p. 44.
[22] The title (already chosen before his death) of the new edition of *RO* III (Cambridge, 1976).

5

THE RANGE AND SCOPE
OF HIS OTHER
SCHOLARLY WORK

CHRISTOPHER BROOKE

To the end of his life Father David remained a prolific writer, and his writings ranged widely over history and theology.[1] It is not easy to find a thread to guide us, but *The Historian and Character and Other Essays* – the collection of his own papers which we presented to him as a Festschrift in 1963 – was deliberately chosen to comprise as wide a variety as possible of his best work, and is a natural starting point.

The Historian and Character includes essays on most of his scholarly interests – on medieval thought and culture, on Thomas Becket, on monastic architecture and monastic historians; and by-products too of his major studies of monastic history. Its range was not all-embracing: it does not include any of his early articles on English literature, on which time had set its mark; nor on mysticism and mystical theology, since much of his early work had been recently garnered in *The English Mystical Tradition* (1961) which was much more than a reissue or new edition of *The English Mystics* (1927). Nor does it include any of the 'essays in Monastic History' in which he had first shown his paces as a monastic historian, since they were repeated in substance in *The Monastic Order*. His most substantial lectures on historiographical themes, by a happy treaty with H.P. Morrison, were assigned to the Nelson volume, and so we were able to find space for all that we chiefly wanted.

Two of the papers in *The Historian and Character* show at their best his work on medieval thought. Of his book on *The Evolution of Medieval Thought* I wrote in 1975, that it 'is one of his more conventional works; it

---

[1] In this chapter the items in *HC* are used to provide a frame to consider the range of his best work. It is deliberately selective – I am particularly aware that I have done scant justice to the theological tracts of his last years.

grew from lectures which undoubtedly influenced a generation of students who attended them more profoundly than one can readily grasp from the printed page'.[2] But when David Luscombe and I studied it closely with a view to preparing the new edition of 1988, our valuation of it rose – not indeed of its details, which needed a surprising degree of correction, but of its broader lines. It was written as lectures and provides an exceedingly lucid introduction; it was written by a man deeply conscious from his own training of the classical background to medieval thought, and he does it rare justice. It is a serious attempt to explain the movements of thought against the background of the cultural heritage and the shifting pattern of schools and universities, the institutional frame within which scholars worked. It has a clarity rarely found in books on such a theme. Yet it remains true that his devotion to St Thomas and his distaste for most fourteenth-century thought gives the book a disappointing conclusion, though one should pause before making too much of this, for he inspired pupils to work on such formidable thinkers as Bradwardine and Wyclif.[3] 'The Censured Opinions of Uthred of Boldon' shows him at work himself in the fourteenth century, revealing the interest and importance of a monastic scholar, a thinker not of the front rank yet of great significance for understanding Oxford and Durham in the late Middle Ages. And 'The humanism of the twelfth century' was one of his most inspired papers. Here a classical learning and a width of culture rare in students of the twelfth-century renaissance revealed to him many aspects of the period which had not been grasped; and it was a remarkable insight for the dedicated, ascetic disciple of the Cistercians, to sketch, in a profound and moving passage, the ground common to St Ailred and Abelard and Heloise. 'Heloise in truth, so far as her own deepest utterances go, has nothing of the Christian in her.'[4] Though I differ in my judgement of Heloise, this sentence makes the more striking his appreciation of her greatness.

The character study of Thomas Becket (his Raleigh Lecture) distilled some of his most brilliant ideas on a theme to which he returned many times in his later years. It was complementary to the Ford Lectures on Becket's *Episcopal Colleagues*; and it was followed by his centenary book and lecture on the martyr.[5] Compared with his massive work on

[2] Brooke 1975, p. 462; for what follows see esp. Knowles 1962a/1988, pp. viii–ix.
[3] And see above, p. 69, on *RO* I.   [4] *HC*, p. 24.
[5] Knowles 1951a, the Ford Lectures for 1949; followed by Knowles 1970a and b. For the most recent study of Becket, see Barlow 1986.

monastic history, the studies of Becket and his circle are relatively slight; yet all who have written since 1949 have been substantially affected by what he wrote. Becket has always had a singular power to stir admiration or hate; and the contrast in A.L. Poole's *Domesday Book to Magna Carta* between the portrait of Becket in the text, which is hostile, and the commendation of Father David's Raleigh lecture in the bibliography, is a good indicator of the influence he has had in checking the harsher condemnations. At the same time it was characteristic of him that he constructed all his work on Becket directly from the Rolls Series *Materials*, which he read and re-read, taking copious notes and attempting to sort out for himself problems of chronology in the quagmire of the correspondence. He generously acknowledged my aid in constructing the appendices to *Episcopal Colleagues*, but they still represent his own contribution on minute, significant points which had helped him to build up the picture of the drama and the character of the contestants. When I came to revise the footnotes for *Thomas Becket* (1970a) I was slightly vexed to discover – two or three years after the publication of Gilbert Foliot's *Letters* – that he was still citing Foliot from the *Materials*. But a moment's reflection brought it home that it was always in the character of his best work that, for all his appreciation of help and criticism, for all his subtle understanding of other scholars' minds, in the end it was his own reading of the sources on which it was based. One of his latest articles (with Anne Duggan and myself) was the reappraisal of an episode and a document in the struggle in which he had detected, by comparison with his own notes and reconstruction, an error of mine.[6]

More obvious than the groundwork was the penetration and the justice of his portraiture. On this all who read with discernment have commented; in the Raleigh Lecture in particular he practised the art later preached in his second inaugural on 'The Historian and Character', and in the grand manner. He showed the development of a curious and difficult personality, and made sense of the personal tragedy of his relations with the king. He has been accused of seeing Henry II in the image of Henry VIII. Very likely he was right to see a likeness; but he had little appreciation of the structure of lay society or the working of patronage. Thus he took it for granted that the bishops were spiritual

---

[6] 'Henry II's *Supplement* to the Constitutions of Clarendon', *English Historical Review*, LXXXVII (1972), 757–71. Dr Anne Duggan has incorporated her very important study of the correspondence in Duggan 1980, and her new edition of Becket's own letters is nearing completion.

pastors with a single overriding obligation; he failed to see the deep tension in Becket as chancellor, servant of the king, and archdeacon, servant of the archbishop, which is revealed in John of Salisbury's letters to him. Since the main lines of advance in studying the dispute seem now to lie in detailed investigation of the sources and in penetration of the social structure, Father David's books and papers are bound to leave younger scholars unsatisfied; but Becket lives in them, and especially in the Raleigh Lecture, as in no other recent writing. Nor can one readily forget the lecture's conclusion, when the clatter of swords and argument is stilled, and the corpse of the archbishop, lying alone in the cathedral, is likened to the corpse of Patroclus, κεῖτο μέγας μεγαλωστί, λελασμένος ἱπποσυναών.[7]

Father David's interest in monastic history had its origin in his early travels with his father; and the one paper formerly unprinted in *The Historian and Character* was an essay originally intended for *The Monastic Order* on 'The monastic buildings of England'. It covers much the same ground as the introduction to *Monastic Sites from the Air*, which he published with J.K.S. St Joseph in 1952. This was the first Cambridge Air Survey, the first major fruit in print of Professor St Joseph's distinguished and original work; and it is primarily an example of his skills – not only in monastic archaeology, for one of the problem photographs at the end led to the uncovering of Yeavering. But Father David's encouragement undoubtedly helped forward St Joseph's work in all its aspects; and his lucid and distilled description of the sites has greatly increased the value of the book both as a guide to many sites and a major treatise on monastic planning. Soon after, a second fruitful collaboration with an eminent archaeologist issued in his book with W.F. Grimes on the London *Charterhouse* (1954), in which Father David's historical learning elucidated the story behind the buildings which had emerged from one of Grimes's most successful excavations in and around the City.

The last three items in *The Historian and Character* are studies of famous scholars. Of Abbot Butler enough has been said, and a little already of Gasquet. It was a singular pleasure to set side by side his portraits of Mabillon and Gasquet. The Mabillon is sober, almost hagiographical; the Gasquet burlesque. But both go much deeper than that. Mabillon's greatness is set off with an account of his failings: of how

---

[7] 'Archbishop Thomas Becket: a character study', the British Academy Raleigh Lecture for 1949, repr. in *HC*, chap. 6, at p. 128.

he was deceived by a forger who by careful study of *De re diplomatica* produced a document to whose authenticity Mabillon himself was prepared to give testimony; of the delinquent brother Denys of whom he could believe no ill.[8] By such means the portrait of the great scholar who was human and fallible and full of charity is given shape and point. On any showing it is remarkable that in the scientific revolution of the seventeenth century the science of history should have owed so much to the holy monks of Saint-Maur. Father David brought out in an unforgettable manner the union of faith and integrity, the passion for learning and candour, quite simply for truth, which marks all that Mabillon wrote and did.

The paper on Mabillon touches the heart of Father David's faith as a historian, and reflects his constant interest in historians and how they worked. This was evident in his understanding of scholarly technique in *The Monastic Order*; manifest in his later lecture on Macaulay; displayed, above all, in the large canvas of his Nelson *Mélange*.[9] Here the Royal Historical Society Presidentials, a quartet of historical enterprises, set out the story of the Bollandists, the Maurists, the *Monumenta Germaniae Historica* and the Rolls Series; and the skill and kindly judgement, not unmixed with criticism, with which he conducted the enterprise, were recognised by the living members of the two institutions which still live – by cordial recognition from the Bollandists, and by election as Corresponding Member of the *Monumenta*.

In the Creighton Lecture, 'Cardinal Gasquet as an Historian', the epic struggle of Coulton and Gasquet is revealed in a vein which Polonius might have termed comical historical, but in faultless taste. He pursues Gasquet's errors with glee: 'he could print a stanza of *In Memoriam* in five or six lines of type without any ascertainable metre or rhyme . . . Gasquet had inherited from his Provençal ancestors little of the Gallic lucidity of thought . . . Towards the end of his life, indeed, Gasquet's capacity for carelessness amounted almost to genius.'[10] He gives free rein to Coulton, but at the last moment pulls him up short: Gasquet was a bad scholar, not – as Coulton supposed – because he was a scheming ecclesiastic, nor because he was a bad man; Gasquet had virtues, even some virtues as a historian; and in a conclusion of notable generosity the comic muse is dismissed, Knowles sets himself firmly by Coulton's side, but Gasquet is given his due. It is beautifully done, and the one notable

[8] *HC*, pp. 235–9.   [9] *GHE*: on the Birkbeck Lectures, see above, pp. 63–4.
[10] From *HC*, pp. 254–5.

weakness is freely admitted: there is no close investigation, nor ever has been, of the debt Gasquet owed to Edmund Bishop, nor any satisfactory explanation of Bishop's readiness to guide and help in a spirit of real friendship a scholar in all points so inferior to himself.[11]

One of his works of collaboration which brought fruits of special use to a wide circle was his joint enterprise with R.N. Hadcock, *Medieval Religious Houses, England and Wales*, the editions of 1953 and 1971.[12] The enlargement of the enterprise to include hospitals and secular colleges and the military orders, and the copious notes which make the later editions a mine of valuable information, were mainly Neville Hadcock's work. But the form of the book, and the inspiration which was later to issue in Hadcock's remarkable pioneering work with Professor Aubrey Gwynne, S.J., *Medieval Religious Houses, Ireland* (1970), owed much to Father David.[13] British medievalists have been too little inclined to collaboration, have even viewed it sometimes with suspicion; yet in serious scholarly enterprise a substantial proportion must be collaborative to be fruitful. Effective joint work in a scholar of Father David's standing involves a measure of modesty, a readiness to listen, a warmth of friendliness, which help to explain the success of *Monastic Sites from the Air, Charterhouse* and *Medieval Religious Houses*; he would have been the first to give for *MRH* the chief credit to Hadcock, but the enterprise came out of an act of humility,[14] and a real wish to be useful, which were his.

This wish played a part also in his one substantial piece of textual work, the *Monastic Constitutions of Lanfranc*,[15] and in his more secondary books – his useful and readable contribution to *The Christian Centuries*; his *Christian Monasticism*; and the theological work of his last years.[16] In

[11] But see *HC* pp. 252–3.   [12] For its background, see p. 55.
[13] There is also an admirable parallel volume for Scotland, Cowan and Easson 1976.
[14] See p. 55.
[15] NMT 1951. The text, which owed much to R.A.B. Mynors, was reprinted with corrections, and a new introduction and notes, in Dom K. Hallinger's *Corpus Consuetudinum Monasticarum*, III (Siegburg, 1967); a new edition by C.N.L.B. for OMT is in preparation. Dom Hallinger was one of a group of continental scholars with whom Father David kept in close touch and to whose ventures he lent a hand; Dom Jean Leclercq was another.
[16] Of the *Christian Centuries*, an international history of the Roman Catholic Church published simultaneouly in Britain, the U.S.A., the Netherlands, Switzerland and France, he was one of the Editorial Board and author of vol. II with Dmitri Obolensky (London, 1969). The second book, also published in 1969, is in the World University Library, and contains an all too brief excursion into the modern history and destiny of monasticism (1969a).

the margin of his work on monastic history there was naturally a group of papers and lectures, of which the eloquent centenary article on St Bernard and the Dr Williams Library Lecture on 'Cistercians and Cluniacs' are characteristic specimens. Both items show his reverence, this side idolatry, though not so far as most of us would be, for Bernard; and in the second he is the monastic judge, who after an appraisal which is cool and kindly, and with a just aside on Cistercian intolerance, finds for the Cistercians on almost all the points at issue.

Yet even more characteristic of his monastic papers is the brief but effective disentangling of the case of 'The last abbot of Wigmore', round which Froude and Gasquet had woven a tapestry of fiction.[17] It is a reminder of the vast amount of original work which underlay his major works.

But it also illustrates the quality he showed time and again of grasping a topic which had been much discussed by previous scholars and giving it a new look. It is instructive to compare his own record with the verdict he had passed on Jean Mabillon, the model of the monastic historian. 'Mabillon stands out from his contemporaries as one of the world's greatest scholar-historians by reason of the vision, the intuition, the creative quality of his mind, by reason of his critical powers, and by reason of his intimate sense of the dignity and obligations of his calling' – nor did he disguise that Mabillon was fallible: there is a most instructive survey of some of his errors 'as a warning and a consolation to lesser folk'.[18] Mabillon was a mighty pioneer, establishing new standards, opening new disciplines; Father David trod paths already partly worn, and never attempted to devise new techniques of research. Yet he had an inspiring combination of critical scholarship, imaginative insight and sense of literary form, with 'the higher wisdom of the great historian'[19] – the sense of his calling in the eyes of God, which made it possible for Father David to renounce all literary recreation, all the alluring intellectual activity of the modern world save those specifically historical and monastic – which have given him a special place among the scholars of the twentieth century.

[17] *HC*, chap. 8. [18] *HC*, chap. 10, esp. pp. 233–4. [19] *HC*, p. 233.

6

DAVID KNOWLES AND PETERHOUSE

ROGER LOVATT

On 15 May 1944 the Governing Body of Peterhouse resolved that Professor Butterfield should convey to Dom David Knowles an offer of an Official Fellowship and a College Lectureship as from 1 October 1944. The offer was accepted and the formal election took place on 20 June.

Father David's election to a fellowship at Peterhouse was a singular event from many different points of view.[1] With the exception of some short-lived, and scarcely encouraging, appointments made by James II, he was the first member of a Catholic religious order since the sixteenth century to hold a fellowship of an Oxford or Cambridge college. At the time when he took up his fellowship he was already 48 years old. He had not previously held any university post and he had no experience of teaching undergraduates. His own degree was in classics rather than history and he was later to stress himself – no doubt with the broad-ranging nature of the Cambridge history course in mind – 'how very little history I knew when . . . brought . . . back to Cambridge'.[2] What is more, his strained relationships with the authorities of his order were already known in the university and any college might well have felt that his election could involve it in the internal affairs of the Catholic

---

[1] My use of the form 'Father David' might seem to require a word of explanation. In a postscript to a letter to me of 17 Oct. 1966 he had written, 'I think Professor K. is a little formal. I don't mind pure David, but if you like to come in line with Christopher Brooke, Billy Pantin, Dick Southern and Richard Hunt (not a bad quartette) who always address and call me Father David I should be agreeable.' Such a suggestion was not to be gainsaid.

[2] D.K. to H[erbert] B[utterfield], 27 Sept. 1964. Butterfield Papers, C[ambridge] U[niversity] L[ibrary], Box Correspondence IJK.

hierarchy in a way which it might be prudent to avoid (as another Cambridge college was to feel little more than two years later).[3] Certainly a distinguished Catholic historian, himself a member of a religious order, was later to visit the college and remonstrate with one of the history fellows for giving refuge to someone who was at odds with the Church. But the election was also unexpected from a narrower, collegiate point of view. A strong tradition of historical studies had existed at Peterhouse for more than forty years when Father David became a fellow – a tradition whose origin dated from the arrival of A.W. Ward as Master in 1900 and that of Harold Temperley as a fellow in 1904 – but in all of this period there had never been a medieval historian amongst the teaching fellows. The novelty was perhaps less striking than it might appear to modern eyes, which take such specialisms for granted, because at that time college lecturers in history at Peterhouse were expected to teach all areas of the syllabus regardless of their own particular expertise. So the distinction between 'medievalist' and 'modernist' was not a decisive one within the college, at least for teaching purposes. Munia Postan had been a fellow since 1935, but he had held a chair for the last six years and had never served as a college lecturer. In any case he seems to have been regarded as an economic historian rather than as a medievalist *tout court*. Hence the election of Father David, 'a specialist in medieval history', could be seen within the college as representing an 'innovation', a real expansion in the historical interests of the teaching fellows.[4] It might also be seen as a change of mood in a more personal sense. During the war years the day-to-day running of the college had largely fallen into the hands of only four fellows, Roy Lubbock, who was an engineer, two historians, Herbert Butterfield and Brian Wormald and a mathematician, Charles Burkill. Two of them, Butterfield and Wormald, had previously been under-graduates of the college, as had the Master, Paul Vellacott. Lubbock came from King's but had been a fellow of Peterhouse for nearly twenty-five years by 1944, and Burkill, originally from Trinity, had been a fellow for fifteen years. The society was tiny and, in social – although not intellectual – terms, parochial. In these circumstances the election to their number of Father David, a monk in conflict with his order and virtually destitute, can scarcely be regarded as predictable.

How had it come about? This was a question which Father David

[3] Cowling 1980, p. 147.   [4] *Peterhouse, 1944–1948*, p. 11.

himself was later to ask Butterfield in specific terms. There can be no doubt that Butterfield himself was the prime mover. Although the two men had been exact contemporaries as undergraduates between 1919 and 1922 they do not seem to have formed any close acquaintanceship at that time. There was a difference of age and of background, and they seem to have moved in quite different social milieux. In fact Butterfield's admiration for Father David appears to date from the years immediately after 1940 when *The Monastic Order* first appeared. To judge from Butterfield's own account of the matter, given some fifteen years later, there were a number of elements to his thinking.[5] He had himself maintained an interest in medieval history, was teaching the subject to undergraduates, and had undoubtedly read *The Monastic Order*. But as part of this continuing interest Butterfield also held frequent conversations with Philip Grierson about matters of medieval scholarship. In the course of these conversations he had got Grierson to talk about Father David and at one point, well before it had become a possibility, had even asked whether it was desirable to enable him to move to Cambridge. 'I still remember his fervent reply', Butterfield wrote in 1959. Subsequently he gained the enthusiastic support of both Zachary Brooke and Munia Postan for Father David's election, but it was Grierson's advocacy which Butterfield later came to regard as crucial. 'The degree of his fervour', Butterfield wrote, 'stands as the first (and at that date the only) outside force acting on the college . . . without him I don't know that I should have ever broached the matter to Zachary. Nobody expected us to make a *medieval* appointment and nobody asked us to do so.' But Grierson was an 'outside force' who would probably not 'have the slightest idea that he played any part in the affair'. He had not taken the initiative but had responded to Butterfield's prompting. It is Butterfield who must be seen as the key figure. And perhaps one particular moment of personal contact might be taken as playing a crucial part in crystallising his views. For in 1943 Father David had returned to Cambridge in order to give a paper to the Cambridge University Historical Society. The Secretary of the Society at that time was Butterfield himself.[6]

Writing in 1959 Butterfield expressed the view that the election of Father David, 'not only a Catholic but a monk', reflected 'some credit' on the fellows of the college, for 'Fellows of Colleges are not always so unprejudiced'. So it may be, but his account of Father David's arrival in

---

[5] For what follows, see H.B. to D.K., 14 Jan. 1959. Butterfield Papers, Peterhouse Treasury.   [6] Morey 1979, pp. 99–100.

Peterhouse – along with the accounts of others who have described these events – was perhaps too bland in passing over the various difficulties which so singular an election was almost bound to provoke. For it is idle to pretend that Father David's first years in the college passed entirely smoothly. The core of the problem lay in his relationship with the Master, Paul Vellacott. It has been said that Vellacott was absent from Cambridge on war service during the negotiations preceding the election, with the implication that his subsequent attitude towards Father David arose from some resentment at not being fully consulted concerning the proposal and at being presented on returning to the college with a *fait accompli*.[7] The evidence suggests that the issues at stake were more diverse, and much more profound. Vellacott had certainly been away from the college on war service, largely in the Middle East, since the end of 1942; but his health had broken down and he appears to have been back in Cambridge by the end of February 1944. A couple of months later the college extended his leave of absence for the whole of the calendar year of 1944 but this decision was taken, not because he was then occupied abroad on war service, but because he was still formally employed by the Foreign Office and also because his illness made it desirable that he should be freed from the administrative burdens of the Mastership. But he took the chair at a meeting of the Governing Body in April 1944 and was accessible until he resumed the full duties of the Mastership rather earlier than planned in October 1944.[8] Hence there can be little doubt but that Vellacott was involved in the discussions concerning the proposal to offer a fellowship to Father David. Hence, also, any later animosities sprang less from the Master's feelings of injured *amour-propre* than from certain temperamental and doctrinal tensions between the two men.

Vellacott was a remarkable man of many gifts and strong character, and he is still recalled more than thirty years after his death with wonder, amusement and even an element of apprehension, by those who were fellows during his Mastership.[9] He had returned to Peterhouse as a

---

[7] Morey 1979, p. 100; Cowling 1980, p. 147.

[8] This sequence of events can be reconstructed from the minutes of the college's Governing Body: 28 Feb. 1944 (3 and 5), 24 April 1944 (6 and 7), 10 Oct. 1944 (1) and 23 Oct. 1944 (Vellacott in the chair).

[9] My account of Vellacott is based on the recollections of his colleagues and, in particular, on two articles by H. Butterfield in the college magazine, *The Sex*, 106, 1946, 5–6, and 114, 1956, 1–4. Valuable material, now in the Peterhouse Treasury, was also collected by Butterfield in preparation for writing his obituary of Vellacott which appeared in *The Times* for 16 Nov. 1954.

fellow in 1919 after distinguished war service. He had risen to the rank of lieutenant-colonel, was mentioned three times in despatches and awarded the D.S.O., but had also been badly wounded and eventually taken prisoner. Indeed his injuries seriously and permanently affected his health. After serving for fourteen years as Tutor (in effect, Senior Tutor) of Peterhouse Vellacott had moved to become Head Master of Harrow School before being elected to the Mastership in 1939 on Harold Temperley's premature death after only a year in office. Vellacott was a highly talented administrator. He had completely reformed – indeed almost invented – the tutorial arrangements in the college and had then gone on to undertake similar work at Harrow, restoring its finances and transforming the whole structure of the school by converting the housemasterships into salaried offices. He was a man of refined sensitivity, attached to the poetry of Keats and the music of Delius. He embodied and demanded the highest standards of life and social behaviour, and his elegance and style became a byword in the college. He caused a sensation when a fellow by installing a private bathroom in the college, and it was rumoured amongst undergraduates that he went periodically to London in order to have his umbrella rolled. In personal relations he could show rare gifts of sympathy, 'a kind of understanding', one of his pupils wrote, 'that it would be difficult for anybody to surpass'. And even those who had no instinctive affinity with him could be surprised, and moved, by his acts of spontaneous kindness and instinctive humanity. Witty and hospitable in private, he was also a highly effective speaker in public, clear, precise and reasonable, with an attractive lightness of touch and a winning humour. But these very qualities had their contradictions. As one who knew him well remarked, he was an administrator rather than a diplomat, and the administrative skills could become perfectionist, meticulous in detail and authoritarian in principle. His methods were 'monarchical', some said; others referred to 'the sergeant-major'. The elegance and style were at times not without artifice, and became what was characterised at Harrow as 'a magnificent fastidiousness'. He would pretend, no doubt half in jest, that he did not know what it was like to ride in a bus, or that he had never set foot on England north of the Trent. The wit could become brusque and wounding. The capacity for imaginative sympathy had its limits, and was replaced by harshness when faced with certain alien areas of life and experience, or certain types of personality. When he returned to Peterhouse after his years at Harrow he was becoming more 'regally remote', forgetting sometimes that he was no longer a Head Master and attempting even to forbid the wives of fellows to attend college chapel – while accepting his defeat in this respect with good humour. Although he was much else besides, he was also – or wished to appear – a conventional English gentleman, deploying an 'unspoken, practical conservatism', distrusting enthusiasm and disapproving of the eccentric and the outsider.[10]

Why did Vellacott come to react against Father David, having earlier agreed to his election? The answer is not straightforward. As a historian himself, Vellacott may have felt that he – rather than Butterfield – should have taken the initiative in recommending a new history fellow. Certainly in the summer of 1944 Vellacott was in very bad health and may simply have found himself unable to resist a proposal so strongly urged on him by both Butterfield and Postan. It is possible that, having been on war service and out of the country for so long, he simply knew little about Father David. Equally, a man so punctilious in his own behaviour, who drove himself so hard in his devotion to the college, may have felt that Father David's regime during the first year of his fellowship, when he almost never attended meetings of the Governing Body and was allowed to be absent from college for as many as four nights a week during term, showed an insufficient sense of obligation towards his benefactors. On another occasion Vellacott complained of the impudence of a young fellow who tried to strike a hard bargain with the college before accepting the office of tutor. It is difficult to weigh these various considerations. Clearly there were differences of temperament and outlook between the two men. But the real basis of the estrangement was almost certainly religious.

Vellacott has been described – perhaps a trifle too harshly – during these years as a 'non-believing Anglican' who adhered to the Church of England 'because it was the Established Church of the State'.[11] On somewhat similar grounds he distrusted Catholicism as sectarian, un-English and prone to enthusiasm. Vellacott wrote very little but it is revealing that what he did write was focused on the reign of James II and on the difficulties provoked by the king's religious policies. In one study he had anatomised the dilemma of a Kentish country gentleman 'not of any unusual intellectual power, but in judgement discerning, in temperament loyal to tradition . . . instinct . . . with the spirit of

[10] Cowling 1980, p. 219.   [11] *Ibid.*, p. 220.

conservatism' when faced with the 'headlong' and 'feverish' course steered by James towards 'an arbitrary and a Catholic monopoly'.[12] Even more prescient in the circumstances was Vellacott's essay, published a couple of years earlier, in which he had described the attempt made by the government of James II in 1687 to force the university of Cambridge to grant the degree of MA to a Benedictine monk, Alban Francis, by dispensing him from the obligation to take the oaths of Allegiance and Supremacy. Vellacott's views came over clearly. James II's policy was 'blind', 'ruthless' and 'unflinching' in its attack on 'the sacred privileges' of the university. The Roman Catholic religion was at that time 'extraordinarily distasteful' to the majority of Englishmen, who had 'a very justifiable fear that their property would be seized and handed over'. And the essay concluded with a conventional coda on the bullying, ignorance and arbitrariness displayed by Lord Chancellor Jeffreys during the eventual legal proceedings against the university.[13] But Vellacott's prejudices were not merely historical. One fellow was told by him that conversion to Roman Catholicism would preclude appointment to senior office in the college. The Master disliked Catholicism, disliked monks perhaps even more and, paradoxically, particularly disliked monks he suspected of enthusiasm and of disobedience to their superiors.

Any subsequent dispute could not of course revolve overtly around such matters. It required a pretext, and the pretext was supplied by the matter of the ration book.[14] The essence of the problem was clear enough. During the academic year of 1944–5 Father David had apparently lived in college for only about three nights a week during term and it was therefore not necessary for him to hand over his ration book to the college kitchens. This situation changed in October 1945 when he became obliged to live in college for five nights a week in term. During this period the college kitchens seem to have been experiencing great difficulty in obtaining supplies and at a Governing Body meeting held shortly before Christmas (when Father David had left Cambridge for the vacation) it was agreed as a matter of general policy that fellows

---

[12] Vellacott 1926, esp. pp. 49, 56. [13] Vellacott 1924, esp. pp. 81, 91, 101.

[14] For what follows, see minutes of the college's Governing Body: 20 Dec. 1945 (17), 18 Feb. 1946 (1), 20 Feb. 1946 (1) and 11 March 1946 (4), together with associated Governing Body Papers, particularly a 'Report of Certain Proceedings', dated 14 Feb. 1946 by the then Junior Bursar, C.E.W. Lockyer. The essential background is supplied by letters from Dr Kornerup to the Ministry of Food of 1 March 1946, and from Lockyer to D.K. of 30 May 1946. Copies in the author's possession.

who dined in Hall on four nights a week should give up their ration books to the college. Accordingly about a month later, after the vacation had ended, the Bursar made a direct request to Father David that he should now let the college have his ration book. At this stage Elizabeth Kornerup intervened on the grounds that she was responsible for Father David's medical care, explaining that his health required special dietary arrangements which in turn made it necessary that she should retain the ration book. After some more fruitless negotiation, including a suggestion from Elizabeth Kornerup that the appropriate number of coupons from the book should be given to the college, it seems that Father David – on her advice – in effect withdrew from the college and returned to London. He remained away from Cambridge, save for fulfilling his teaching engagements, until the matter finally came to a head at a meeting of the Governing Body on 18 February 1946. At this stage Father David attempted to resolve the problem by suggesting that the residence requirements attached to his college lectureship might be relaxed, presumably by returning to something like the arrangements of the previous academic year, so that the necessity to hand over his ration book would not arise. There was lengthy discussion and eventually the meeting was adjourned for two days. At this adjourned meeting a statement from Father David was read, he withdrew, and the Governing Body then unanimously agreed not to relax the conditions of residence attached to his lectureship, moderating its decision only slightly by agreeing that his ration book need not be transferred to the college until the beginning of the next Full Term (23 April 1946). This resolution was then conveyed to Father David who returned to the meeting and stated that he would agree to abide by it.

It seemed like defeat. But the actual outcome was rather different. A forceful and elaborately detailed medical case was presented to the food rationing authorities by Elizabeth Kornerup, and the matter was even referred to the Ministry of Food. The previous limitations on the supply of food eased slightly. The Governing Body found itself able to relax to a small degree its rules about the number of meals which could be taken without a ration book being handed over. And a compromise was eventually agreed – without doing too much violence to the facts of the case – by which Father David was to be regarded as a 'non-resident fellow'. In a sense everybody won. The college's residence requirement remained in force. Father David was permitted to take four dinners a week in Hall. But he kept his ration book. Even Paul Vellacott was no match for the combination of obfuscation and tenacity that Elizabeth Kornerup could deploy in the defence of her charge.

At a deeper level perhaps nobody won. In one sense the whole issue was a storm in a teacup, an archetype of the kind of personal ill-feeling that can so readily develop within the small community of a college fellowship. But storm it certainly was, at least in the life of the college at the time. It was almost unprecedented, then as now, for a matter to be so vexed that the Governing Body should feel it necessary to adjourn its proceedings and then resume them two days later. The Master, who was in particularly bad health at the time, intervened in the discussions in sharp terms, treating Father David – according to one eye-witness – 'like a criminal'. Vellacott's personal animus was unmistakeable. In the course of the dispute it would seem that not only did he imply that Father David's word was not to be trusted but he also argued that the car crash he had experienced in 1928 had permanently affected his capacity to perform his college duties.[15] By all accounts Father David conducted himself with reticence, dignity and charity. Indeed many years later he acknowledged that Vellacott was 'a sincere Christian' while still recalling his 'ruthlessness of purpose and acidity of speech'.[16] As far as the precise issue was concerned Father David may well have been partly in the wrong, but it is hard not to see him also as to some degree a pawn between the implacable figures of the Master and Elizabeth Kornerup. What is more, unlike the proverbial storm, the underlying tensions did not rapidly relax. Almost exactly a year later, on 25 January 1947, Father David was elected to the chair of medieval history vacated by the death of Zachary Brooke. The election meant that his teaching fellowship automatically lapsed, although he naturally became eligible for election into a professorial fellowship. As a purely stopgap arrangement the university agreed that Father David could continue with his college teaching for the remainder of that academic year and, on this condition, the Governing Body allowed him to retain his rooms in college and to continue to take free meals. But his fellowship had terminated and he naturally ceased to attend meetings of the Governing Body. It is difficult now to establish the precise nature of the negotiations which then took place. Most were no doubt informal and consisted of no more than private discussions amongst the fellows of other colleges. But it does

[15] D.K. to Vellacott, 16 Feb. 1946. Copy in the author's possession. See above, pp. 15, 40–1.
[16] Dom Adrian Morey to H.B., 13 Oct. 1977. Butterfield Papers, CUL, Box Correspondence IJK.

seem to have been known elsewhere in Cambridge that Father David's election to a professorial fellowship at Peterhouse was by no means a foregone conclusion. This was in itself unusual. A teaching fellow elevated to a chair can normally expect a professorial fellowship in his own college. It was a sign that earlier problems had not entirely been forgotten. Two or three other colleges apparently considered the possibility of inviting him to join them but the suggestions came to nothing. Father David's own college, Christ's, did not wish to jeopardise its long standing links with Downside. Elsewhere there was reserve about electing a Roman Catholic monk. But it was only when a month had passed after his promotion, and only when the situation threatened to embarrass the college, that the fellows of Peterhouse finally agreed to elect Father David to a professorial fellowship, and even then – as the minutes of the Governing Body precisely (and unusually) specify – the proposal was approved only 'by a majority'.[17]

Subsequently resentments did fade away. The college's fellowship expanded. The appearance of the first volume of *The Religious Orders* in 1948 further established Father David's scholarly distinction. He himself did nothing to exacerbate ill-feeling, and others may well have seen little point any longer in nursing old grievances. But while personal relationships eased, Father David retained a sense of these earlier difficulties. More than twenty years later he still recalled how he had ventured to suggest in 1949, in connection with the college's celebrations to mark the third centenary of the death of its former fellow, the poet Richard Crashaw, that a commemorative plaque might be set up in the ante-chapel, but that the proposal had been immediately quashed when the then Dean had simply remarked, 'Crashaw was a Roman Catholic'.[18] Yet Crashaw had himself played a large part in raising the funds for the completion of that same chapel. In so far as the collective religious sentiment of any body of fellows can be characterised it is true to say that throughout these years there survived an earlier tradition of – largely implicit – anti-clericalism and of hostility to Roman Catholicism. Hence it was no doubt a concern not to appear to proselytise within the college – combined with his habitual reticence and perhaps a reserve arising from his own relations with the ecclesiastical authorities – that explains Father David's otherwise unexpected failure to offer a word of direction or spiritual comfort to a close colleague who only a

[17] Peterhouse Governing Body minutes of 27 Jan. 1947 (9), 10 Feb. 1947 (1) and 24 Feb. 1947 (1). See also, Morey 1979, p. 102 and, more precisely, Cowling 1980, p. 147.
[18] *Peterhouse, 1972*, p. 3.

few years later was himself moving towards the Catholic Church. True, direction was not sought, and current social conventions frowned upon unprompted discussion of personal religious matters, but his silence in this respect was articulate. For many years Father David felt that these religious issues made it impossible for him to preach in the college chapel and in particular to deliver the sermon at the college's Commemoration of Benefactors, and it was not until 1972, almost ten years after leaving the college, that he finally overcame this sense of inhibition.

These were petty events. Probably they played only a limited part in Father David's early life at Peterhouse. Even less do they seem to have affected his academic activities. But temperamentally he was not proof against personal animosities of this sort and it is misleading to suggest that his first years in the college represented a completely untroubled haven after the years of exile and loneliness at Ealing and Warwick Square. Subsequently the college undoubtedly did come to represent such a haven. But how far was this necessary for the fulfillment of his spiritual and intellectual life? That is the really important question to be put concerning his years in the college. And the answer is far from clear-cut. What did Peterhouse come to mean to him? As far as I know, he referred publicly to the matter on only three occasions, in the prefaces to two volumes of *The Religious Orders* and in the sermon which he preached at the Commemoration of Benefactors in 1972. In the preface to the first volume of *The Religious Orders*, dated April 1947, he acknowledged his indebtedness to all those who 'in one way or another, have brought it about that the book should have been completed and this preface written at Peterhouse, the ancient and venerable foundation of Hugh of Balsham, bishop of Ely and monk and sometime subprior of the cathedral monastery of St Etheldreda'.[19] The sentiment was conventional enough and, although he was clearly conscious of the Benedictine origins of the college, he mentioned Hugh of Balsham only once in the body of the text and then in passing. The inattention was surprising for the book dealt in some detail with the attempts made by the Benedictines to found a house of studies in late thirteenth-century Oxford. Father David did not dwell on the paradox that simultaneously one of the leading Benedictines of the day was founding a house of studies at Cambridge, but a house intended for secular clerks.[20] More

---

[19] *RO* I, p. xiii.
[20] *Ibid.*, pp. 25–7, 105. For similar inattention in the same context, see Mayr-Harting 1988, p. 321 n. 4.

deeply pondered – and more personally felt – was his ambiguous judgement, also in the preface to the same volume, on monks who 'capitulated to the spirit of the age and took part in the intellectual life of the country by frequenting the universities'.[21]

In his sermon at the Commemoration of 1972 Father David spoke more directly about the college, although his words were naturally coloured by the nature of the occasion.[22] In the manner of the medieval preacher he took the history of the college as an *exemplum*, illustrating and embodying the Christian's faith in the Communion of Saints. Most of his congregation, he suggested, 'must surely at one time or another have felt the individuality, the identity, of this small community of ours, that it should have led its continuous, busy life since the days when Edward I was king, and Dante a boy in Florence, never the victim of mergers or takeovers or development, and that in this chapel daily worship has continued in term-time for more than three centuries'. On a purely secular level the conclusion was clear enough. 'We are not just a list of names, not mere class-mates or messmates, but a family with ancestors who built and worked for us, as we now build and work for the present and future.' But this perception was merely a shadow, almost a simulacrum, of the church's historic faith that 'we who believe in Christ, whether here or in the beyond, are all one body in the Communion of Saints, and that we can in unseen ways help with our prayers, and be helped in turn, by those who have gone before us . . . The Commemoration of Benefactors reminds us of another unity of spirit, that between the Christians of today and those of past years on the real level of eternity . . .'

Closely considered, the sermon also spoke on a more personal and specific level. While recalling the earlier lack of sympathy towards Catholicism shown by some of his colleagues, which had previously made him feel unable to preach this particular sermon, Father David ventured gently to remind his congregation, in words which required no partisan flavour to make their point, of the role which the Catholic tradition had played in the life of the college. The service of Commemoration was in itself 'a survival of a universal custom in medieval religious houses, where in many abbeys the names of benefactors were enshrined in a book laid upon the altar on festal days'. And in alluding to what Herbert Butterfield had described as the

[21] *RO* I, p. ix.
[22] The text of this sermon is printed in *Peterhouse, 1972*, pp. 3–6.

'historic moment' of Peterhouse, the days of Wren, Cosin and Crashaw, he added for himself the name of the college's Jesuit martyr, Henry Walpole. But particularly there was conveyed his sense of the beauties of things past, of the mean spirit and blinkered vision of iconoclasm. In a passage which has echoes at many points in his writings, private as well as public, but which to one hearer at least recalled most sharply his *éloge* on the sack of Durham Cathedral Priory, Father David described how glorious the college chapel had been for a brief moment in the 1630s, when it revealed 'a glittering display of candlesticks, basins, chalices, patens, thuribles and the like, with silken vestments, eastern altar and a rich liturgy'. It manifested 'a transient and poignant beauty of holiness' which had now 'vanished from our walls at Peterhouse'.

This intense awareness of beauty, and especially of its precariousness, and an associated sense of a college which had grown organically over many centuries without 'mergers or takeovers or development' was to colour many of Father David's attitudes. From 1945, only a year after his arrival in the college, he had occupied a set of rooms in Gisborne Court, a small, quiet and somewhat withdrawn court, built in the 1820s in a simple Tudor Gothic style and placed to the rear of the main college buildings. The set was not monumental in any way but it was quite substantial, with a large hall, a dining-room and a keeping room. It was furnished simply and modestly, almost shabbily, and without any strong impress of personal mannerism, not quite austere but both uncluttered and well worn. It was comfortable but certainly no abiding city – as the *prie-Dieu* in the hall reminded any visitor. Father David was greatly attached to these rooms, not least because of their setting. They were situated on the first floor, and from the windows of both the dining-room and the keeping room in summer scarcely a building or a road could be seen. In part they faced the college's own garden where in the spring apple trees blossomed and daffodils covered the ground. In another direction they looked out over Coe Fen, the medieval common pasture of Cambridge, often bright with daisies, buttercups and dandelions and still populated with cows during the summer. This penetration of green fields so far into the centre of Cambridge was – and still is – a rare survival, giving the rooms almost a rural air. And the daffodils of spring never failed to move him. Even in recollection, after his retirement from the college, he could write, 'The May daffodils in the Grove . . . must be lovely – they are my favourite flower, as I think they were Shakespeare's – anyhow he gave them one of his most beautiful lines'.[23]

This later affection for the college, and contentment within it, can be seen in other, and more prosaic contexts. On only one occasion, and then for only one term, does he appear to have taken sabbatical leave from the college although he was a fellow for nineteen years. Of course, other considerations came into play. Father David disapproved of the gadabout monk, the *gyrovagus* of the Rule, and the Benedictine virtue of stability never entirely lost its meaning for him.[24] But a sense of being at ease in the college also played its part. This is equally apparent in his involvement in college business. For nineteen years he attended meetings of the college's Governing Body. Some professors amongst the fellowship were notoriously inert, others volatile. Certainly Father David often wrote his correspondence during meetings, but he also participated judiciously in discussion. During these years many issues were raised, many schemes adumbrated. But he lent himself to no proposals for changing the face of the college, and still less did he initiate any. His only consistent theme was to deprecate what he regarded as unnecessary or extravagant expenditure. For the rest, he did not see the college as being in need of any radical reform. And when such a scheme for reform was pressed his response took on an unusually explicit character. In 1947 the university was faced with the problem of planning its future, post-war shape after the temporary influx of ex-servicemen had disappeared. The government of the day wished to expand substantially the total population of university students, by as much as a half or even twofold. At the same time a group of scientific professors in Cambridge argued that the university should make its own particular contribution to this development by greatly increasing its numbers of research students especially in the sciences. Logs were being rolled. But, as colleges were responsible for admissions and were therefore in a position to control the implementation of any such policy, they were naturally asked by the university for their views. In response one of the scientific fellows of Peterhouse produced a plan for drastically reducing the number of undergraduates in the college and for making an even greater increase in the number of research students. As a result the overall

[23] D.K. to R.L., 21 April 1964 'in festo S. Anselmi'. Compare Stacpoole 1975, p. 76.
[24] For D.K. on this theme, see Knowles 1929, pp. 76–80. Also, Stacpoole 1975, pp. 72, 82 n. 22 and Morey 1979, pp. 64–5.

size of the college would grow and its composition would dramatically change. The issue was central to the whole future character of the college and prolonged discussions took place at the Governing Body between July and November 1947.[25] Father David made his own views plain. He valued the distinctively small size of the college. He wished to maintain its membership at a maximum of 150 and he described the pressure to increase numbers as 'mechanical and irrational'. He also enquired, with a note perhaps of sharp realism, whether there was any serious likelihood of such a scheme for reform being put into effect. His instinct was to preserve a simple community of undergraduates and fellows. The ablest undergraduates would naturally go on to do research in Cambridge but he had little sympathy with the concept of a substantial 'third estate' of graduate students, many of them drawn from universities outside Cambridge. In particular he felt that research students were often, as it were, semi-detached members of the college, with loyalties to their laboratories and to external supervisors. The undergraduates on the other hand formed part of a coherent, organic collegiate community, a community of teachers and taught. As Father David put it, the undergraduates of the college did not even 'know the Research Students of the college by sight, though they do know the Fellows'. It was a clear – and at the time widely held – view of collegiate life, looking backwards perhaps rather than forwards and possibly not unaffected by the fact that Father David had himself never undergone any period of formal post-graduate training, but a view which was none the less coherent as a social and intellectual ideal.

At the time of his retirement from Cambridge in 1963 he reflected on the university and the college with the same air of contentment, 'I made no move whatever to go to Cambridge nineteen years ago and had there no abiding city. I had the good fortune to meet with a group both at Peterhouse and in the Faculty of History, of unusually good and just men . . .' And lest one should think that he was showing more tolerance towards his academic colleagues than he did to errant monks, he added, 'In this I think I was exceptionally fortunate. Academics elsewhere . . . are not always noted for the good qualities I met with.'[26] Writing to Butterfield he put his feelings more personally, 'As I have said to all and sundry at all times, I have always counted my membership of the Society

---

[25] A full abstract of these discussions at meetings held on 6 July 1947 and 27 October 1947 is amongst the Governing Body papers in the Peterhouse Treasury.

[26] Morey 1979, p. 106.

of Peterhouse the greatest of the many pieces of good fortune that Cambridge has brought me, and it is to you first and foremost that I owe that happiness.'[27] Father David had expressed a somewhat similar sentiment, although in a more precisely revealing form, some four years earlier, at the end of his preface to the third volume of *The Religious Orders*, where he acknowledged the importance of the help given by his college – and other Cambridge – friends in bringing the massive historical undertaking to completion. He defined their role in some crucial words from St Matthew's Gospel, *Hospes fui et collegistis me*.[28] The words are crucial both for what they say and for what they do not say. Their implications need to be considered with the same care with which they were undoubtedly written. They describe one of the corporal works of mercy. They accompany the other gospel counsels to feed the hungry, to clothe the naked and to visit the sick and the imprisoned. But they are the corporal works of mercy, not the spiritual; nor do they imply intellectual sustenance. What Cambridge, and above all Peterhouse, primarily represented for Father David was a temporary and corporal refuge.

Of course he profited in various ways from the academic stimulus provided by his colleagues in Peterhouse, but this often took place on a limited, almost technical, level or on the basis of a general intellectual affinity. In the first category must be counted the assistance given to him by Munia Postan. The monastic economy – the organisation of monastic estates – was not a subject which naturally attracted Father David. He had dealt with the topic in an almost perfunctory fashion in *The Monastic Order*, partly he explained on the grounds that 'the economy of the monastic estates was not in origin different from that of lands owned by lay proprietors, and belongs rather to the economic than to the religious history of the country', and partly because the 'intensive study in the last thirty years has been directed rather to the later centuries of the medieval period, when the records become more abundant'.[29] No doubt personal empathy also played its part. However, this situation changed in the first two volumes of *The Religious Orders* where the monastic economy received much fuller attention. To some extent this was the natural result of the fact that, as Father David had himself pointed out, much more work had been done on the subject during this later period. But it

[27] D.K. to H.B., 1 Oct. 1963. Butterfield Papers, CUL, Box Correspondence IJK.
[28] *RO* III, p. xi: Matt. 25:35, 'I was a stranger and you took me in.'
[29] *MO*, p. 441 and n. 3.

is also not unreasonable to see Postan's influence at work here. His assistance is explicitly acknowledged in the prefaces to both of these volumes and it is clear from the text that his articles on the chronology of labour services and on the population decline of the later middle ages had been influential in giving a theoretical and synthetic edge to Father David's own thinking on the subject. Equally it is clear that Postan had helped Father David in the detailed understanding of the complexities, indeed illogicalities, of monastic estate accounting.[30] But Postan's role was not unique in this respect. First in time was R.A.L. Smith. Smith, who had taken an external degree at London University from Brighton Technical College, had been a pupil of Eileen Power, and to a lesser extent of Postan, while holding a post-graduate scholarship at the Institute of Historical Research and before moving in 1939 to Trinity College, Cambridge. But Smith's association with Father David, which was later to grow into a close friendship, had developed independently in the later 1930s and it was through him that Father David first came to a detailed appreciation of the financial administration practised by the great Benedictine houses during the thirteenth and fourteenth centuries.[31] Similarly, although the relationship was much less close on a personal level, Father David gained much from the work of Miss Elizabeth Halcrow at Oxford on the economy of Durham Cathedral Priory. Hence Durham looms large in his account of the matter, although it is also clear that his admiration for Miss Halcrow's work sprang at least in part from its 'wide range' and from her refusal to confine herself to accounts and estates. She had approached the cathedral priory in the round and could provide information as readily on the holiday homes for the monks and on the money-lending activities of the priors as on the priory's rents and leases.[32] So Munia Postan's influence was recognisable but it was exercised largely in matters of detail or in areas marginal to the main themes of the books. Equally it was not exclusive, and it was certainly not decisive in any fundamental sense. Indeed, given the essential differences of temperament and outlook between the two men, it is difficult to see how it could have been otherwise.

Paradoxically Father David's affinities with another professorial

---

[30] *RO* I, pp. xiii, 37 n. 1; *RO* II, pp. ix, 9 n. 2, 13 n. 1, 320 n. 1. See also Postan 1937, and 1949–50.

[31] *RO* I, pp. xiii, 36 n. 3, 49 n. 1, 56 n. 3, 314 n. 2. See also, Smith 1943, p. xi and Smith 1947, pp. 9–22 and *passim*.

[32] *RO* II, pp. ix, 246 and n. 3, 310 and n. 2, 327 n. 1. Also, Halcrow 1949, 1955a, 1955b and 1957.

fellow of the college, Denis Brogan, sprang from a deeper source. The exuberant, omniscient Professor of Political Science, overflowing with anecdote and reminiscence was a powerful figure in the social life of the fellowship. Brogan's interests in modern France and America were remote from those of Father David. Even more alien might have seemed his apparent tough-mindedness, the worldly and contemptuous wit and the vigorous anti-clericalism, matched though they were by profound sympathy and sensitivity. But these were superficial matters. Brogan's immense learning provided many unexpected areas of common interest. As a young man he had read 'the *Patrologia*, Hroswitha and *De Consideratione*, and Bernheim's *Quellen*', and he could cheerfully correspond with Father David on topics as diverse as the exact date when Cardinal Gasquet's grandfather had fled from revolutionary France or the historical malpractices, to say nothing of the sympathies with the *Action Française*, of Dom Besse, a monk of Solesmes. Brogan also admired Father David's literary style, 'up to the very highest French standards – as good as Sainte-Beuve!', and was even persuaded by his essay to take a less unfavourable view of St Bernard. But central to their relationship, at least to Father David, was the fact that Brogan was a lapsed Catholic, and lapsed perhaps more in observance than in totality. Away from what he saw as the pomposities and inhibitions of England he had even been known to attend Mass. Butterfield himself was to stress how there was 'something ineradicable' in Brogan's Christian education, even though 'he never quite brought the whole of his mind into unity with itself'.[33] Naturally it was this aspect of Brogan's character which spoke most deeply, although not exclusively, to Father David: 'I was always impressed by the readiness with which, as a lapsed Catholic, he welcomed me at Peterhouse . . . He retained, in fact, a considerable and very just respect for the Church he had left – I never penetrated to the real reason or occasion of his leaving her – was it the Oxford-Balliol agnosticism . . .? I always hoped that he would come back to Christ at the end . . . Another attractive trait was the absence of any overbearing use of his wit and vast memory. With Ronnie Knox I always felt a sense of inferiority and that having neither Eton nor Balliol behind me, and being slow of wit, I was being written off. Denis never gave me that feeling and in return I had a real affection for him.'[34]

---

[33] Brogan to D.K., 24 June 1963 and 27 June 1963; both letters in the author's possession. Also, the sermon preached by Butterfield at a Memorial Service for Brogan, printed in *Peterhouse, 1974*, pp. 14–17.

[34] D.K. to H.B., 5 June 1974. Butterfield Papers, CUL, Box Correspondence IJK.

Yet no other fellow of the college was as close to Father David as Herbert Butterfield. Butterfield had first recognised his distinction and had brought him to Peterhouse. Father David never forgot this debt, 'I always remember you and Pamela [Butterfield] at Mass *inter amicos et benefactores* and shall continue so to do.' And years after leaving the college, on Butterfield's 70th birthday, he could write in the same vein, 'My gratitude will always remain, for it was you who led me back to Cambridge and to Peterhouse.'[35] There was a deep rapport between the two men – yet never an intimate personal friendship – in many areas of substantial intellectual and religious importance, although of course their precise fields of study were in superficial respects as far apart as were their nominal religious affiliations. Butterfield himself stressed his 'personal indebtedness and attachment' to Father David 'at the profoundest level of all', a bond which was 'greatest of all in a realm of spiritual things in which differences of Church seemed to be no obstruction'. Their 'instinctive sympathies' and 'similarities of assumption and disposition' have been delineated at length elsewhere, and there is no need to accept every nuance of this account to recognise that both men were part of 'the anti-liberal theological movement of the twenties – that rejection of rationalism, humanitarianism and liberal innocence . . .'[36] Father David may have regarded Butterfield at times as 'too much of a lawyer', that is, too inclined to plunge into the type of controversy, academic as well as historical, which he instinctively shunned.[37] But this was largely a difference of temperament. The affinities were apparent at many different levels, in different moods and on different topics. There was a common interest in Lord Acton, his correspondence and his controversies. Indeed Father David was uncertain whether the palm amongst Cambridge historians ought not to be awarded to Acton rather than Maitland.[38] There was a shared stance on the academic politics of the faculty and the university. When Butterfield became Vice-Chancellor Father David rejoiced 'in these days of technology . . . to think that the representative of the University will be someone to whom material values and achievements are not every-

---

[35] D.K. to H.B., 1 Oct. 1963 and 9 Oct. 1970. Butterfield Papers, CUL, Box Correspondence IJK.

[36] H.B. to D.K., 27 Sep. 1963; in the author's possession. Cowling 1979, p. 596, and Cowling 1980, pp. 129–55, 205–50, esp. pp. 194, 199.

[37] D.K.'s judgement is recalled by Professor Hugh Kearney.

[38] D.K. to the Secretary of the Cambridge University Press, 25 Oct. 1965. Butterfield Papers, CUL, Box 13.

thing'. And when Butterfield ceased to hold this office Father David pleaded with him to return to membership of the History Faculty Board, adopting a tone of gentle waspishness which did from time to time characterise his letters and conversation, 'The two speakers who occupy three-fifths of every debate are Elton and Kitson [Clark] – both very able . . . – but both extremely narrow in their interest. All the other modernists have a slant of some kind away from "straight" history.' And this feeling was reciprocated. Looking back on his career in Cambridge Butterfield emphasised how Father David had been 'so effective in our midst for the right kind of History'. When other members of the Faculty sought to reduce the number of general lectures on European History given by Butterfield, on the curious grounds that they were both too elementary and also too attractive to the under-graduates, Father David was vigorous in his support, ' . . . if you changed your course a great loss to history teaching here would ensue. I do *not* believe that this year you rob others – and even if you did, it seems to me paradoxical to cut down your best apple tree in the hopes that stunted ones in the other corner of the orchard will grow better . . . you have a right (if not a duty) to follow your call.' There were letters of friendly good humour concerning old acquaintances, 'One of my surprises in life was to learn that [G.P.] Gooch was an Old Etonian. He had a perfect disguise.'[39] And there were letters raising the deepest of spiritual issues, phrased in a tone which combined affection and admiration with unmistakeable candour. In 1951 Butterfield asked Father David to read the text of his Durham lectures which were to be published in the following year as *Christianity in European History*. Father David thought the first two lectures of the three 'wholly satisfying' and 'eminently just'. Yet his own more rigorous – and expert – spirituality still found difficulty with Butterfield's occasionally homespun sentiments:

> . . . you appear sometimes to equate sanctity with gentle[ness] and speak of the Christian's self-effacement as if it were something purely negative – the opposite of self-assertion. . . . yet surely the ideal Christian – the saint – effaces himself in order that God's will and truth may be made manifest in him, and Love shows itself not

[39] D.K. to H.B., 29 Sep. 1959, 5 April 1961, 22 Feb. 1957, 23 April 1971. Butterfield Papers, CUL, Boxes 78 and Correspondence IJK. H.B. to D.K., 27 Sep. 1963; in the author's possession.

only in kindness but in fortitude and even in severity. Our Lord spoke of and to the scribes and Pharisees with a fearful severity which was at the same time Love – Love for them, that they might see their fault, and love for those whom they were leading astray – and we cannot say Yes, but He was God, any more than we can say the same when we see Him consoling the widow of Nain . . .

And the matter-of-fact although characteristic, metaphor employed could not mask the directness of his judgement on the last lecture:

I felt that there you were batting on a far more sticky wicket and did not give quite the same sense of having got hold of the bowling . . . it is the old difficulty that a Christian, whether on the balance a sinner or a saint, may act sometimes *qua* Christian . . . and sometimes not. And there is the other old difficulty that the highest Christian virtues are (or may be) quite hidden, without any effect upon anybody save just one or two in a domestic circle. The Mother of Christ, for example . . . loved Our Lord and did His will at least as well as any given Apostle – yet she certainly never did anything spectacular like St Paul – or Florence Nightingale.

But more fundamental than any such reservations was an essential unity of outlook. Father David picked on one remark of Butterfield in the second lecture as 'altogether admirable' – 'hold fast to Christ and to spiritual things while retaining great elasticity of mind about everything else'. It exactly echoed a principle which Butterfield had expressed a couple of years previously at the conclusion of his *Christianity and History*, 'Hold to Christ, and for the rest be totally uncommitted.'[40] A decade later Father David was to reflect on the whole sweep of medieval monastic history in words which reveal an almost uncanny identity of sentiment, alike in their rejections as in their assertions, with those used earlier by Butterfield:

When once a religious house or a religious order ceases to direct its sons to the abandonment of all that is not God . . . it sinks to the level of a purely human institution, and whatever its works may be, they are the works of time and not of eternity. The true monk, in whatever century he is found, looks not to the changing ways

[40] D.K. to H.B., 19 Oct. 1951. Butterfield Papers, CUL, Box Correspondence IJK. Butterfield 1949, p. 146, and 1952, p. 42.

around him or to his own mean condition, but to the unchanging, everlasting God, and his trust is in the everlasting arms that hold him.[41]

Another ten years later, in an essay on St Augustine written as a contribution to Butterfield's *Festschrift*, Father David distinguished two strands in Butterfield's thinking which he characterised as 'Augustinian' but which the context makes it permissible to conclude he himself found especially sympathetic. The first was that Butterfield's judgements had 'as their foundation his consciousness of the sinfulness of all men, even if he might not accept Augustine's celebrated and terrible phrase, *massa damnata*, for the human race of old'. The second was that Butterfield had room in his 'world-view' for the saint who – like Augustine – 'escapes from the circumstances of his world by a conversion that sets him above circumstance'.[42]

The echoes of these views in Father David's own writings are clear and frequent. But sympathy and affinity are not the same as intellectual stimulus, indeed they may well be its opposite. There is no evidence that Father David's own thinking was changed in any profound respect by his prolonged association with Herbert Butterfield, or in general by the nineteen years of his fellowship at Peterhouse. Indeed, for all sorts of reasons it would have been surprising if such a change had been effected. The preface to *The Monastic Order* was dated 25 March 1939, more than five years before he returned to Cambridge. There is a consensus (from which I would not dissent) that this volume represents the high point of his historical writing. Other volumes, perhaps especially the third volume of *The Religious Orders*, come close to it, and there are a multitude of particular passages in his later works which must be counted amongst his finest achievements. Yet in the scale, the coherence and the power of its vision, the sense of discovery and of awakening, *The Monastic Order* was never to be surpassed. But the book owed nothing in any immediate sense to Cambridge. In one obvious direction its antecedents lay at Downside. It was at Downside in the summer of 1929 that he had first combed through Domesday Book in order to establish the value of monastic lands, and it was also there that he had opened the uncut pages of the Rolls Series in pursuit of the monastic chroniclers.[43] Fittingly, the first fruits of this work were published as a series of articles

---

[41] *RO* III, p. 468.   [42] Knowles 1970b, p. 19.
[43] See above, pp. 47–8, 55; Stacpoole 1975, p. 87; Morey 1979, pp. 119–22.

in the *Downside Review* between 1931 and 1934, and these articles were incorporated, sometimes *verbatim*, in the relevant parts of *The Monastic Order*.[44] Yet the origins of the book also lay in Downside in a more complex sense. For what gave passion and intensity to *The Monastic Order* was not Downside but Father David's conflict with Downside, that is, both his vocation towards a more austere observance and the loneliness and exile at Ealing which this vocation had ultimately produced. Hence when we are told that the work was 'the fruit of a Benedictine cloister and not a Cambridge court', we may fully accept the second half of this judgement while insisting that the first half, although self-evidently true, also misleads in its blandness.[45] However for the moment it is necessary to stress only three features of *The Monastic Order*, that it represents the supreme statement of Father David's historical position, that it was written by him in conditions of personal turmoil and that at no point in its creation could he have had any sense of a future at Peterhouse.

When Father David arrived at Peterhouse in 1944 he was already 48 years old. *The Monastic Order* had been finished more than five years previously and the first volume of *The Religious Orders* was already well under way. Indeed he was later to describe the book as being merely 'completed' at Peterhouse.[46] In all important respects the clay was already fired. Some have discerned Father David's essential intellectual and religious positions as clearly articulated in embryo at an even earlier date, in *The English Mystics* of 1927 and *The Benedictines* of 1929, and as having been given decisive form in 1930 with his reading of Garrigou-Lagrange at Quarr Abbey. From this point of view 'his meaning had been expressed long before his major writing had been written, perhaps even before it had been conceived, in works which were not in any ordinary sense history'.[47] Be that as it may, an unmistakeable slackening of tension is apparent after 1940, when the three volumes of *The Religious Orders* are compared with the initial statement articulated in *The Monastic Order*. In part this was dictated by the nature of the sources themselves. *The Monastic Order* was based on the broad sweep of twelfth-century chronicles and monastic biographies which themselves naturally invited a coherent and unified response. By comparison the sources for the later volumes tended to be more administrative in nature, often

[44] Knowles 1931a, 1931b, 1932a, 1932b, 1933b, 1933c, 1933d, 1934c.
[45] See above, 15–17, 37–41; Stacpoole 1975, p. 72. [46] *RO* I, p. xiii.
[47] See above, pp. 31–3; Stacpoole 1975, pp. 20–4; Cowling 1980, p. 137.

visitation records or the proceedings of the general and provincial chapters of the various orders. The result was that certain governmental themes came more to the forefront, control replaced creation, and the handling became more episodic and less dominant. Similarly, where *The Monastic Order* had been concentrated on the monks, the Benedictines followed in turn by the Cluniacs and the Cistercians, the later volumes had also to embrace both the friars and the canons and this was bound to entail a certain dilution of focus and coherence. Finally there can be no doubt that Father David himself gradually came to feel less at ease with his subject matter. Well before the close of the Middle Ages he saw that the 'normal spiritual temperature' of monastic life had been 'lowered', an 'indefinable spiritual rusticity' had taken hold and the 'Catholic religion was being reduced to its lowest terms'. The religious life had degenerated into 'an occupation, an apprenticeship to a craft' rather than 'a dedication . . . to the imitation of Christ', and the members of the religious orders had become 'men that were settled upon their lees'. The contrast with the 'splendours of the dawn and noonday' was acutely felt and could not but affect the tempo of the writing.[48] Of course this relaxation of tension was only relative. It was not incompatible with the production of passages of the greatest power and sharpest intensity of feeling. The portrait of Thomas de la Mare is unsurpassed amongst the many biographical studies of monks which appear in all four volumes. Father David wrote nothing more moving than his account of the last days of Durham or of the martyrdom of the London Carthusians. And the present writer may be permitted to express a particular admiration for the gentle dismantling of Erasmus and the exquisitely sensitive interpretation of the evidence on monastic observance produced by Henry VIII's visitors.[49] But the general picture of monastic life in late medieval England was derived from, and based upon, a standard which had been established by 1940 in *The Monastic Order*. Everything subsequently flowed from that. Everything was judged by reference to it. Perhaps it did represent the hypothetical 'age of perfection' criticised by Galbraith but its normative role in all of Father David's later writings on the subject cannot be doubted for a moment.[50] It would be hard to argue that his historical achievement was

[48] *RO* II, p. 364; III, pp. 459–61, 464. For a fuller account of the contrast between *MO* and *RO* I, II and III, see above, pp. 48–9, 66–9.
[49] *RO* II, pp. 39–48; III, pp. 129–37, 141–56, 222–36, 268–303.
[50] Galbraith 1961, esp. pp. 100, 102.

on any deep intellectual or spiritual level substantially the product of his nineteen years at Peterhouse.

Of course the argument might be phrased in more mundane and practical, although scarcely less essential, terms. It is easy to overlook the financial security which his fellowship – and still more his professorship – brought to Father David. The publication of *The Monastic Order* had been a source of expense rather than profit. He had no regular income, only occasional fees for examining. In effect he was destitute. As he wrote to Butterfield at the beginning of his fellowship, 'I have scarcely any furniture of my own. I occupy rooms in a friend's house . . . and only books, etc., are mine.'[51] Hence it might be felt that his years at Peterhouse gave him the security and stability necessary for the completion of so massive an undertaking. Certainly he came to be at ease within the college and this in turn had its effect on his outlook. Those who knew him well at this time record how his attitudes seem to have 'mellowed and the old bitterness to have gone', how he escaped from the 'deep, withdrawn reserve of the early 1940s' and began to mingle 'freely in combination room and committee' displaying 'genial good humour'.[52] Certainly too, his initial undertaking expanded considerably in scale. When *The Monastic Order* was written Father David envisaged that only one further volume might cover the remaining period of monastic history until the Dissolution. In the event three more volumes appeared. But the increasing size of the work is more readily seen as the outcome of an increasing amount of source material than as the fruit of some more relaxed and congenial manner of life.

It misunderstands the nature of Father David's imperatives to imagine that external circumstances of this sort could substantially affect the progress of his work. *The Monastic Order* was written at Ealing Priory in conditions of deep personal strain and distress, during a period which he was himself to describe as one of 'real agony . . . a nightmare'.[53] His scheme for a contemplative foundation separate from Downside had come to nothing. He had in effect broken off all relations with his abbot and was living in enforced exile from his mother house. Many of the things which meant most to him had been lost. He could no longer share in the rich liturgical life of a large community. Most of his closest confrères had (as he saw it) deserted him for Worth, Quarr and elsewhere.

---

[51] See above, p. 62. D.K. to H.B., 21 Aug. 1945. Butterfield Papers, CUL., Box Correpondence IJK.

[52] Morey 1979, p. 110; also, above pp. 19–20.   [53] Morey 1979, p. 82.

A lover of the countryside, he found himself in London suburbia. The personal toll was dramatic. Father David was himself aware of it. 'Come to Ealing still', he wrote to one of his oldest Cambridge friends, 'but not to see me as in the past'.[54] He moved into a state of almost complete withdrawal, never speaking unless spoken to, sitting apart when the community gathered together and avoiding as far as possible all social contacts, whether those of teaching or of friendship. Yet it was against this background that *The Monastic Order* was born. Indeed it would not be difficult to trace in detail the echoes of this state of private destitution, and of its origins, in the work itself. *The Monastic Order* was the product, in worldly terms, of personal despair. Its existence of itself invalidates any presumption of a causal relationship between ease of personal circumstance and intellectual achievement. Certainly Father David himself saw the relationship as actually working in an opposite direction. In a revealing passage in his memoir of R.A.L. Smith, published in 1947, he envisaged the experience of personal suffering almost as part of the essential qualifications for the mature historian. While recalling how Smith's charm flowed from his 'simplicity' and 'innocence of mind' Father David also added that he had endured 'no intense mental or emotional crisis such as may lead, if happily resolved, to the wisdom and consideration of deep sympathy . . . it may be that he still had to learn from hard experience a more severe, yet not less sympathetic, criticism of character.' And in a sentence whose personal resonances are only too clear, Father David went on, 'Life to him [Smith] was still something of a successful adventure; perhaps he was not always aware that others did not find it so, and that what seemed to him a passing episode was to them an aching memory of what had not endured.'[55] It is not necessary to accept the view that in his later writings Father David slipped into 'a condition of blandness and relaxation' to feel that, whatever else Peterhouse may have meant to him, he was not dependent on the security that it provided to produce his finest work.[56]

Two further points might be made with regard to the influence of his years at Peterhouse on Father David's intellectual life. The first arises from the way in which he saw his historical task. Speaking later about his early years in the college, he said, 'I felt that . . . it was right to appeal to as wide an audience as possible, not with apologetics but with history in which Christianity was taken for granted as true. Hence breadth rather

---

[54] *Ibid.*, pp. 87–8.   [55] Smith 1947, p. 20.   [56] Cowling 1980, p. 148.

than depth . . . I have felt all my life . . . that scholarship is a real apostolate.'[57] This was a public rather than a purely academic function. It was manifested in his powers of synthesis, his ability to transmute other men's writings and the breadth of his view – the capacity to see six centuries as a whole and to sustain what was essentially a single theme through detail and diversion over four volumes and some two thousand pages. But there was an inevitable price to be paid for this achievement, the opposite side as it were of the same coin. The range and the sweep naturally tended to preclude some of the more precise, technical forms of scholarship which one might naturally associate with the professional university scholar. At one point Father David avowed his 'amateur status as an historian'.[58] Faced with the work of Denifle and Ehrle, he felt 'on the level of scholarship, the sense of utter unworthiness that contact with a saint might bring on the level of virtue'.[59] He argued that he was not set in the mould of some types of academic historian, 'I cannot hold a candle to a Stenton or a Douglas or a Powicke or a McFarlane – *nedum* to a Maitland – as a "professional" historian; I have made no important discoveries and changed no patterns.'[60] In an obvious sense the judgement was self-deprecatory to the point of caricature. The four great volumes had transformed understanding of medieval monastic history and, judged by any criterion, were superb works of scholarship. Yet there were elements of truth in Father David's disclaimer. His intellectual apprenticeship as a historian had been served, not at university, but at Downside, at the feet of Edmund Bishop, Cuthbert Butler and Hugh Connolly. Indeed as a historian of medieval monasticism he was largely self-taught. Something of this cast of mind is exemplified in his attitude towards the study of manuscript sources. Father David's reluctance to immerse himself in unpublished source material has often been stressed, exaggerated even, as would be shown by a glance at his edition of Lanfranc's *Monastic Constitutions* or at his initial work of compilation for *The Heads of Religious Houses*. Yet there is some substance to such a view and the reasons for his reluctance were various. He was conscious of the fact that he lacked any formal training in the disciplines of palaeography and diplomatic (and was perhaps inclined to undervalue them). At the outset he was determined not to weaken his vow of stability by travel, and therefore chose to work on the topic of English monasticism prior to 1216 because he believed that

---

[57] Stacpoole 1975, p. 19.
[58] *Ibid.*, p. 72. On the matter of 'amateurishness', see also above pp. 48–9.
[59] Stacpoole 1975, p. 19 n. 3. [60] Morey 1979, p. 117.

the subject could adequately be studied by reference to the printed sources which were available to him at Downside. The examination of manuscript material would have involved absence from the community.[61] Later his reasoning changed, although the conclusions remained very similar. At both Ealing and Cambridge he took 'considerable soundings in unpublished manuscripts' but decided that, while such research was desirable in order to write the history of an individual house or to give a full account of the monastic economy, for his own more wide-ranging purposes it was not worth the diversion of effort. As he said, 'It was "either-or"; and I judged that what activities I had could be used more profitably as they have been'.[62] Indeed he claimed that scholars were inclined to make a fetish of manuscript studies, often to the detriment of absorbing the printed sources. It was partly a matter of his own judgement, partly a matter of temperament and training, but it did exemplify a kind of detachment from the more specialised and technical aspects of professional historical study. This detachment was apparent in many contexts, some trivial and some less so, in his reluctance to frequent the Public Record Office until the 1950s and in his reservations about attending international academic conferences. One would not look to his major works for the development of new techniques of historical research, nor were they the product of any organised, collective historical enterprise. He was essentially self-moved, and in many important respects at odds with the general tone of the historical milieu which greeted him at Cambridge. Some of Father David's writings were a direct outcome of his teaching. *The Evolution of Medieval Thought* sprang more or less directly from a course of lectures. But he was never, so to speak, a fully paid-up member of the professoriate. Or rather, he was more than that. Primarily he was a priest and a monk. And from this point of view the academic environment which he encountered at Peterhouse, and in the university at large, had little to offer him in strictly professional terms.

What is more, this detachment was physical as well as intellectual in nature. It is often assumed that Father David's years at Cambridge represented a break with his immediate past, a new and independent episode in his life. This was not so. Before his arrival at Peterhouse he had been living in London for the previous five years with the companionship of Elizabeth Kornerup. This arrangement was not entirely transformed in 1944. During his nineteen years in the college Father

[61] Stacpoole 1975, p. 72; Morey 1979, pp. 121–2.   [62] Stacpoole 1975, pp. 87–8.

David adopted a regular and consistent regime. He lived in his rooms in Gisborne Court during weekdays in term time, but at weekends and during the university vacations he normally returned to the care of Dr Kornerup, usually at the flat in Warwick Square. His time was therefore roughly equally divided between Cambridge and London, with London perhaps having a slight predominance. This dichotomy is clearly seen in the details of his life in college. On the one hand, as a bachelor fellow, he dined in Hall during term much more regularly than most of his contemporaries, who were largely married men. From this point of view he was a visible and active member of the collegiate community. But he rarely attended two of the more important meetings of the college's Governing Body each year, one to discuss undergraduate examination results and the other to consider admissions to the college, because these meetings were held outside term either in mid-summer or just before Christmas. Similarly, after his retirement from Cambridge, he returned to Dr Kornerup at Wimbledon or Linch. Above all, wherever he was and regardless of surroundings, many hours were spent in prayer. There was the regular recitation of his office and, whether heard or – latterly – said, the daily Mass. Against this background Peterhouse was a passing episode, 'no abiding city' even in the most physical sense, and during all of his years as a fellow of the college a large part of him was elsewhere. The notion of home has a particularly immediate meaning for a Benedictine monk but we should not assume that the college fulfilled this role in Father David's life.

Finally, and in parenthesis as it were, one might just glance at the opposite side of this relationship. What did Father David give to the college? Of course, and above all, he lent immense intellectual distinction. The combined presence of Denis Brogan, Herbert Butterfield, Munia Postan and Father David undoubtedly made Peterhouse for a while the most distinguished college for historical studies in either Oxford or Cambridge. But different observers might attach different importance to the contributions of each of the four individuals. In some respects Brogan and Butterfield had a more public stance. For a time every sixth-form student of history had a copy of *The Whig Interpretation of History* at his elbow, and every intelligent layman was familiar with the journalism and the broadcasting of Denis Brogan. The work of Postan and Father David was less widely known. Conversely, their reputations amongst their professional colleagues may well have stood higher than those of Brogan or Butterfield. But what did their collective reputation mean for the college in tangible terms? Professors did not normally give supervisions (or tutorials) to undergraduates, and after 1947 no informed schoolboy would have applied for admission to Peterhouse in the expectation of being individually taught by Father David. But not all applicants for admission are well-informed, and a former admissions tutor might reflect that the pattern of applications to any college takes shape in mysterious fashion. Legend, prejudice and ignorance are well to the fore. What, however, is clear and also perhaps surprising is that none of Father David's research students was a member of his own college. He supervised the research of many and their relationship with him formed a bond much stronger than the normal link between student and supervisor. But the circle was in no way based upon Peterhouse. Partly this was because he shied away from casting himself in the teutonic mould as the head of an organised research seminar. The uncoercive nature of his direction of research has been rightly stressed by many.[63] Partly it was a function of the collegiate nature of Cambridge which inhibited the concentration of research activity in this physical sense. Cambridge graduates who worked with Father David naturally remained in their own colleges. Those from elsewhere did not expect that their relationship with him would be coloured in any decisive way by membership of his own college. But the fact remains that there was no Peterhouse school of medieval history under the direction of Father David.

What was important to the college, although only briefly, was that for three years, between 1944 and 1947, Father David regularly taught Peterhouse undergraduates, starting in 1944 with only four pupils a week but increasing in 1946–7 to about a dozen. They were a more than usually mixed group. Many had been hardened by several years of war service. Their interest in academic matters had often diminished. Some were anxious to obtain a degree as soon as possible and to launch on their delayed careers. Others were straight from school, callow and inhibited. Some were freshmen, new to academic life; others were in their third year, more confident in the college than was their teacher. They were not even united by common intellectual concerns. At that time the history fellows of the college were not expected to specialise in their teaching. They were assigned pupils for the whole of an academic year and were

[63] Morey 1979, p. 103; also above p. 21 and below pp. 129, 132. The present writer can amply confirm this from his own experience. For a list of Father David's research students, see below, Appendix III, pp. 157–8.

required to teach whatever subjects their pupils might happen to be studying during that year. The justification for the system was clear enough. The options in the syllabus were then more limited than they were later to become. The volume of historical literature had not expanded to its present size. And it was held that a trained, intelligent historical sense could illuminate – often in fresh and unexpected ways – areas of study which lay outside its own particular expertise. But Father David had read classics as an undergraduate and his historical experience had begun, not with the broad demands of the tripos, but by immersing himself in Domesday Book. Now he was to find himself cast in the role of an expert on eighteenth-century France, seventeenth-century English constitutional history or the history of Political Thought.

Yet his supervisions (or tutorials) followed a regular – if not invariable – pattern. Each week at their appointed time his pupils would climb the spiral staircase to his rooms bearing their essays.[64] They would knock on the door and wait for it to be opened. It was a solecism, provoking an unusually explicit rebuke, to open the door for oneself and enter. His rooms struck many as spartan, even in the austere post-war years. There were few books and few personal possessions. In the bleak winter of 1947 the only heating was produced by an inadequate and antiquated electric fire. Even so, some suspected that the heating was provided for their benefit rather than Father David's and at the first onset of warmth he was quick to ask his pupils to turn off one of the bars. Normally Father David would read the essay himself, sometimes aloud. It was a technique which could be used to devastating effect. One of his pupils, given to writing a rather purple prose, still recalls how Father David 'embarked on one of my more impressive passages, came to the end of the page, turned over, read on for a line or so, then stopped and apologised, "I am so sorry, I seem to have turned over two pages".' The criticism was oblique, implied rather than overt, and this muted tone characterised Father David's reactions. In this area, as in others, he avoided confrontation. A freshman whose first essay was on the subject of the Reformation unwittingly launched an attack on both the teachings and the 'auth-

---

[64] For what follows I am indebted to a number of Father David's undergraduate pupils who have kindly shared with me their recollections of his teaching, particularly Arnold Allen, Brian Anderton, Francis de Carteret-Bisson, John Cannon, George Gale(†), Frank Glyn-Jones, F.J. Griggs, Hugh Kearney, F.A. Larcombe, Graham Presland, L.D. Stockwood, Bryan Swingler, Hugh Watts, Ken Webley, John Wendon and Peter Woods.

oritarianism' of the Catholic Church. It was only later, to his own mortification, that he was disabused of his assumption that his supervisor was an Anglican priest. Father David, partly anxious no doubt not to embarrass a freshman, had simply passed over the subject without comment. In fact much of his criticism of his pupils' essays focused on matters of style and clarity of argument. Certainly his own distinction as a writer lay behind this sensitivity, but it also reflected his long previous experience as a schoolmaster and perhaps also his ignorance in detail of the subjects he found himself teaching. At the least he could ensure lucidity and elegance of expression. But by some this innate reticence and the concentration on style were regarded as unhelpful. A few complained – probably not without reason – that he was not *au fait* with the current literature on the topics he was covering, that he was insufficiently dominant or forthcoming, expecting his pupils to suggest their own essay topics and in general failing to go out to meet them, as it were, on an intellectual level. In a word some felt that they got little out of him as a teacher. Certainly he had no *view* of teaching. His supervisions were unsystematic and discursive, as likely as not when opportunity presented to turn into a disquisition on Browning's poetry or an enquiry into the distance between the basins of the Cam and the Thames. He treated his pupils as adults. He did not give strong direction or seek to impose himself. And there were areas where his mind was closed. One undergraduate who had thrown himself into Hegel and Toynbee met incomprehension when he sought to discuss their writings, and another, excited by hearing Bertrand Russell speak, was disconcerted to find him dismissed as a 'madman'.[65] Doubtless there were other reasons at this time why Father David should also have been reluctant to talk about religious matters, even with a pupil who was a devout Catholic.

Yet it is noticeable that such criticisms were often made by the ablest, the most demanding of his pupils. Many others responded quite differently. For every one who found Father David withdrawn and unforthcoming, there were others who recall him as 'kind, encouraging and indefatigably good humoured' or as 'self-evidently a benign and good-hearted man' who could laugh at himself and 'laugh at others, with the faintest whiff of malice'. Father David did not wear his heart on his sleeve. Equally the reactions of his pupils reflected their own

---

[65] Compare Knowles 1962b, p. 223.

temperament as much as his own. So ambiguities and contradictions abound. One who regarded him as 'an austere, detached, somewhat forbidding figure' could still take the unusual step in those more formal times of inviting him to tea in his own lodgings. Another recalls Father David's comments on his work as 'authoritative' yet 'paradoxically tentative'. And a pupil who described the criticisms of his essays as 'reticent and low key', was still left feeling that his work was 'hopelessly inadequate'. Nevertheless some general impressions emerge of a teacher who was diffident and forbearing, gentle, calm – almost hesitant, and tolerant of weakness while not glossing over inadequacy. His supervisions seemed to one in retrospect more like 'friendly chats' than 'forceful education'. Yet, as a particularly perceptive pupil discerned, Father David was not entirely relaxed, 'taut rather than tense . . . a man with no chink in his armour'. Looking back, 'I think he was a man living right out on the edge of self control.'

Armour there certainly was. The measured quality of Father David's relations with his pupils was a protection against the intensity of relations with Downside and with Elizabeth Kornerup. And the armour was effective. Undergraduates are quick to caricature their teachers but Father David was never remotely a figure of fun. Nor, like some, did he demean himself by cultivating undergraduates: 'we would not have expected that or wished it from Dom David'. In general there was an air of formality, of rectitude, about his teaching. The supervision was important and should be taken seriously. He did not, like Denis Brogan, continue writing his correspondence while his pupils read their essays. Rather he 'made it politely clear that one was expected to do things properly and not seek by "cleverness" to conceal that one hadn't done the spadework one ought to have done'. One of his pupils who was normally taught at 9 o'clock in the morning, but was confined to bed with an ankle injury, found that nevertheless Father David came to his bedside at the appointed time to conduct the supervision. Equally, error – and particularly stylistic infelicity – was there to be corrected. One able undergraduate, subsequently to become a distinguished journalist, made the mistake of presuming on his ignorance of the English railway system. The response was withering but the experience saved the pupil 'countless times from writing some piece of rubbish which sounded good and expert and wasn't'. Others, whose recollection of the factual content of Father David's teaching is now fading, have never forgotten learning from him that the word 'however' is a signpost to the reader and should therefore normally be placed near the beginning of a sentence, or that metaphors should illuminate and not obscure the writer's meaning.

Yet sometimes the armour would momentarily be removed, particularly where the pupil had something in common with Father David, an interest in cricket, a shared knowledge of the west Midlands or even a common social background. Then the mood might soften and there would be surprisingly candid asides, often involving personalities. To one pupil he confided, in slightly conspiratorial fashion, that St Bernard must have been a *very* difficult man. Another he regaled with a hilarious account of the personal clumsiness of the great Anglo-Saxonist, F.M. Stenton. Occasionally he would lapse into a slightly self-conscious argot, familiar to all close readers of his books, as when Anne Boleyn was dismissed as 'really a rather cheap little whore'. A pupil who ventured, when faced with his enormous and old-fashioned typewriter, to ask him about his technique of writing received an unexpectedly revealing response:

> He explained that he would first digest his material and then write direct into the typewriter with three or four sheets of narrative; the fourth or fifth sheet would then be 'the purple passage', a phrase which he used with mischievous glee. He said he maintained this rhythm throughout the text for he feared he might lose the attention of his readers.

And for some there were acts of considered, intimate kindness which went well beyond any normal relationship between teacher and pupil. One undergraduate lent Father David a copy of G.M. Trevelyan's *English Social History* which was then reprinting and scarce. When the book was returned he was moved to discover that it now bore the author's signature on the dedication page. As an unspoken token of his gratitude Father David had taken the book to Trevelyan himself to be inscribed. Another pupil found in his pigeon-hole on one day which had a particular personal resonance for him a copy of *The Imitation of Christ* inscribed 'From M.D.K.' and with the words 'Where is the profit, and what is the worth in the sight of God, of aught that is not love of God?'

Public perceptions of Father David amongst the college's undergraduate community naturally varied greatly. There was knowledge of the break with Downside and of the relationship with Elizabeth Kornerup and, fuelled by the indiscretions of a colleague, gossip quickly gave a lurid gloss to the matter. Less predictably, amongst a group of undergraduates who were largely not his pupils but who were closely interested in public affairs, Father David became something of a political totem. The group was unsympathetic to the new Labour government of 1945, 'hostile to the world that we then imagined Harold Laski and his ministerial acolytes wished to create'. For them the election of a monk to a fellowship of the college 'seemed an important gesture of defiance against the newer world to be run by LSE levellers'. But others saw a more private man, 'a small dark clad, clerical collared figure walking lightly across Gisborne Court' who was not fully part of their Cambridge life, a man who was 'away from the college a good deal', who was frequently 'going off early tomorrow'. The college was 'no abiding city' and some, who were his fellow Catholics, were aware of this and aware also that the face which he presented to his pupils, diffident, often benign, sometimes gently exigent, at times even apparently relaxed, was in important respects a mask. Behind it lay deeper issues which transcended the academic world and which could find no articulation in it. A few of his pupils had some sense of this, 'when he heard Mass in the Catholic Church he kept himself small and very much at the back of the congregation as if painfully aware of his exclusion'. Or, again, 'whenever one went to morning Mass at the church in Lensfield Road, right at the back, behind the screen, was always the small figure of Dom David. Forbidden to say Mass or to communicate, he never lost his faith. In a way, it seemed wrong that *I* could receive – but then, of course, mine was the greater need.'

In a number of ways Father David came closer to some of his undergraduate pupils than he did to many of his colleagues amongst the fellowship. There were a variety of reasons for this. From January 1947 he was a professor and therefore formally precluded from holding any major administrative office, such as tutor or bursar, within the college. But, even had he been able to do so, his regular absence from Cambridge during weekends and vacations, his age, his background, his temperament and abilities and particularly his massive commitment to the completion of the four volumes of monastic history, would have made a close involvement of this sort in the life of the college unlikely. Perhaps also the memory of earlier conflicts inhibited him, particularly as some of the other participants remained amongst the fellowship. It may have been no accident that one of his most decisive interventions in college affairs, or at least the one best remembered, occurred after Paul

Vellacott's death at the end of 1954, when the fellows were faced with the problem of electing a new Master. The college statutes of course laid down formal rules for the conduct of an election but these rules were restrictive and in particular imposed a tight timetable on the proceedings. What was required was some informal machinery by which fellows' views could be clearly expressed before the constraints of the statutory procedure came into force. To resolve the problem Father David suggested to his colleagues that they might care to follow the arrangements for electing an abbot which were practised within Benedictine communities. His suggestion was adopted and in the event, appropriately enough, Herbert Butterfield was elected Master. Father David would have savoured the thought that in this respect at least the college's Benedictine founder was proving to cast a long shadow. Finally there can be no doubt that his habitual reticence – the wish to avoid confrontation and sometimes even familiarity – was at times carried to lengths where it could be misunderstood. When a close colleague sent a copy of his new book to Father David, a major work which had occupied him for some fifteen years, he was justifiably disconcerted to receive a note in return with the laconic – if consoling – comment, 'You must have thought a lot', merely accompanied by a rebuke for having referred to a minor character in the book as young when he was at the time in fact middle-aged.

This is not to imply that in general his relations with his colleagues were cool. By the time of his retirement he was regarded within the college with widespread respect and affection. But the fellows of any college are not a homogeneous group, and Father David aroused a variety of different responses. The secular were bewildered by his evident calling. Some sensed that they were in the company of one whose loyalties and preconceptions were entirely alien to them. The literary-minded enjoyed his range of allusion and the style of his conversation and writing. His fellow historians might have taken a professional attitude towards his work. All could value his restrained wit and be conscious of his distinction. A few were close to him and were regaled during his absences from Cambridge with a correspondence which combined rigorous judgement with a wit which could extend to farce. One brief note recommending a candidate for admission to the college might begin surrealistically, 'If you had this letter yesterday, so to say, don't trouble to read what follows', adding by way of explanation, 'I wrote it and stamped it, but could not find it at post-time, nor since', and then conclude with a brisk reflection on a notable recent history of a particular monastery, 'It seemed to me first-class within its terms of reference, viz. a religious house without visible religion (like Geoffrey Elton's Reformation)'. In another letter the judgement was similarly brisk on *The Mirror of Simple Souls*, a mystical text whose author, Margaret Porete, was burnt for heresy in Paris in 1310, and which – according to Father David – had been over-valued by those whose wish to emphasise the achievements of women writers in the Middle Ages outran their theological discretion, 'It [*The Mirror*] says all the things that the anti-mystics have always accused mystics of saying, and isn't much practical help even when orthodox'. Ironic good humour was always present: 'Next week I go to Oxford to . . . examine a Franciscan for the D.Phil. What would St Francis have made of that – a thesis on Franciscan poverty?' And an account of a visit to Linch by the distinguished monastic historian Dom Kassius Hallinger rose to hilarity, 'an unexpected mixture of a high spirited rather elephantine cleric and a dedicated scholar who emerged from a Morris Mini without any notice or warning with the greeting – "Professor Knowles? (Dr Livingstone, I presume?) I want to know what you think of the relationship of the Paris MS and the Regula Magistri".'[66] Such letters embroidered his Cambridge friendships, but these were not in any way confined to his own college.

Father David was a man of complex character and his colleagues naturally responded to those elements in his make-up which spoke to them. As the scholastics warn us, and as he was himself only too well aware, '*Quidquid recipitur, secundum modum accipientis recipitur.*'[67] But the fact that he was a man of many parts, diversely talented, should not be the final judgement, should not be deployed as a way of evading his own priorities. In an obvious sense his spiritual life was not open to the world in the same sense as his writings or his public demeanour. But this ought not to lead us merely to acknowledge it in passing or to treat it as just one other facet of his protean nature. Of course his writings cover many themes and contain many felicities. His memories of the broader cultural enthusiasms of his earlier life were often recalled and their resonances echoed on in his later works. But the substance was more demanding.

[66] D.K. to R.L., respectively 25 Oct. 1973, 21 April 1964, 20 Oct. 1974 and 15 Sept. 1968.
[67] See Knowles 1961, p. 12, and 1962b, p. 232: 'We modify to suit our capacity everything that we receive'.

The last words of the third volume of *The Religious Orders* are a conclusion in the fullest sense. They are not just the final sentences. They are a statement of the only meaning that ultimately mattered to him.

Above all, in purely human terms, Father David was his own man. Throughout his mature life and in varying circumstances he preached detachment. This was not just a detachment from the more obvious forms of worldliness. It was merely symptomatic that he read no novels after 1930, that he essentially ceased to listen to music, that he visited the theatre only twice and then to see two Greek plays, that he virtually abandoned foreign travel, and that he watched television on only two occasions in his lifetime. And it was in the same vein that he rejected a range of nostrums, whether romanticism, self-expression, literature as religion or rationalism. Even the beauties of nature, which meant so much to him, had 'nothing to do with the deeper life of the spirit'. Rather renunciation was a positive act, '*Unum est necessarium*, the mind and heart wholly free for God'.[68] This theme was insistent and demanding, repeated at different times and in different contexts, but never varying. In 1931 he wrote to a confrère of his faith

> . . . that the way of renunciation, of the Cross, is the only one – and that the renunciation must be of ourselves – affections, hopes, activities. It is also that there is no place at all in the scheme for development of private interests, of 'self-realisation'. I have no defence to offer, e.g., for my tour in Greece. It just should not have been done. That it was pleasant, and amassed a store of pleasant memories, is nothing. God just did not want it and who knows what I missed – not only in Masses not said but in what I might have done for other people had I not gone . . . Superficial, peripheral happiness is never a test of anything once the edge of the supernatural has been passed. The test is unselfishness and detachment . . . God never fails to bless the least sacrifice, even if it is merely making a virtue out of necessity . . . Until we have so been through fire and water that we can be in this world *tamquam nihil habentes et omnia possidentes*, loss is better than gain.[69]

And more than thirty-five years later he was writing to another confrère in almost identical terms.

---

[68] Stacpoole 1975, pp. 76, 83, 50; Morey 1979, p. 115. See also Abbot Sillem's judgement, above pp. 29–30, 44–6.   [69] Stacpoole 1975, pp. 22–3.

Activity, not least because it may be good in itself, at least in appearance, can so easily be a flight from God, a denial of part of the heart of Our Lord. I know it so well myself. True spirituality is the choice of the unseen, the essentially supernatural, God, in place of what is merely natural, the created.[70]

Intellectual activity was no different from any other.

Haste, rush, the accumulation of work never in the long run does spiritual good. It may be necessary now and then, and *solid work* has a great spiritual value – but once it becomes absorbing, or an escape from oneself or from God, then it is a mere sounding of brass and does not do any spiritual good; and any talk of 'charity' or 'merit' is just hot air.[71]

Hence it followed,

The old misquotation *laborare est orare* is terribly false in the common sense of the words . . . work is never a substitute for prayer and overwork is (in the monastic, spiritual context) always self-love.[72]

Father David's own academic duties were to him, 'just what they are – the day's stint of work – not the *Opus Dei*, the *unum necessarium*'.[73] And for the monk the imperative was overwhelming.

A monk cannot throw himself utterly into anything. The lines of his life, the interruptions of the day and the loss of energy caused by the office and spiritual duties must always keep him in check. It is part of his obedience and of his poverty that he cannot call his life or his time his own.[74]

Thirty years later the need for a 'monasticism of the soul' was no less exigent.

The true monk, in whatever century he is found, looks not to the changing ways around him or to his own mean condition, but to the unchanging everlasting God, and his trust is in the everlasting arms that hold him. Christ's words are true: He who doth not renounce all that he possesseth cannot be my disciple.[75]

---

[70] *Ibid.*, p. 33. [71] *Ibid.*, p. 50. [72] *Ibid.*, p. 33. [73] *Ibid.*, p. 50.
[74] Knowles 1929, p. 90. [75] *Ibid.*, p. 78; *RO* III, p. 468.

Certainly Father David changed after his arrival in Peterhouse in 1944. He became more relaxed. Old passions naturally cooled as time passed. Twenty years spent amongst professional academics could not but take their toll. He acquired some of the mannerisms of the caste. His interests expanded. Public distinction and prolonged association with *l'homme moyen sensuel* had an effect. But these were superficial matters. He never forgot the proper place of intellectual activity in the life of the monk. And we totally misunderstand him if we imagine that he could be essentially influenced by any purely secular body of men. What the college meant to him was perfectly and precisely summed up in his own words. The house of St Peter was a refuge, a source of stability and companionship. *Hospes fui et collegistis me.* Of course this was important to him. We do not diminish his affection for the college by recognising that there was another house whose deeper claims on him he explicitly acknowledged, '*Unam petii et hanc requiram, ut inhabitem in domo Domini omnibus diebus.*'[76]

On the day before his death Father David wrote two letters, one addressed to me and one to my wife.[77] The lightness of touch was still there. There was a request that I should lend to the University Press my copy of the first printing of the third volume of *The Religious Orders*, unless you have 'spoilt your copy in fury'. But the hand was tremulous and thoughts were directed to the last things. His mind had now turned to a monastic ideal of long standing, which had never lost its hold over him, the Carthusian Order. This eremetic, and most austere, of monastic orders, *nunquam reformata quia nunquam deformata*, had first attracted him when still a novice and for many years subsequently he had contemplated a Carthusian vocation. The superiority of the Carthusian calling had been explicitly acknowledged in *The Monastic Order* and its claims were still as compelling for him in 1969.[78] He had chosen a portrait of Prior John Houghton as the frontispiece to the last volume of *The Religious Orders* and his account in that volume of the deaths of the monks of the London Charterhouse stood as an exemplar of monastic observance: 'When bishops and theologians paltered or denied, they

---

[76] Stacpoole 1975, p. 19; Ps. 26(27):4, 'One thing have I desired . . ., that will I seek after; that I may dwell in the house of the Lord all the days of my life.'

[77] D.K. to R.L. and D.K. to M.L., both of 20 Nov. 1974.

[78] *MO*, p. 224; Knowles 1969, pp. 122–3, 198–9. For his earlier attachment to the order, see Stacpoole 1975, pp. 89, 22, 24, and Morey 1979, pp. 35–6, 42, 50, 54, 129–32. Also, above pp. 29–30, 43–4.

were not ashamed to confess the Son of Man. They died faithful witnesses to the Catholic teaching that Christ had built His Church upon a rock.'[79] And it was an incident arising from the sufferings of the London Carthusians that he now recalled. During their imprisonment in Newgate they were given succour by the adopted daughter of Sir Thomas More, Mistress Clement, who had endeavoured to let food down to them through a hole in the roof of the prison. Forty years later when Mistress Clement lay dying in exile in Bruges she repeatedly told those with her that she could not stay long for the fathers of the London Charterhouse stood around her bed, calling her to come away with them.[80] It was this detail of this story, embodying an ideal which reached back not to Cambridge or his college but to the days of his noviciate, which was in the forefront of Father David's mind on the day before his death: 'I hope they will be near me with their prayers as they were at the bedside of Mistress Clement.'[81]

[79] *RO* III, p. 236.   [80] *RO* III, p. 236, n. 1.

[81] Many of my colleagues have helped me, often quite unwittingly, in the writing of this essay, but I am particularly grateful to Maurice Cowling, Martin Golding and Brian Wormald. Patrick Higgins generously guided me through the voluminous Butterfield papers in the CUL. That the work has seen the light of day at all is a tribute to the painstaking assistance and cheerful forbearance of Christopher Brooke.

7

DAVID KNOWLES AND HIS PUPILS

DAVID LUSCOMBE

Knowles's lectures in the Mill Lane lecture rooms in Cambridge introduced him as a teacher to succeeding generations of undergraduate students reading History and sometimes other subjects besides. He always got to the lecture room before the hour and stood on the podium, grim of face, sombrely dressed in clerical black with the obligatory black academic gown, and waited until the due moment. He appeared to meditate but inscrutably. The mouth was thin and tightly closed, the eyes dark, his hair sparse but bright silver. But then it was time to start and he would smile, not ingratiatingly but charmingly as if he were immensely glad to see us all. And he would speak in that high, slightly bleating voice which Angus Wilson so exactly described in *Anglo-Saxon Attitudes* when introducing Father Lavenham, 'the great Benedictine scholar'. And we would take notes.[1]

Knowles came to Cambridge as a Fellow of Peterhouse in 1944. His first course which he put on in 1945–6 was a final-year Special Subject. This was on St Francis of Assisi. For Daniel Waley, now celebrated as a historian of medieval Italy, who had the year before first seen Assisi as a soldier and who had scarcely read a book for over five years, it was a marvellous experience to be thrown straight into the enthralling problems set by the Thomas of Celano *Lives* and the *Legenda trium sociorum*. Rosalind Clark was another who took the new Subject in

---

[1] *Anglo-Saxon Attitudes: a Novel* (London, 1956) p. 44. It is not I but other former pupils and friends of Dom David who have provided whatever is of value in this chapter. My thanks go to Rosalind Brooke (née Clark), Christopher Brooke, Giles Constable, Keith Egan, Philip Jebb, Hugh Lawrence, Gordon Leff, Daniel Waley, Michael Wilks – and above all and most especially to Hugh Brogan. I call Dom David in this chapter by his surname simply because I seem to remember that this was how many of us spoke of him colloquially.

1945–6. C.R. Dodwell, later Professor in the University of Manchester and distinguished historian of medieval art, took it in 1946–7. Among those who followed in 1947 was Christopher Brooke, whom Rosalind later married. Knowles was appointed University Lecturer in August 1946, and Professor of Medieval History early in 1947, and henceforth a wider variety of lecture courses was put on by him, and he was heard by undergraduates in different years of their course (see Appendix II, p. 156).

My own earliest opportunity to hear Knowles lecturing came in 1957 towards the end of my first year as an undergraduate when it was customary to prepare for an examination in medieval European history. In the third term many of us sought him out without too close a regard for the imminence of our examinations. While preparing for an entrance scholarship examination in English at King's College two years before, I had read the published version of his Ford Lectures on *The Episcopal Colleagues of Archbishop Thomas Becket* (1951a); and after diverting from English to History during my first year in the university, I settled, like many others, into reading sections of the large volumes of *The Monastic Order* and of *The Religious Orders* which provided me with accounts – easily followable and adequately full – of the European dimension of medieval monastic history as well as of aspects of European intellectual history which all helped towards the first-year examination paper. In the late 1950s and early 1960s the lecture courses Knowles offered to students of the outlines of medieval European history focused specifically on the history of monks and friars and on the history of medieval thought. He did not lecture on the development of the medieval English church, in spite of the Ford lectures, nor on the medieval mystics on whom he had published a book in 1927 which was revised into a new book that appeared in 1961. His courses of eight lectures on The Orders of Monks and Friars in the Middle Ages and (from Easter in 1957) on Some Figures in Medieval Thought bridged two of Knowles' main historical interests, for all the thinkers were either monks or friars and many of the monks and friars were also thinkers. The lectures also gave Knowles full scope to present character studies, in fulfilment as it were of the reflections enshrined in the inaugural lecture on *The Historian and Character* which he had given as Regius Professor in 1954 and which was well known to undergraduates through being widely available for sale in pamphlet form in the local bookshops. His speech was such a clear pane of glass that one thought only of the persons in view and as they were so deeply interesting and as he made clear a world with which we were mostly and largely unfamiliar his audiences were quietly very appreciative. But they were probably also slightly specialised audiences as students of history go; to learn about William the Conqueror or King John or about medieval tradesmen or farmers one turned elsewhere, to Edward Miller for example. But Knowles did put before us the features of the age and the times of the persons on whom he dwelt. The piercing originality of the mind of Anselm of Canterbury was seen to have been assisted by his geographical mobility and especially by his Norman monastic setting; Aquinas's career in Naples, Paris, Cologne and Rome presented him with pressing opportunities to harmonise and synthesise on an ambitious and vast scale the speculative achievements of ancient Greece and Rome, of medieval Islam and of Christian tradition. Knowles presented these and other figures as they appeared to an ecclesiastical or rather a religious eye; but the historical vista was always richly full and instructive. However, the qualities pursued by any lecturer appear as defects to at least part of an audience; he spoke slowly enough for one to be able to write down nearly all of what he said and it could be urged that in his anxiety to be perfectly lucid and perfectly fair he made Anselm and Francis and the rest a little too approachable. But he owed some of his esteem to his practical recognition of the fact that there were many in the room who needed all the help that they could get if they were to perform adequately in the Tripos and also to those unexpectedly delicious moments (no doubt carefully rehearsed) as when he told us that Aquinas was so fat that a semicircle was cut into the dining table to enable him to reach his food (laughter). And slowly, with slightly puzzled smile, Knowles continued: 'But when you think about it, it's hard to see how this would help' (louder laughter).

Knowles had taught his Special Subject on St Francis in years before I arrived in Cambridge. A Special Subject in History involves the detailed study of a select body of historical source material together with a consideration of the critical problems this raises in reconstructing and in evaluating a historical topic. As a Special Subject the study of Francis and the early Franciscan friars had offered to students the opportunity to explore the life of a truly exceptional religious genius and to weigh the tensions and the controversies that this genius aroused and over which no later judge can pass a final objective verdict. For as Knowles had written in *The Religious Orders in England* in 1948,[2] the origins of the Franciscan friars abound in highly complex problems that are at once

[2] *RO* I, 114.

religious and also historical and scholarly. And as such they had attracted and still continued to attract eminent scholars from many nations, and they had also for long generated a vast technical literature of their own. The passions aroused for and against St Francis and the friars both in the late Middle Ages and in the Age of Romanticism, and involving both those who were members of the Catholic church and those who were not, and also those clergy who were and who were not members of the orders of friars, did not appear to perturb him. Such tensions he put into perspective by a concentration upon the critical study of the literary monuments of the early Franciscan life. But at the same time Knowles called attention to the persistence of deeper biographical and spiritual problems that critical techniques alone cannot lay to rest.[3] He once identified three defining characteristics of a Special Subject. First it must be interesting and significant in itself. Secondly, it should have a sufficiency of sources, not too little, not too much. And thirdly, these sources should be sufficiently discordant to involve labour in their reconciliation. And he distinguished this labour into two kinds of criticism, ordinary criticism which requires decision between conflicting sources (harmonisation, rejection, resolution) and high criticism which considers the authenticity of documents. To illustrate the former type of criticism he cited Eusebius's labours on the Four Gospels; to illustrate the latter he referred to the so-called Higher Criticism pursued within circles of Biblical scholars in the past century. As a definition of a Special Subject this may not be perfect because in modern (as distinct from medieval) history the morass of documentation defies the principle of 'not too little, not too much' and also the nature of the evidence often allows very little necessity to apply 'higher criticism'. And even if the definition is limited to special studies in medieval or ancient history it would no doubt need to be qualified when the evidence taken into account is not exclusively literary. But although it is easy to enumerate differences in other fields of historical teaching, the central aim of a Special Subject remains that of giving undergraduate students sustained experience of the problems involved in the use of primary sources. The St Francis subject did that.

At first sight Knowles's later Special Subject on Cistercian Origins and the Controversies of St Bernard with the Cluniacs, with Abelard and with Gilbert de la Porrée may seem to breach his stated intention by

---

[3] Cf RO I, chap. xi.

offering too great a variety of focus and topic. I followed this course in 1958–9 along with a good forty or so other students. The title was certainly a long one. But it was in reality held together by a concentration upon the study of a critical moment in the evolution of Benedictine monasticism when the order of Cistercian monks was formed, and when that order grew to prominence under the leadership of the remarkable Bernard of Clairvaux. And if Bernard's career seems too vast and varied for detailed study at an undergraduate level, it was in fact made possible through concentrating upon his controversies only with the Cluniacs and with the men of the schools. The subject was interesting and significant in itself in so far as it focused on a dramatic turning point in the development of European monasticism, one when monasticism experienced sharp reform and growth and yet began to feel a threat to its intellectual and cultural hegemony consequent upon the advance of ways of thought that were in time to be associated with the development of universities. Moreover, it involved great men, for Bernard, the two Peters and Gilbert were all in their different ways leaders of their time. The sources too were discordant and fully reflected the reasons that brought Bernard into so many quarrels. As for 'higher criticism' there was ample scope; the complex set of primitive documents relating to the foundation of the Cistercian order teemed with problems of authenticity and interpretation. The scholarly literature concerning these documents that had appeared during the 1940s and 1950s was severely technical; it was mostly devoted to distinguishing the successive stages of the evolution of the earliest Cistercian programme or way of life. This was not the stuff to inspire large groups of university students then or indeed in any age. But there was in that literature an uneasy awareness that though the Cistercians ably proclaimed their fidelity to a Rule, Cîteaux had started in an act of disobedience and revolt. And the tension between conformity and disorder contains some of the ingredients conducive to even a little undergraduate study. The early Cistercians, although they aimed to restore what they saw as a faithful respect for the provisions of the Rule of St Benedict himself, invented an articulated order of houses set apart from traditional abbeys by their subordination to a ruling general chapter of their own abbots meeting together.

Furthermore, Robert of Molesme, the first abbot of Cîteaux, had been concerned enough to find a way of restoring the values and the observances for which Benedict had legislated that he had removed himself with various companions and supporters from more than one previous monastic abode. To all appearances he had broken his vow of stability. It was therefore in circumstances of some respectful excitement just before the examinations began in the summer of 1959, in fact within a few days of the examination paper itself, that Knowles received and made available to us a copy of a paper written by the Belgian scholar Charles Dereine who showed that a breakaway group of monks would be able to protect itself against censure in the lifetime of Robert because his contemporary Pope Urban II had specifically allowed such an exodus or migration if it was undertaken, as the Cistercians themselves claimed, in pursuit of an *arctior vita* or stricter way of life.[4] Knowles guided us to think that Dereine's contention was definitive.

There could have been no students of this Special Subject who were unaware that Dom David was a monk and very few who were unaware that he had been under some sort of a cloud for parting company with his monastic community at Downside. Knowles, although educated in the Classics at Christ's College, was manifestly not a home-grown Cambridge don and if the proximate roots of his scholarly interests – Cuthbert Butler for example or Edmund Bishop perhaps – were hidden to most, it was clear enough that the general source of his inspiration was the Benedictine tradition. He made comments sometimes that seemed to emerge obliquely from his own monastic past as when he once said, à propos of entry into the religious life, how well populated convents of women had been in Austria at the turn of the last century – a comment that seemed to reflect some talk in the cloister rather than in academe. And when he remarked with what seemed like a shiver how dreadfully cold Romuald and other eleventh-century hermits must have been in their caves in the Apennine mountains in wintertime or when he dwelt grimly on the austerities Bernard of Clairvaux imposed on himself during his first two years as a monk, eating only beech leaves and nettles and vomiting almost every night on account of a weak stomach, one sensed a personal preoccupation or perhaps horror creeping in to the exposition. But Knowles himself never once as far as I know allowed the experience of his own crisis to obtrude. Enough was known for students to realise that they were being introduced to the study of a monastic reformation by one who had striven to change his own monastery and had then left it. We gossiped about this, naturally, but on the basis of

[4] Dereine 1959. For a recent comment on these scholarly problems see Holdsworth 1986.

threadbare surmise and virtually no facts – though one witty don had allegedly put it about that Knowles would not go back to Downside until he received apologies from a pope and a cardinal, both unfortunately dead. The rumours stimulated our interest but there was never a moment when Knowles uttered even the briefest of comment on the modern church that could be related in any way to his own past difficulties. He strikingly exemplified the intellectual chastity which he praised as the essence of scholarship and which kept him, especially in his formal teaching, away from everything that was irrelevant to the matter in hand.

In his rooms in Peterhouse, Knowles occasionally brought together after his lectures small groups from the larger Special Subject audience to hear papers presented by one or other member of the class. The discussions were flat and uninspiring as Knowles made only the slightest of efforts to direct or promote discussion. He did, however, show to us an adjoining room where he had collected together all the sources and articles and 'where you may go whenever you wish'. This was generous as the room was within his suite, the collection was immensely convenient, and we came and went at all hours of day and evening. From time to time in this room he also entertained smaller groups of, I suppose, three or four students to lunch. He had not always done so, and in his earlier years in Cambridge when he was less relaxed and times were harder his hospitality was restricted. But his teas were sumptuous and when he offered in 1947–8 to invite Rosalind Clark (who was then his research student) to come to tea to meet Christopher Brooke (who was then taking his Special Subject) but then either forgot or repented of his offer, Rosalind – who was to become Christopher's wife – felt doubly disappointed! But by the late 50s he had people to tea and gave fine lunches as well, though he himself avoided the wine that was available. On such occasions, not then unusual in Cambridge, all felt diffident on gathering but conversation could take off and run in surprising directions. The ownership and occupants of The Albany in London seemed to be the most pressing matter of interest when my turn came to be invited and I still have not come to terms with the evident fascination and considerable knowledge shown about London's millionaires over the table that day.

In his last years before retirement Knowles turned from teaching a Special Subject to teaching what was known as a Specified Subject, that is, a year-long course of lectures given to students under supervision within their own Colleges and not requiring very prolonged exposure to original sources. The course was on The Intellectual History of Europe, 1000–1350 and was followed in 1962 by the appearance of Knowles's book on *The Evolution of Medieval Thought* (1962a). The main theme of the course was the currents of speculation and enquiry that had descended from ancient Greece and Rome into the medieval Christian west. As an approach to the history of medieval thought this owed much to the earlier work of such giants as Etienne Gilson and Fernand Van Steenberghen, and the debt was acknowledged freely, but Knowles added his own knowledge of classical thought, which he had studied as an undergraduate, his own knowledge of Catholic and scholastic theology which he had studied in Downside and in Rome, his own knowledge of the medieval mystics and, incomparably, his own biographical sketches of the leading figures. He addressed himself primarily to undergraduate students of History, and not, as his Continental models did, to students of Philosophy, and in so doing he enlarged the boundaries of historical study – as R.L. Poole and F.M. Powicke had also tried to do in Oxford earlier. The lectures always began with the reading of a written introduction and they usually closed with a somewhat hastier reading of a prepared conclusion, but the bulk of the delivery, even if he had a full script with him, was almost colloquial and easy for the note taker. Knowles was seldom dry; his evenly pitched, delicately modulated voice clearly indicated by a slight change of tone when something humorous was coming, as it periodically did. His asides carried weight and still do. When May McKisack's welcome volume on the fourteenth century appeared in 1962 in the Oxford History of England Knowles promptly but mildly drew the attention of the class to the absence from it of any treatment of what is by any standard of judgement a signal feature of that age, the debates and activities of the English schoolmen. He correctly drew attention, even though there was nothing an undergraduate could immediately do about it, to the absence of a full study of the medieval English cathedral schools as well as to the unlikelihood that Dr Eleanor Rathbone, for all her marvellous discoveries and huge collection of material, would ever complete and publish one. In 1961 Knowles published his book on *The English Mystical Tradition*. This contained the substance of the Sir D. Owen Evans Lectures given at the University College of Wales, Aberystwyth, during the session 1959 to 1960. On February 23, 1961, an anonymous reviewer of the book in *The Times*, while recommending the delightful accounts of such medieval figures as Richard Rolle, Walter Hilton, Julian of Norwich and Margery Kempe, also declared his unhappiness that a Regius Professor in a University dedicated to the pursuit of truth should have his work published with the 'imprimatur' and 'nihil obstat' of the Roman Catholic censors. The comment caused a stir and until early March the correspondence columns of *The Times* witnessed strong expressions of divergent views by a series of often public and well-known figures, including some leading colleagues in the historical profession; and the published correspondence terminated with a leader in which the writer acknowledged that the divide between Roman Catholics in Britain and their Protestant and other thoughtful neighbours had been sharply and vehemently laid bare. Knowles himself must have suffered some pain, although at least on this occasion ecclesiastical authority could not look at him askance. However, he made no public comment at all, not, that is, until one morning in Mill Lane he began a routine lecture on medieval thought by slowly saying 'this lecture hasn't been seen by the censors in Westminster'. Tension evaporated under the pin-prick of humour and the audience burst into applause.

Some of the research students allocated to Knowles for supervision had taken one or other of his undergraduate courses; others came to him having previously studied elsewhere. The relationship between a research student and his supervisor is always fraught with danger, especially if the one or the other gives an appearance of too much or of too little interest in the topic being attempted or in the pursuit of precision and depth of scholarship as compared with comprehension and perspective. In his early years in Cambridge Knowles must have been extremely reserved except with intimate friends. His first research student, Rosalind Clark, presented him with the added problem of being a woman. She had been enthralled by his Special Subject lectures on St Francis in 1945–6 and had inwardly noted a chance remark made by Knowles that more work was needed on Brother Elias. When she had succeeded in convincing her Director of Studies, Dr Helen Cam of Girton College, of her commitment to research, Dr Cam rang Father David up. 'This was', so Rosalind Brooke recalls, 'in 1946; it was winter, fuel was short; Father David was in his London flat under the keen eye of Elizabeth Kornerup; and he was just running the water for a bath. At the other end of the phone Helen Cam, full of persuasions; beside him the bathwater, threatening to lose its warmth'. The only escape was to say yes, and this he duly did. It was too soon after Knowles's entry into academic life for the best of his counsel and guidance to be given, and he had never been a research student himself. Dr Brooke was by no means the last of his students to have to find her way feeling pretty much unaided and feeling very insecure. Nor did she dare to admit to him her perplexities and problems. The sparseness of his comments on sections of written work submitted to him then and later was legendary; one of the longest comments I received was: 'I have read this with interest and, I hope, without permanent deterioration of eyesight.' But as the seemingly interminable stage of finding one's bearings in a scholarly fog began to draw to a close it did become possible to count blessings. He implicitly set an unrivalled standard by sheer example and reputation and one could never forget that he had written at least something on one's own topic, be this Plotinus or Augustine Baker or almost anything in between. He liked to discuss, if rather briefly, the work of those he called 'real' masters, such as Gilson or Martin Grabmann, as well as of those whom he thought were not. He ran no seminar and provided for graduates no forum and no succession of visiting speakers yet he was enterprising in writing letters of enquiry or introduction to other scholars who might give advice or share knowledge – and vigilant in finding out what ensued. So a circle of informed helpers was progressively formed. As Gordon Leff (PhD 1954) puts it:

> as a research supervisor he admirably combined the difficult balance between giving a lead and allowing one one's head. Not the least among his virtues – and not the most common among eminent people – was his capacity to listen. Although, in retrospect, I think he was too favourable and encouraging . . . he gave me the invaluable sense that I was writing for a sympathetic and responsive audience which made me try to raise my game . . . As no doubt most of those who knew him discovered, he was far more than a mere supervisor. He would never immediately begin an encounter with the latest state of one's work but would talk about a wide range of subjects: railways, places, sometimes other people, his own (less personal) experiences. Over the years they built up into a stock of impressions. He was also extraordinarily

hospitable; the, at first appearances, rather unworldly figure showed himself quite able to cope with the outside world in his pied à terre in Warwick Square or at Linch in Hampshire, including driving me to and from the station.

Matching a student to a topic he seemed to manage well. In the seminal studies that were devoted to the papacy and the friars, and to scholasticism and the universities, by H. Denifle and F. Ehrle nearly a century before, and which they published in their astoundingly wide-ranging *Archiv für Litteratur- und Kirchengeschichte des Mittelalters* (7 volumes, 1885–1900) Knowles found a host of subjects (he called it a quarry) inviting considerable exploration and still holding out the promise of substantial new advances. And so it proved. He was proud of what appeared under his editorship in the Second Series of *Cambridge Studies in Medieval Life and Thought*. Not all of these volumes were written by his pupils nor were all derived from topics first critically explored by Denifle and Ehrle, but two were.[5] And the culmination of having one's work published in his Series gave several of his students a start that might otherwise have been much harder. Once he had got a student into a position of competence he was a willing referee of applications for posts, not only writing testimonials but taking steady initiatives to find out what appointing committees really wanted, to match the person to the post. His letters, nearly always handwritten, kept one abreast of his view of the prospects and increasingly included a personal touch. He gently converted apprenticeship into friendship – and friendship that endured.[6]

Such friendships were fostered not least during the conversations he

---

[5] These are Brooke (R.B.) 1959 and Luscombe 1969. Knowles published a memorable study and appreciation of 'Denifle and Ehrle' in *History* 54 (1969), pp. 1–12. He told me once that Ehrle's studies (*Archiv*, 6 and 7 (1892 and 1900)) of Pedro de Luna (Benedict XIII) still deserved to attract a student into research.

[6] In a letter to me dated 1 Oct. 1972 he wrote: 'I reckoned the other day that at least 7 of my old research students are now in chairs, with one also who is Director [of the Department of Manuscripts in] the British Museum, your fellow Kingsman. And among those who followed classes or were college pupils are at least 3 more professors and the Headmaster of Winchester'. 'Research students', he also wrote, 'are in every way a most rewarding part of academic life. To see the gradual development of talent and judgement, and to follow and to try to forward a career, which usually implies a marriage and a new family to know or hear about, is perhaps the most abiding pleasure of a senior position.'

had while sitting on the left side of his desk and in front of a small but rather ornate crucifix. They were never long but they were never hurried. Many topics were closed to him – television, cinema, the radio among them, as well as Sunday newspapers, very nearly all novels and no doubt many other seemingly necessary adjuncts to a student's life. But he made an exception to listen each year to the carols broadcast from King's College on Christmas Eve and he expected me, as a Kingsman, to get to him a copy of the printed programme in advance. As this programme rarely arrived at the College from the University Printing House until 23 December, and as he was by then invariably in his cottage in the depths of Hampshire, and as it also reached him in time, it could be said that he inspired miracles, at least in Post Offices. Other topics, such as prayer and religious practice, the monastic experience and the contemporary church, were no doubt closed topics to some of his pupils, but – and especially if they were fellow Christians or priests – it was easy to raise them and he was invariably forthcoming although always brief. That he was a Catholic priest could never be put out of one's mind, but utterly faithful to Catholic doctrine though he was, his openness to students with different persuasions was quite unfeigned. He was plainly critical of those university bodies in the 1950s, the McCarthy period, which had not accepted his recommendations on behalf of a candidate with Marxist views. Conversely, at the end of the 1960s when he staunchly defended Pope Paul VI and his encyclical *Humanae vitae* on contraception, and thereby distanced himself from the overwhelming mass of expressed lay and educated opinion in England, he did not press his views on individual colleagues nor allow the difference to disturb friendships. The precise hindrance that kept him away from public appearances in churches and chapels was not clear to students; for many years he said daily Mass quietly on weekdays in St Bonaventure's friary on the other side of Trumpington Street from Peterhouse and on one occasion at least, this being the funeral in 1964 of his friend, the historian Outram Evennett of Trinity College, he did preach at Fisher House, the home of the Catholic Chaplaincy. On the other hand he would freely accept invitations to tea or dinner with students and he would speak to a College Historical Society. That he was active and knowledgeable in Faculty and University matters could not go unnoticed but he always withdrew from Cambridge at weekends, and the sight of his black-suited, black-hatted frame carrying a small suitcase was a regular one on Friday and Sunday afternoons between Peterhouse and Cambridge railway station via Hills Road and the Catholic Church there. People were discussable. He was not (by my time at least) at all 'buttoned up' nor excessively discreet. Come 25 May, the feastday of Pope Gregory VII, he might make fun of how he felt he should go round to Trinity College and serenade Walter Ullmann under his window. Whenever he spoke of 'the police' one had to remember he meant the Vatican. He had a treasure house of remarks about colleagues such as S.T. Bindoff – 'the slowest speaker ever heard' – and Bruce Dickins (who was seldom out of cycle clips) – 'there are two of him, one always in the foyer or catalogue room of the UL and the other on a bicycle in King's Parade'. He could get huffy at times. One year the examination questions paper for the Intellectual History course (he had not set it and this was no printing error) asked candidates to comment on the doctrine of *rationes sensuales*. He was manifestly hurt over this confusion by a colleague of Augustinian teaching on *rationes seminales*.

As retirement drew near and the realisation grew that he could not continue to live as before in Peterhouse his sadness and disappointment were acute and well shown once at least by the speed with which a screwed-up piece of paper met an unoffending wastepaper basket in his room.

To many outside Cambridge who had not been his pupils there came opportunities to hear Knowles lecture. He gave, for example, his Presidential addresses to the Royal Historical Society in Crosby Hall in four successive years.[7] When he spoke thus on the Maurists in the gathering twilight of one December evening, it felt, according to Professor C.H. Lawrence, 'like listening to a reincarnation of Jean Mabillon'. Knowles was no expert on diplomatic nor was he really a manuscripts man but Mabillon, as well as being the founder of the study of palaeography and diplomatic and the author of *De re diplomatica* (1681), was a great monastic historian and Knowles was his most worthy successor. Many, like Hugh Lawrence, had not been in his stable but became close to him, reticent though he was, through shared interests and the crossing of professional paths. M.J. Wilks's celebrated study of *The Problem of Sovereignty in the Later Middle Ages* also illustrates this for it began as a PhD dissertation on Augustinus Triumphus and on fourteenth-century views of papal monarchy, Walter Ullmann being

---

[7] Published in *Transactions of the Royal Historical Society*, Fifth Series, 8 (1958), 147–66; 9 (1959), 169–87; 10 (1960), 129–50; 11 (1961), 137–59; and republished in *GHE*.

the supervisor. Knowles came in as an examiner along with E.F. Jacob. It was not the practice to tell a candidate how he got on but Professor Wilks vividly remembers 'how at the last moment, as I shakily groped for the door handle, a little hand patted me on the shoulder and a whisper advised me not to lose any sleep about the result. It was a great kindness. And somehow or other we were friends from then.' In 1963 the work was published, in rewritten form, in *Cambridge Studies*.

In 1962 he gave the Birkbeck Lectures in Cambridge. These are public lectures in ecclesiastical history and are not tied to any course of study. His title was *Problems in Monastic History*. The audience he gained was comparatively senior and moderately sized. He dealt with two problems, the first being the Rule of St Benedict and the extent to which Benedict still was owed credit for its content. His purpose in this was to examine and appraise the debates on this among scholars – and he spoke of them in terms of bombers and disposal squads and fire-fighters who had been at war with each other on many fronts for decades. Surprisingly, in view of this imagery and of the displacement of St Benedict from his traditional position as a solitary genius, Knowles did not draw any parallel with the destruction in 1944 of the buildings at Benedict's monastery on Monte Cassino or with their resurrection afterwards. There was and is a general recognition that his account of the issues is important and was highly desirable as at that time it was impossible for any historian not working closely in the field of sixth-century monastic literature to know what to believe or where truth might lie. The second problem was the primitive documents of the Cistercian order. This had been the core of his Special Subject recently but now he aligned the scholarly discussions over the beginnings of the reformed Cistercian way of life with those concerning St Benedict and the earliest documents of the traditional monastic order. Both topics had 'a real importance in religious history' and as well 'much of the perennial appeal of the historical mystery, not to say, of the detective story'.[8] Like the Rule, the Cistercian *Carta Caritatis* had long been 'recognised as one of the very few epoch-making and revolutionary pieces of monastic legislation',[9] but, and again like the Rule, a careful comb-out of the manuscripts had transformed understanding and it had come to appear to be a composite document or rather bunches of documents unfolding at various dates, not the work of a single sophisticated mind showing a

---

[8] These lectures were also published in *GHE*. See here p. vi.   [9] *GHE*, p. 201.

sudden flash of foresight and genius. Like St Benedict, Stephen Harding, the English abbot of Cîteaux who had always enjoyed the distinction of inventing the constitution of the Cistercian order, was having his wings clipped by modern cutting tools. In some ways the scalpels of historical criticism seemed to threaten all positions, especially for a monk, but out of the dissolution of received certainties and cherished beliefs had come a positive stimulus to work over the whole field of monastic life and institutions in the early sixth century and to re-examine also the nature and process of reform around the year 1100. Benedict had lost part of his claim to a unique position among monastic spiritual writers but he could 'now take a more truly historical place as an eminent member of a series or group of sixth-century legislators'.[10] And more generally Knowles concluded by saluting 'the achievements of the spirit of enlightened critical skill. With no assistance save the documents under consideration, scholars of today have uncovered the real course of events which had been hidden for eight' – and one should add, in case of the Rule, thirteen – 'centuries under a delusive appearance of simplicity.'[11]

In the following year, 1963, Knowles retired. We dined together in King's on the day he gave his last university lecture and he said he was sure that not a single pupil had any idea that it was his last appearance. But in a certain sense the Birkbeck Lectures were his farewell statement for in his other courses he had not been moving into any new fields of teaching. They offer a contrast with the pronouncement he made in his Inaugural Lecture on becoming Regius Professor. There he had sung of the joys of studying character, not documentary problems. And in much of his teaching he had delighted audiences with biographical portraits of medieval figures. And not just of medieval ones, for to celebrate the centenary of Lord Macaulay's death he gave on his own initiative a public lecture on 30 November 1959 which attracted a large and packed Cambridge audience, one that was thrilled to a rare degree by an outstanding salutation to a great historical talent. George Macaulay Trevelyan was present and was the first to shake Knowles's hand in warm congratulation as he stepped down from the platform. Knowles (like Trevelyan in this at least) had made his reputation chiefly through writing history on a panoramic scale and in the grand manner, because he largely saw history as literature, 'to be', that is (as he said of Macaulay's achievement[12]), 'not merely well ordered and well written,

---

[10] *GHE*, p. 190. See p. 63, n. 44. [11] *GHE*, p. 223. [12] Knowles 1960, p. 13.

but perfectly designed and clearly and attractively written'. He was also a sources man, and all his best books were written from sources, including unpublished ones, but he could be critical of scholars who allowed textual scholarship to take them over – as he thought had happened to Grabmann in his later years. He could be quite critical of the work being done on medieval sources at the Pontifical Institute of Medieval Studies in Toronto, not on account of its technical quality or importance or of any lack of ability among the scholars who worked there but because what was published in the journal *Mediaeval Studies* appeared to be *too* concerned with texts for texts' sake, *too* centred on their discovery and edition and discussion.

The Birkbeck Lectures, however, remind one that Knowles was as concerned with documentary problems as with the study of character. As Christopher Brooke has written,[13] when he had been at Downside and preparing *The Monastic Order*, Knowles laid the foundations of this work by a thorough study of Domesday Book, of the volumes in the Rolls Series and of monastic chronology. When in Cambridge later, his increased opportunity to teach and lecture enabled him to give more public prominence to his underlying concern with the basics of historical and textual criticism. Characteristically he drew a favourite parallel when summing up the debates about the Rule of St Benedict: 'I can think of no other text', he said, 'where the same frustrating hesitations occur save in that crux of Franciscan studies, the Legend of the Three Companions, where something of the same situation occurs – two or more non-literary writers using a common store of earlier material'.[14] And he pointed to the need for further study of language and the preparation of concordances. Perhaps surprisingly he never published a study of early Franciscan documents, on which he had taught, yet he did publish a masterly study of the Benedictine Rule, which had not been part of his regular teaching or courses of study. To some extent his discussions of the Rule and of the primitive Cistercian documents led him away from the study of character for in reality he was dealing with situations in which the study of individual character had to be suspended in the interests of getting nearer to the truth about groups and about largely anonymous writings. But it would be wrong to think that his directions were changing. In his teaching he was more able to show the rigorous and technical documentary basis on which all without

---

[13] Above pp. 47–9, 55–7.   [14] *GHE*, pp. 193–4.

exception must construct their own expositions, as he had also done. He experienced and demonstrated both the power of imagination and the reward of toiling with the sources. We learned much about the former through reading his works and thus were never in danger of losing sight of the paramount value of the human spirit when we came, as he had often done, to tackle the latter for ourselves.

APPENDIX I

Two chapters of the *Monastic Order in England* were omitted from the book when it was published in 1940 (see p. 62); of these, one, on monastic buildings, was revised for *RO* III and finally printed in *HC* (chap. 9); the other, on Gilbert of Sempringham, has never seen the light. It is one of the very few finished pieces of his historical writing which have not been printed: the only others known to me are scripts for lectures most of which were replaced by other work of his own or other scholars and not in a form suited to publication. Much has been written on the Gilbertines since 1940, and Father David would have set about the task differently if he were writing now; yet it is so characteristic a piece, and its original purpose and setting of such interest, that we have felt it appropriate to print it here – a missing fragment of one of his masterpieces, yet also complete and coherent in itself. When he wrote it, the canonisation dossier of St Gilbert, incorporating the early *Life* of the saint, was known in print only from the substantial extracts in the nineteenth-century edition of Dugdale's *Monasticon Anglicanum*. Father David studied the manuscripts and edited the letters which describe the revolt of the lay brothers of Sempringham (Knowles 1935). In 1943 Raymonde Foreville published a partial edition in Paris (Foreville 1943); and finally in 1987 the full text, with English translation and commentary, has become available in the complete edition by Raymonde Foreville and Gillian Keir in the Oxford Medieval Texts (Foreville and Keir 1987). This has rendered Father David's references obsolete and some of his notes from the MSS unnecessary. I have left the quotations in the footnotes but altered all the references to Foreville and Keir 1987; I have left out some notes and observations no longer appropriate and made some minor corrections; but new editorial matter is marked by square brackets.

C.N.L.B.

GILBERT OF SEMPRINGHAM

DAVID KNOWLES

i

The order of Sempringham, which in its male branch is reckoned among the canonical institutes, might be thought to fall outside the purview of a monastic history. Apart altogether, however, from the interest attaching to the only medieval religious order of purely English origin, the multiple relation of Gilbert and his nuns with the various monastic bodies, his own great indebtedness to the Cistercian statutes, and the fact that his nuns followed the rule of St Benedict make a brief account of the founder and his work appropriate here.

The documentary evidence on which such an account must rely is unfortunately scanty in the extreme. Gilbert must have written very many letters in his long life, and it is known that he composed a history of his foundations which would provide invaluable information; both these sources have disappeared, save for insignificant fragments, and there are surprisingly few detailed references in contemporary literature to the actions of one who lived far beyond the common span and was for more than half a century a venerable and venerated figure. This absence of personal, contemporary detail is, however, remedied in part by the information given by a *Life*, written soon after Gilbert's death by one of his intimate disciples; it is a lengthy document, containing a number of passages of great insight and eloquence, as well as many pages of diffuse and irrelevant morality, and it provides a considerable, though by no means complete, account of his life and character.[1]

[1] The *Vita, Canonizatio, Miracula* and *Epistolae* [comprising the canonisation dossier of St Gilbert] are preserved in three MSS, viz. British Library Cotton Cleopatra B. i, Harleian 468, and Oxford, Bodleian, Digby 36. A considerable part of the *Vita* and *Canonizatio*, together with the *Institutiones*, is printed in the *Monasticon*, ed. J. Caley,

Gilbert was born at Sempringham, a village of south Lincolnshire lying between Grantham and Boston, *c.* 1089; his father, Jocelin, a Norman knight of property, had married an English wife of lower degree than himself.[2] It is perhaps not wholly fanciful to trace to this fusion of blood Gilbert's ability to frame elaborate constitutional documents while at the same time remaining altogether free from the doctrinaire, and excelling in intimate personal direction. As a boy he was awkward, if not positively deformed;[3] he was also lazy, and it was only after strong remonstrance on the part of his family that he was roused to cross the Channel in search of learning. There he acquired, besides the mental formation which made him responsive to the legal and institutional revival of the continent, that control over himself and that zeal for religion which distinguished him ever after. Returning to Sempringham, and not yet a priest, he first showed his talent for organisation and his capability of inspiring devotion by gathering together the neglected children of the neighbourhood and teaching them letters and discipline. Like Vincent de Paul in a later century, whom he resembles in more than one respect, Gilbert looked always to the immediate need, and allowed the event to shape the development of his projects; it was only when a work was in being that he clothed it with an ordered rule, and throughout his life he allowed fresh needs to evoke ever fresh dispositions.

Shortly after his return to England, his father gave him the churches of Sempringham and Torrington; Gilbert appointed curates, and himself lived for a time with the priest of his native village. His influence began to make itself felt among the people: so that wherever they went, parishioners of Sempringham were recognisable by their devout bearing.[4] After a time (the *Life* gives no more precise information) he

H. Ellis and B. Bandinel, VI, 2, as an intercalation between pp. 946 and 947 [pp. i*–xcix* in the edition of 1830, i*–lix* in the reprint of 1846]. But the letters do not appear there, and many passages are omitted without any indication. [For the complete text see now Foreville and Keir 1987, here cited, which see also for recent literature]. Dr Rose Graham's valuable *S. Gilbert of Sempringham and the Gilbertines* (London, 1901) contains an excellent account of the saint and his institute; the author had consulted the manuscript authorities referred to above. The letters are printed in full as an accompaniment to an article by the present writer [Knowles 1935].

2 Mater uero ortu Anglica, a parentibus fidelibus inferioris tamen conditionis originem trahens (Foreville and Keir 1987, pp. 10–11).

3 Corporali scemate incompositus et incultus (pp. 12–13).

4 Nam quocumque basilicam intrassent, discerni poterant a ceteris parochiani[s] de Sempringham per orationum deuotionem et inclinationum humiliationem, quas eos

attached himself as a clerk to the household of the bishop of Lincoln, Robert Bloet (1094–January 10, 1123) and his successor Alexander 'the magnificent' (July 22, 1123–February, 1148). Neither of these prelates had a good reputation, though it is probable that Alexander, at least in his later years, deserved a milder judgment than he has received from most historians; Gilbert, for his part, afterwards told his sons that he lived a stricter and more sparing life in the bishop's household than ever afterwards, and Alexander warmly supported the rising order of his sometime clerk. An incident that belongs to this period of his life throws light upon both the manners of the times and Gilbert's own ascetic practices. A visiting bishop chanced to share a room for the night with Gilbert and the bishop of Lincoln. He was sleepless, and all night long he watched the changing shadow cast on the wall by Gilbert as he alternately stood and knelt in prayer. When morning came he rallied his host on the tumbler he kept in his bedroom.[5]

After some years, Alexander insisted on ordaining his clerk priest against his desire, and took him for confessor. Meanwhile, Gilbert had been concerned with the needs of some young women, his parishioners at Sempringham. These had received his spiritual teaching, but could find no opportunity of practising it in its fullness. Nunneries, as has been seen, were as yet few in England, and in Lincolnshire itself none at all existed. Gilbert therefore, with the encouragement of Alexander, determined to bestow his patrimony upon the construction and endowment of a convent attached to the parish church at Sempringham; as the life of the community began informally there is some doubt as to the precise date of the foundation, but it was probably *c.* 1131.[6] The original group of nuns numbered seven, among whom we know one to have been the daughter of the house where Gilbert had first lodged, and it was his intention that the community should not increase, but the

---

docuerat prelatus eorum Gilebertus (pp. 18–19). [But a parochianis is the more likely reading, so that Gilbert's disciples are distinguished from the other parishioners of Sempringham.]

[5] Vidit idem episcopus, in pariete opposito ad lumen lucerne, effigiem hominis per totam noctem nunc ascendentem, nunc descendentem in umbra, . . . putans autem fantasma esse . . . Inuestigans tamen diligentius quid hoc esset, inuenit uirum Dei ante suum grabatum stantem et orantem, et manus sursum genua deorsum crebro ponentem deprehendit. Quod mane facto referens episcopus arguit iocose hospitem suum quia saltatorem haberet in thalamo (pp. 22–3).

[6] The land was formally given and adequate buildings erected *c.* 1139, but the community had been in existence some years previously.

needs of others, and the success of his ministration, led him to change his resolve.

He had at first made arrangements for girls of the village to fetch, carry and purvey for his nuns; it became gradually clear that it would be more satisfactory for these girls themselves to be under religious discipline, and the second branch of the order – that of the lay sisters – came into being with a strict rule of life. Gilbert himself tells us that this was done at the suggestion of William, first abbot of Rievaulx, who happened to stay with him while upon a journey.[7] Next, it was found that, as the houses grew in possessions, regular labour was needed to safeguard the cultivation of the land and the collection of the revenues. Here again the Cistercian influence was at work, for Gilbert was solicited by those who had seen or heard of the white lay brothers at work, and wished to imitate their example. He therefore attached *conversi* to his nunneries.[8]

The order grew with unexpected rapidity, patronised by Alexander of Lincoln and later by King Henry II. For a time Gilbert was alone in his responsibility for the spiritual and temporal administration, helped only by his lay brothers. Feeling himself unable to control the growing body, and greatly admiring the Cistercians, who had often stayed with him upon their journeys, he crossed to France in 1147 and proposed to the General Chapter at Cîteaux that the Cistercians should make themselves responsible for his order. It was no ordinary year in the history of Cîteaux. Eugenius III was present in chapter,[9] and during its deliberations the thirty and more houses of the Savigniac obedience were received under its jurisdiction. It is not surprising, therefore, that the fathers were averse to further commitments, and especially to one which would involve responsibility for women and lay brothers.[10] Gilbert was

---

[7] *Institutiones, Monasticon,* vi, 2 (1830), p. xxix*, (1846), p. xix*: Consilio abbatis primi Rievallis, per me transeuntis, et propositum meum laudantis.

[8] *Institutiones* (1830), p. xxx*; (1846), p. xix*: Assumpsi mihi mercenarios, dans eis habitum religionis qualem habent fratres Cistercienses. Cf. *Institutiones* (1830), p. lix*; (1846), p. xxvi*: Eo tempore . . . venerunt monachi de ordine Cisterciae . . . cum quibus venerunt laici ad laborem promptissimi . . . Quod audientes plurimi de communi laboriosorum genere nobis servientes in victu paupere, obtabant Deo vivere apud nos in eorum ordine. Cf. *Vita,* pp. 40–1: Hos (sc. Cistercienses) enim ceteris habuit, ex frequenti hospicii susceptione, familiariores, quos et iudicauit aliis religiosiores, quia erant recentiores et regule arctioris.

[9] Ubi (sc. in capitulo) forte tunc aderat bone memorie papa Eugenius (pp. 40–1). This gives us the date.

[10] Dominius autem papa et abbates Cistercie dixerunt sui ordinis monachos aliorum religioni, et presertim monialium, non licere preesse (pp. 42–3).

therefore confirmed in his administration by the pope himself. Eugenius, so the author of the *Life* informs us, was profoundly impressed by him. The pope had recently deprived William Fitzherbert of the see of York, and still more recently confirmed the disputed election of Henry Murdac in his room. After meeting Gilbert he is said to have declared that had he known him earlier he would have made him archbishop of York.[11] As for Bernard and Gilbert, the admiration was mutual and the Englishman was fortunate enough to meet at Clairvaux another saint, Malachy, archbishop of Armagh, who was soon to end his days there.[12]

Unsuccessful in his attempt to gain help from Cîteaux, he had to devise other means. Communities of women, living a severe and enclosed life, clearly needed enlightened and constant spiritual direction. Gilbert therefore decided, after his visit to Cîteaux, to add a fourth member to his order by grouping together a number of chosen priests as canons who should be chaplains to his nuns. He therefore drew up statutes, which were approved by Eugenius, and built his first double monastery, and the full Gilbertine order was in being. All in it centred upon the nuns; the lay sisters and brothers existed to minister in things temporal, the canons in things spiritual.

ii

The Gilbertine order belongs to that group of new institutes, characteristic of the first half of the twelfth century, for which elaborate written constitutions were composed dealing almost entirely with external, accidental aspects of the life. By contrast with the Camaldolese, the Vallombrosians and the Carthusians, whose rule of life was merely a translation into writing of standing, primitive custom, the Orders of Grandmont, Fontevrault and Sempringham had long and intricate regulations, smelling somewhat of the lamp, and bearing only indirectly upon the spiritual life. The difference between the two groups of rules is, indeed, not unlike that between the political constitutions of the older states of Europe before the eighteenth century, and those elaborated in the studies of political theorists and applied to various countries of Europe and America from the epoch of the Encyclopedists onwards.

[11] Doluisse fertur papa Eugenius, quoniam uirum antea non nouisset, eo quod uoluisset, ut dixit, illum sullimasse in archiepiscopum Eboracensem . . . si fama meritorum eius illi prius innotuisset (pp. 44–5).
[12] Beatis quoque Malachie Hyberniensi archiepiscopo et Bernardo Clareuallensi abbati in illo itinere adeo factus est familiaris (pp. 44–5).

The contrast, therefore, between the simple, practical aims and basic principles of Gilbert's order and its intricate framework and machinery is very great. His institute, as has been said, existed primarily for the nuns; they are the centre round which the whole system turns. His legislation shows little originality and contains no pregnant spiritual principles. For the rules governing the inner life of his communities he was content to take over what already existed. The nuns received the Rule of St Benedict, the canons that of St Augustine and the lay brothers a very slightly modified version of the Use of the lay brothers of Cîteaux.[13] Gilbert's written contribution consisted almost entirely in the careful and ingenious planning of a double monastery which should give no occasion for scandal, and in the elaboration of a scheme of government by Master and general chapter which gave the nuns a real voice in the settlement of their own affairs. Here, as elsewhere, the Cistercian constitutional documents are expressly referred to as exemplars that have been followed,[14] but he had also studied the practices of Grandmont and Fontevrault.

The same eclecticism shows itself throughout the liturgical books as well as in the constitutions. Gilbert borrowed and adapted, he did not create. As his biographer says, he built upon the foundations of the Rules a structure derived from the customs of various monastic houses and churches, and the Gilbertine Missal and Breviary, based principally upon those of Cîteaux, contain a number of elements drawn from other sources.[15]

---

[13] Monialibus regulam beati Benedicti, clericis uero regulam sancti Augustini tenendam proponens (pp. 48–9) . . . Clericatui beatus presidet Augustinus, monachatum precurrit sanctus Benedictus (pp. 52–3). *Institutiones* (1830), p. xxx*; (1846), p. xix*: Ut in vigiliis et jejuniis [canonici] vitam secundum regulam Sancti Augustini tenerent. *Institutiones* (1830), p. lix*; (1846), p. xxxvi*: Fratres nostri laici in modo victus et vestitus sequantur formam fratrum ordinis Cisterciae, qui morantur in grangiis. Cf. also the charter of Alexander of Lincoln for Haverholme [1139] when the nuns' future was uncertain [*English Episcopal Acta*, I, *Lincoln 1067–1185*, ed. D.M. Smith, London, 1980, no. 37, pp. 24–5]: He vitam artam, vitam sanctam, vitam scilicet monachorum Cistersensis religionis arripientes, quantum illius sexus valitudo permittit . . .

[14] *Institutiones* (1830), p. xcvi*; (1846), p. lvii*: Volumus Cisterciensis capituli vestigia sequi.

[15] *The Gilbertine Rite* has been edited for the Henry Bradshaw Society (2 vols., 1921–2) by Canon R.M. Woolley. The editor remarks (pp. xxv–xxvi) that 'The Use is, generally speaking, Cistercian. The body of the Missal is evidently copied directly from the Cistercian Rite . . . but on the other hand a considerable amount of variation [shows] great eclecticism as to the sources from which the various forms were derived.'

The details of all these arrangements belong rather to the history of the order itself and to archaeology than to a general account of monasticism. The Gilbertine constitutions have none of the simple and logical strength of the *Carta Caritatis*, nor do they enunciate any principles of the religious life. Yet the success of the order was great and immediate. Women naturally shared with men in the remarkable awakening of the period, and hitherto no provision had been made for them. Many of those who had brothers at Rievaulx or Kirkham must have longed to follow the same call, and in the Gilbertine houses they could find, at the hands of the Master and his most trusted canons, the most enlightened doctrine and direction of the age. Doubtless, as so often in the history of the Church, the fervour and devotion of the women was a potent influence upon their masters: in the grotesque metaphors of Gilbert's biographer, 'the rhinoceros teaches the ewe gentleness . . . and the tortoise follows the eagle to the stars'.[16] Certainly no religious fact of the time is more weightily attested than that of Gilbert's supreme competence in the spiritual direction of women. The long and eloquent eulogy devoted to his memory shortly after his death by the historian William of Newburgh[17] does but echo the testimony of the most eminent of the bishops of England and of Henry II, forwarded to Alexander III at a moment when Gilbert was under a cloud of calumny.[18] Henry II also, we are told, who twice showed himself a staunch friend in a crisis, never failed to honour him, and whenever he was at court on business connected with his houses, went to his lodging and asked his blessing.[19] Unfortunately, we can form no idea of the

---

[16] Ibi rinoceros docet ouem mansuetudinem . . . ibi damula canem, et alauda uenatur accipitrem, et testudo aquilam comitatur ad astra (pp. 52–3).

[17] William of Newburgh, *Historia rerum Anglicarum*, ed. R. Howlett, in *Chronicles of the Reigns of Stephen etc.*, 4 vols., Rolls Series, 1884–9, I, 54–5. Venerabilis Gillebertus, vir plane mirabilis, et in custodia feminarum gratiae singularis . . . meo judicio palmam tenet inter omnes quos instituendis regendisque feminis religiosam operam impendisse cognovimus . . . potensque est in terra nostra semen ejus, et generatio ejus benedicetur in seculum.

[18] Roger of York (pp. 152–3): uirum innocentem et per quem Deus multa et magna et usque ad tempus eius inaudita operatus est in medio nostri. Henry of Winchester (pp. 144–5): lucernam sanctitatis eius et odorem deuotionis eius, qui longe lateque diffunditur, fame preconio creberrime persensimus. Henry II [(pp. 142–3, on the whole group of letters): commendant personam et sanctitatem uenerabilis uiri Dei, magistri G. de Sempingham, et singularem fructum utriusque sexus quem fecit in domo Domini . . .]

[19] Pp. 92–3: [Queen Eleanor too rejoiced that her sons, the future kings, also had his blessing.]

peculiar quality of his influence. He does not appear to have composed any spiritual treatises, and no Gertrude or Hildegarde arose among his daughters; the only two anecdotes which show him in contact with the nuns obscure rather than reveal the picture.[20] The aged ascetic, tireless in his severity towards himself, whose most distinguishing quality was guileless simplicity,[21] and whose energy was directed to every kind of work of charity, does not at first sight give evidence of possessing the intuitive sympathy of a François de Sales, still less the clear analytic vision of a John of the Cross. Yet the fact of his influence is beyond dispute. At the time of his death, besides numerous hospitals for lepers and orphanages, Gilbert had founded more than a dozen houses,[22] of which some ten were 'double' monasteries of nuns and canons, three were of canons serving hospitals and other works, including at least one, that of Old Malton in Yorkshire, which was to serve primarily as a kind of retreat-house for canons alone, where they might learn and practise the life of prayer that they were to teach to the nuns.[23] All the nunneries had a considerable staff of lay brothers, besides a large community of nuns. The cardinal legate Hugh, writing to Alexander III in 1175, reckoned the total number of the latter as high as fifteen hundred[24] and the author of the *Life* put the total aggregate at two thousand and two hundred.[25] This, perhaps, was an exaggeration, but at some early period of the history of the order, probably *c.* 1190, it was found desirable to put a limit to the numbers of nuns and lay brothers by assigning quotas to the fourteen existing houses; the total allowed was 594 canons and lay brothers and 980 nuns: the total is a little over that given by the legate for the nuns.[26] Several of the houses contained more than a hundred nuns,

20 Cf. Ailred's account of Gilbert's attitude towards the nun of Watton [*PL* 195, 789–96; see esp. G. Constable in *Medieval Women*, ed. D. Baker (Oxford 1978), pp. 205–26], and the anecdote given by Gerald of Wales, *Opera*, ed. J.S. Brewer et al., 8 vols., Rolls Series, 1861–91, IV, 185.   21 [See esp. pp. 62–9.]

22 [DK noted that 'there is some discrepancy in the sources' in counting the number of houses: this is discussed in detail in Foreville and Keir, pp. xxxii–xxxv, with an account of later foundations on pp. xxxvi–xxxix. There were in fact ten double houses by 1189 and three of canons; there was also a large hospital at Clattercote.]

23 Cf. Gilbert's letter to Malton, pp. 164–7.

24 Circiter mille quingentas esse dicantur (pp. 348–9).

25 In quibus, ut estimamus, duorum milium et ducentorum uirorum et religiosarum mulierum collegia in obitu suo reliquit (pp. 54–7; cf. pp. 128–9, 192–3, 250–1).

26 [The figures are given in the *Institutiones* (1830), p. xcvii★; (1846), p. lviii★, but are not without problems: see Foreville and Keir 1987, p. xxxiii.] If not Gilbert's this decree would seem at least to date before [the 1190s], the date of foundation of Shouldham [and Bridge End], which do not appear in the list [see Foreville and Keir 1987, p. xxxvi].

the largest being that of Watton in Yorkshire, which held 140 nuns and seventy lay brothers, besides a small staff of canons.

All contemporary witnesses unite in praising Gilbert's nuns. Ailred of Rievaulx, in at least two passages, describes at some length their fervent life and illustrates a principle of mystical theology by describing the experiences of one of the sisters.[27] At about the same time Gilbert of Holland addressed to one of their houses, probably Sempringham, several of his sermons on the Canticle.[28] Some years later, there is the evidence of the bishops already alluded to, and that of the cardinal legate, who had visited Sempringham and was loud in his expressions of admiration.[29] Later still, there are the words of William of Newburgh already quoted. Even Gerald of Wales and his friend Walter Map, otherwise so ruthless in their criticism of religious, leave the order of Sempringham untouched, and speak of the simple candour of the founder.[30] Unfortunately, as has been said, no written monument has survived of all this fervent life; the nuns, it is probable, were mostly of the middle and poorer classes of the country villages and therefore attracted little attention; no eminent leader or mystical writer arose among them, and with the exception of an isolated prioress here and there, even the names of Gilbert's earliest and most favoured daughters have perished. To aid us in estimating the quality of their spiritual doctrine we have only the incident, repellent to modern sentiment, of the nun of Watton as related by Ailred, and the account, also given us by Ailred, of the mystical experiences of a Gilbertine house which, though more satisfactory, is itself not wholly free from ambiguity.[31]

iii

Until long after his foundations had succeeded and multiplied the Master had refused to become technically a member of his own order, through unwillingness to profess obedience to a Rule drawn up by

---

[27] Ailred, *Sermo III de Oneribus* (PL 195, 370): Scio in monasterio virginum, quae sub venerabili et cum summa reverentia nominando sancto patre Gilberto uberes pudicitiae fructus quotidie transmittunt ad coelos. Cf. [similar] language in the treatise *De Sanctimoniali de Wattun* (PL 195, 789–90).

[28] *PL* 184, 11–252 [but I do not know the grounds for Father David's statement].

[29] Quarum quidem conuersacio, ut pura uobis [Alexander III] loquar consciencia, magis potest et uerius dici esse in celis quam inter homines (p. 349).

[30] Walter Map, *De Nugis Curialium*, i. 27, ed. and trans. M.R. James, C.N.L. Brooke and R.A.B. Mynors (OMT, 1983), pp. 114–17. [Map in fact makes no specific comment on Gilbert, but the absence of criticism is remarkable.]   [31] See n. 27.

himself. He was at last persuaded by his sons to do so, in order to avoid confusion and intrigues after his death, and made his vows to one of his first canons, Roger, prior of Malton, who became the order's second Master. Roger's priory of Old Malton in Yorkshire was itself one of the later developments of Gilbert's idea; it was founded, as has been mentioned, for canons alone, without any nuns to direct, in order that they might learn in solitude and full religious observance something of the life they were to teach others.

When Gilbert was already an old man, the object of universal veneration and, as it might have seemed, beyond the reach of calumny, he had to pass through two exceedingly distressing experiences. The first, an attack from without, was due to his loyal support of Becket. Gilbert had been on terms of warm friendship with both king and archbishop, but in the controversy he stood by the latter; when the archbishop fled from Northampton [in October 1164] he was guided and entertained by Gilbertines on his way to the coast;[32] it was not unnatural, therefore, when all the relations and friends of Becket were being proscribed, that the Master should be accused of sending money to the exile in France. The charge was false, and Gilbert, owing to his reputation for holiness, was offered the occasion of clearing himself upon oath. This he refused to do, fearing that it would be interpreted as a declaration against Becket and his rights. He was therefore kept for trial in London and was only saved, when sentence against him seemed imminent, by the direct action of the king, who sent a message that proceedings were to be stayed until he had made personal investigation into the charge.[33]

The second attack, which followed shortly after, must have been far more painful, for by it not only were his personal character and the reputation of his order blown upon, but he had to suffer from the ingratitude of sons to whom he had given everything, and to lose the confidence of Becket, for whom he had risked so much, and of the pope. The occasion was the revolt of a group of lay brothers, which took place c. 1164–5.[34] As has been said, the lay brothers, in Gilbert's original scheme, occupied a position of great importance in the order. In this they

---

[32] Pp. 70–5, and p. 70 n. 2; *Vita S. Thomae Auct. Anon. I* [Roger of Pontigny], *Materials for the History of Thomas Becket*, ed. J.C. Robertson and J.B. Sheppard (Rolls Series, 1875–85), IV, 53–5.   [33] Pp. 74–5.

[34] For a fuller account of this episode by the present writer, see Knowles 1935 [now revised in Foreville and Keir 1987, pp. lv–lxii; for the chronology, pp. 343–4; for the documents, pp. lxxxiv–xc, 76–85, 134–67, 346–9].

resembled the lay brethren of such orders as the Grandimontines rather than those of Cîteaux; in the former, as in some other contemporary enclosed orders, their function was to relieve the choir religious not only of manual work, but of the cares of administration, and it would appear certain that Gilbert borrowed this conception when framing his own institute. During the early years, therefore, and indeed perhaps throughout Gilbert's life, all the external business of the order was carried on by a few trusted lay brothers, under the direction of the Master, the canons being wholly occupied in spiritual ministrations at the nunneries and hospitals. Thus these men, of lowly origin and quite illiterate, were incessantly travelling from place to place on errands of weight, and it is only by bearing in mind their responsible position and also the fact that they had been members of the order before the canons, that their jealousy of the latter can be understood,[35] as also the audacity and success which distinguished the first movements of their revolt.

For the narrative of this strange affair we are dependent upon a few lines of Gilbert's lost history of his foundations, preserved by his biographer, and a collection of undated letters and papal documents.[36] It is natural to suppose that the malcontents received encouragement in their designs from the unsettlement prevailing in the Church in England during the Becket controversy, and also perhaps from the suspicions which had attached to the Master; it was certainly the archbishop's absence that made their initial success possible; but of all this the sources say nothing. The trouble began among a small group of lay brothers, including some of those who had been longest in the order; the ringleaders were a certain Ogger the Smith and one Gerard, to whom Gilbert had given supreme charge of the temporalities. The characters of these men had altogether degenerated; they had become extravagant, dishonest and immoral. In addition to jealousy of the canons, they exploited a certain discontent at the severity of their rule which had spread among the lay brothers of some of the houses. When the evil ways of Ogger and Gerard came to the notice of the Master, he took steps to correct them, whereupon the rebels proceeded to the papal court, at the time in France, and charged Gilbert with having seriously changed the nature of their life. They also asserted that the close proximity of nuns and canons had led to grave moral lapses.

[35] Cf. pp. 78–9. Cf also Gilbert's words: Insurrexerunt aduersum me et canonicos nostros . . . (pp. 78–9).

[36] Besides the [fifteen] letters printed in Foreville and Keir 1987, pp. 134–67, 348–9, [and the narrative at pp. 76–85, there are] two letters of Becket, *ibid.* pp. 346–8.

Besides approaching Alexander III, the lay brothers obtained access to the exiled Becket, and their accusations found credence in both courts. The pope gave Ogger a letter instructing Gilbert to make important constitutional changes (as the letter has disappeared there is no means of telling what these were)[37] and Becket wrote in general terms rebuking the Master and urging submission to the papal mandate. The return of Ogger to England, however, called forth an impressive defence of Gilbert from a group of the leading bishops – Roger of York, the Cluniac Henry of Winchester and the black monk William of Norwich – to whose solicitations were added those of Henry II. Such weighty representations could not be ignored, and Alexander took the usual course of appointing judges delegate with certain instructions in either province, three of the four being Gilbert's friends. The two enquiries were held, and at both Gilbert and his rebellious subjects were present. At both, the innocence of the Master and of the canons was triumphantly vindicated; a few small changes were made in the customs, and all the lay brothers, save Ogger and a few others, made unconditional submission. The pope subsequently confirmed the fullest powers to Gilbert, and it was not till 1186–9 that the Master, in the presence of Hugh of Lincoln, consented to mitigate some of the severity of the Rule for the lay brothers.[38] The whole episode, which did no permanent harm to the order and which gave striking proof of the veneration in which Gilbert was held, served to show that the attempt to transfer to illiterate lay brothers the cares of administration was unwise and unworkable; it is noteworthy that only a few years later, in the mid-1180s, the powerful lay brothers of Grandmont organised a still more formidable revolt.

iv

At the time of the revolt [in the 1160s] Gilbert was already approaching eighty years of age, and his advocates did not fail to urge this as a motive for consideration, begging the pope to do justice to an old man who

---

[37] Gilbert says (pp. 78–9): nimis seuerum mandatum et sententiam crudelem aduersum nos dedit.

[38] Pp. 116–19. [The dispute opened *c.* 1164–5 and the pope sent instructions for the lay brothers to be disciplined in 1169; but the final settlement did not come before 1178; even after that the mitigations referred to in the text had to wait until the late 1180s. Foreville and Keir 1987, pp. lv–lxii, 343–4.]

would soon have left the scene of his labours. Against all likelihood, the Master survived for twenty years, outliving the bishops who had befriended him, and dying a centenarian. In his last years he handed over his administrative duties to Roger of Malton, whom he designated as his successor. His biographer gives a vivid and detailed account of Gilbert's way of life in this last phase; it was austere in the extreme, though he was full of tolerance and tenderness for others. He is pictured to us as an old man, withered, and thin, with skin like parchment clinging to his bones,[39] recalling in more than one respect the vivid phrase used by Teresa of Avila of Peter of Alcantara, an old man 'like the roots of trees'. Towards the end, he became completely blind, and there is a touching yet noble description of his anxiety to be carried in a litter from house to house, where he refused to relax any of his regularity and, as once a young man in the bishop's bedchamber, rose and knelt in prayer throughout the night.[40] He refused, also, to eat outside the common refectory. 'Gilbert', he said, 'shall not give to his successors the example of eating dainties in a private room.'

At last, when he had reached his hundredth year, he felt his end approaching and received the last sacraments on Christmas night, 1188.[41] He was at Newstead in Lindsey, and his chaplains, fearing that powerful clients might detain the dying saint on the road in order to bury him in some private church or the monastery of another order, decided to carry him with all speed and by devious routes to Sempringham. Arrived there, he took farewell of all; then he lay alone, with only Roger his successor sitting by his bed. The biographer[42] tells of his last moments in words that attain a high degree of solemn beauty:

> After he had for long been silent, as one about to draw his last breath, and no one had spoken to him for long, nor could he himself either see or hear anyone – realising in spirit (so we think) the presence of the one who sat by him, he repeated in a low voice, but slowly, distinctly and intelligibly the verse of the psalm: 'he

[39] Mirari posses et misereri si uideres senilis corporis membra uix ossibus coherentia, concussis humeris et collisis dentibus, subtracto tam naturali quam accidentali calore, multotiens contracta (pp. 64–5).

[40] Pp. 86–91. If discovered [out of bed at night and prostrate in prayer], he made a show of blaming his bedding. Cumque a comitibus sic iacens repertus fuisset, quasi culpauit eos quod stratum eius uespera male parauissent (pp. 88–9). [41] [Pp. 120–1.]

[42] [Identified by Raymonde Foreville as Ralph de Insula, the sacrist of Sempringham: Foreville and Keir 1987, p. lxxv.]

hath dispersed, he hath given to the poor' [Ps. 111 (112): 9], and going back upon it, as if explaining it, he said: 'he dispersed to many; he gave, he did not sell; to the poor, not to the rich', and he added: 'on thee now lies this duty' . . . Even so did Paul glory in what he most trusted, when the time of his dissolution was at hand, saying: 'I have fought a good fight, I have finished my course, I have kept the faith' . . . and David, the saintly king of Scots, when death stood at his door, repeated seven times the verse of the psalm in which he put his hope: I have done judgement and justice, deliver me not to those that traduce me.'

On the next day . . . the Sabbath dawned; the time for him to rest from his labours. 'The night had passed and the day was at hand', for he could truly say: 'the darkness shall not comprehend me nor tread me down'. It was the hour of morning Lauds, the hour of the outgoings of the morning, nor were there wanting stars of the morning to praise the Lord . . . On that Sabbath, the day before the nones of February,[43] in the year of our Lord's nativity 1189, when night was changing to day and Lauds were being sung by the community, he passed from the darkness of this world and earthly toil to true light and to eternal rest, an old man past a hundred and full of days, to dwell in the house of the Lord and praise God unto eternity.[44]

He was buried at Sempringham in a tomb visible to both canons and nuns, and it was not long before miracles were reported. In 1200 Hubert Walter was approached and in 1201 sent a report to Rome, in the hands of two canons, accompanied by a commendatory letter. The process of canonisation had by this time been fully elaborated, and the pope sent a mandate to the archbishop to erect a commission of the bishop of Ely and the abbots of Peterborough and Wardon to examine the evidence.

[43] 4 February.

[44] Pp. 120–5 [DK's own translation]. Postera die que preteriri non poterat illuxit sabbatum, tempus scilicet quo requiesceret a laboribus suis. 'Nox precessit, dies autem appropinquauit', quia dicere potuit: 'Non me tenebre comprehendent nec conculcabunt me' [Rom. 13: 12; cf. John 1: 5; Ps. 138 (139): 11–12]. Hora erat matutinarum laudum et hora exitus matutini; nec deerant que Deum laudabant astra matutina [cf. Ps. 64: 9 (65: 8); Job 38: 7] . . . Sabbato ergo illo . . . cum nox immutaretur in diem, dum celebrarentur laudes a conuentu, a tenebris huius seculi et laboribus mundi ad ueram lucem requiemque eternam migrauit, plus quam centennis senex et plenus dierum, habitaturus in domo Domini et Deum in secula laudaturus . . .

The commission met, and was assisted by many other prelates. Their report was sent to Innocent III, who solemnly canonised Gilbert in January 1202 at Anagni, and himself composed the collect for his Mass and Office, as he did also for St Wulfstan of Worcester. [On 13 October 1202] the body of the new saint was solemnly exhumed and translated.[45]

---

[45] [Gilbert's canonisation was in fact a turning point in the elaboration of such processes; hence the double enquiry ordered by Innocent III. See Foreville and Keir, pp. xc–c; the narrative is on pp. 168–97; the letters about the process on pp. 198–263; the posthumous miracles are on pp. 264–335 – the whole *Book of St Gilbert* indeed is a dossier intended to support and justify the canonisation.]

APPENDIX II
DAVID KNOWLES'S LECTURE COURSES AT CAMBRIDGE, 1945–63

From *Cambridge University Reporter*, January 1945 and October 1945–62. These lists, strictly speaking, are forecasts, not records of lectures given; but we have no reason to suppose that any of the courses was abandoned due to ill health or leave.

1945, Lent Term, Intellectual Movements in the Middle Ages, 1200–1400

1945–8, Michaelmas and Lent Terms, Special Subject on The Life of St Francis and early Franciscan History

1946–8, Easter Terms, (The) Medieval Church and Culture

1948–55, 1959–63, Michaelmas and Lent Terms, (The) Intellectual History of Medieval Europe, 1000–1350

1949–56, 1960–3, Easter Terms, (The) Orders of Monks and Friars (in 1949 and 1950 given dates 1000–1350)

1955–9, Michaelmas and Lent Terms, Special Subject on Cistercian Origins and the Controversies of St Bernard with the Cluniacs, with Abelard and with Gilbert de la Porrée

1956, Lent term, he joined Professor Guthrie and others in a course on Ancient and Medieval Philosophers

1957–9, Easter Terms, Some Figures in Medieval Thought

APPENDIX III
DAVID KNOWLES'S RESEARCH PUPILS

We give name, college, faculty, dates of registration and the title of the thesis. The closing date in each case is that in which the PhD was conferred. The titles often passed through various vicissitudes: the form given here is that in the Catalogue of Dissertations in the University Library Manuscripts Room. We shall be very grateful for any corrections and additions to this list.

Clark, R.B. (now Mrs Brooke), Girton (History), 1946–50, 'Brother Elias, and the government of the Franciscan Order 1217–1239'

Waley, D.P., King's (History), 1947–50, 'Mediaeval Orvieto; the political history of an Italian city, 1157–1334'

Mayne, R.J., Trinity (History), 1950–5, 'Cardinal Humbert of Silva Candida'

Vaughan, R., Corpus (History), 1951–4, 'The relationship and chronology of the historical manuscripts of Matthew Paris'

Leff, G.H., King's (History), 1951–5, 'A study of Thomas Bradwardine's *De Causa Dei* and its relation to contemporary Oxford thought'

Robson, J.A. (now Sir John Robson, KCMG), Caius (History), supervised by E.F. Jacob, 1952–7, by D.K., 1957–8, 'A study of Wyclif's *Summa de Ente*, and its relation to contemporary Oxford philosophy'

Clover, Mrs V.H., New Hall (History), 1957–62. 'The correspondence of Archbishop Lanfranc: a critical edition with notes and historical introduction'

Kelly, M.J., King's (History), 1959–63, 'Canterbury jurisdiction and influence during the episcopate of William Warham, 1503–1532'

Luscombe, D.E., King's (History), 1959–64, 'Peter Abelard's following and the influence of his theology in the early scholastic period'

Egan, K.J., Downing (History), 1959–65, 'The establishment and early development of the Carmelite Order in England'

Blumenthal, H.J., Trinity (Classics), 1960–4, 'Plotinus' doctrines of the embodied soul'

Lunn, D.M.C.J., Fitzwilliam (History), 1967–70, 'The origins and early development of the revived English Benedictine Congregation, 1588–1647'

OXFORD D.PHIL.

Lovatt, R.W., Balliol (History), 1960–5, 'The influence of the religious literature of Germany and the Low Countries on English spirituality, 1350–1475'

In addition, three other Cambridge research students embarked on theses under his supervision which were not completed; and some others received informal advice and supervision without being registered research students, e.g. Giles Constable and Christopher Brooke.

BIBLIOGRAPHICAL
REFERENCES

For earlier biographical studies of David Knowles, see esp. Morey 1979; Brooke 1975; W.A. Pantin in Knowles, *HC*, pp. xvii–xxviii; Stacpoole 1975–6. There is a select bibliography in Morey 1979, pp. 155–62; a full bibliography to 1962 in Knowles, *HC*, pp. 363–73 (by Giles Constable, with the author's help); Dom Stacpoole has edited a continuation to 1974 in Stacpoole 1975 and 1976. A few articles privately printed for Peterhouse have not been listed here (see pp. 83–99).

Abercrombie, N.A., 1959, *The Life and Work of Edmund Bishop*, London, 1959

Bailey, C., 1936, *Francis Fortescue Urquhart, a Memoir*, London, 1936

Barlow, F., 1986, *Thomas Becket*, London, 1986

Bishop, E., 1918, *Liturgica Historica*, Oxford, 1918

Brooke, C.N.L., 1971, *Medieval Church and Society*, London, 1971
1975, 'David Knowles', *Proceedings of the British Academy*, 61 (1975), 439–77

Brooke, C.N.L., and W. Swaan, 1974, *The Monastic World*, London, 1974

Brooke, R.B., 1959, *Early Franciscan Government: Elias to Bonaventure*, Cambridge Studies in Medieval Life and Thought, New Series, 7, Cambridge, 1959

Bulst, N., 1973, *Untersuchungen zu den Klosterreformen Wilhelms von Dijon (962–1031)*, Bonn, 1973

Butler, E.C., 1919, 1924, *Benedictine Monachism*, 1st edn, London, 1919; 2nd edn, London, 1924; reprint with foreword by David Knowles, London, 1961
1922, *Western Mysticism*, London, 1922

Butterfield, H., 1949, *Christianity and History*, London, 1949
  1952, *Christianity in European History*, London, 1952
Cassian, *Collationes*, ed. E. Pichery, *Conférences*, I, Sources Chrétiennes, 42, Paris 1955
Caussade, J.P. de, 1959, *Self-Abandonment to Divine Providence*, trans. A. Thorold, ed. J. Joyce, with introduction by David Knowles, London, 1959
Chibnall, M., 1967, 'Monks and pastoral work: a problem in Anglo-Norman history', *Journal of Ecclesiastical History*, 18 (1967), 165–7
Clark, K., 1977, *The Other Half: A Self-Portrait*, London, 1977
Constable, G., 1964, *Monastic Tithes from their Origins to the Twelfth Century*, Cambridge Studies in Medieval Life and Thought, New Series, 10, Cambridge, 1964
Cowan, I.B., and D.E. Easson, 1976, *Medieval Religious Houses, Scotland*, 2nd edn., London, 1976
Cowling, M., 1979, 'Herbert Butterfield, 1900–1979', *Proceedings of the British Academy*, 65 (1979), 595–609
  1980, *Religion and Public Doctrine in Modern England*, Cambridge, 1980
Darlington, R.R., 1933, 'Aethelwig, abbot of Evesham', *English Historical Review*, 48 (1933), 1–22, 177–98
Darlington, R.R., ed., 1928, *The Vita Wulfstani of William of Malmesbury*, Camden Third Series, 40, London, 1928
Dereine, C., 1959, 'La fondation de Cîteaux d'après l'*Exordium Cistercii* et l'*Exordium Parvum*', *Cîteaux*, 10 (1959), 125–39
Duggan, A., 1980, *Thomas Becket: a Textual History of his Letters*, Oxford, 1980
Dunn, M., 1990, 'Mastering Benedict: monastic rules and their authors in the early medieval West', *English Historical Review*, 105 (1990), 567–94
Foreville, R., 1943, *Un procès de canonisation à l'aube du xiiie siècle (1201–1202): Le livre de saint Gilbert de Sempringham*, Paris, 1943
Foreville, R., and G. Keir, eds., 1987, *The Book of St Gilbert*, OMT, Oxford, 1987
France, J., ed., 1989, *Rodulfi Glabri Historiarum Libri Quinque*, [with] *Vita domni Willelmi abbatis*, ed. N. Bulst, J. France and P. Reynolds, OMT, Oxford, 1989
Galbraith, V.H., 1961, Review of *RO* III, in *English Historical Review*, 76 (1961), 98–102
Garrigou-Lagrange, R., 1922–3, *Perfection chrétienne et contemplation selon S. Thomas d'Aquin et S. Jean de la Croix*, 2 vols., Paris, 1922–3

Green, B., 1989, 'David Knowles's first book', *Downside Review*, 107 (1989), 79–85

Hadcock, R.N., *see* Knowles, M.D., and R.N. Hadcock

Halcrow, E.M., 1949, 'The administration and agrarian policy of the manors of Durham cathedral priory', B. Litt. thesis, Oxford, 1949.

    1955a, 'The decline of demesne farming on the estates of Durham cathedral priory', *Economic History Review*, Second Series, 7 (1955), 345–56

    1955b, 'The social position and influence of the priors of Durham as illustrated by their correspondence', *Archaeologia Aeliana*, Fourth Series, 33 (1955), 70–86

    1957, 'Obedientiaries and counsellors in monastic administration at Durham', *Archaeologia Aeliana*, Fourth Series, 35 (1957), 7–21

Heads: Knowles, D., C.N.L. Brooke and V.C.M. London, *Heads of Religious Houses, England and Wales, 940–1216*, Cambridge, 1972

Holdsworth, C.J., 1986, 'The chronology and character of early Cistercian legislation on art and architecture', in Norton and Park 1986, pp. 40–55

Jerome, St, *Lettres*, ed. J. Labourt (Collection Budé), I, Paris, 1949

Jones, J. 1988, *Balliol College: A History, 1263–1939*, Oxford, 1988

Kemp, B.R., 1980, 'Monastic possession of parish churches in England in the twelfth century', *Journal of Ecclesiastical History*, 31 (1980), 133–60

Kirby, D.P., 1965–6, 'Bede's native sources for the *Historia Ecclesiastica*', *Bulletin of the John Rylands Library*, 48 (1965–6), 341–71

Knowles, M.D., 1919, 'A preface of Mabillon', *Downside Review*, 38 (1919), 53–7

    1924a, 'The religion of the Pastons', *Downside Review*, 42 (1924), 143–63

    1924b, 'Italian scenes and scenery', *Downside Review*, 42 (1924), 196–208

    1926, *The American Civil War: A Brief Sketch*, Oxford, 1926

    1927, *The English Mystics*, 1st edn, London, 1927 [*see also* Knowles 1961]

    1928, 'The thought and art of Thomas Hardy', *Dublin Review*, 183 (1928), 208–18

    1929, *The Benedictines*, 1st edn, London, 1929 (a 2nd edn, considerably revised, was publ. in St Leo, Florida, 1962)

    1930–1, 'A Greek August', *Downside Review*, 48 (1930) 291–314, 49 (1931), 102–23

1931a, 'Essays in monastic history 1066–1215. I. Abbatial elections', *Downside Review*, 49 (1931), 252–78

1931b, 'Essays in monastic history 1066–1215. II. The Norman plantation', *Downside Review*, 49 (1931), 441–56

1932a, 'Essays in monastic history 1066–1215. III. The Norman monasticism', *Downside Review*, 50 (1932), 33–48

1932b, 'Essays in monastic history 1066–1215. IV. The growth of exemption', *Downside Review*, 50 (1932), 201–31, 396–436

1933a, 'Contemplative prayer in St Teresa', *Downside Review*, 51 (1933), 201–30, 406–33

1933b, 'Essays in monastic history 1066–1215. V. The Cathedral monasteries', *Downside Review*, 51 (1933), 73–96

1933c, 'Essays in monastic history. VI. Parish organisation', *Downside Review*, 51 (1933), 501–22

1933d, 'The monastic horarium 970–1120', *Downside Review*, 51 (1933), 706–25

1934a, 'Contemplation in St Thomas Aquinas', *The Clergy Review*, 8 (1934), 1–20, 85–103

1934b, 'The excellence of *The Cloud*', *Downside Review*, 52 (1934), 71–92

1934c, 'Essays in monastic history 1066–1215. VII. The diet of Black Monks', *Downside Review*, 52 (1934), 275–90

1935, 'The revolt of the lay brothers of Sempringham', *English Historical Review*, 50 (1935), 465–87

1940, *The Religious Houses of Medieval England*, London, 1940 [revised as Knowles and Hadcock 1953, 1971]

1947, *The Prospects of Medieval Studies: An Inaugural Lecture*, Cambridge, 1947

1948, 'Dom R.H. Connolly, 1873–1948', *Journal of Theological Studies*, 49 (1948), 129

1951a, *The Episcopal Colleagues of Archbishop Thomas Becket* (The Ford Lectures, Oxford, 1949), Cambridge, 1951 [corrected repr., 1970]

1951b, 1967, ed., *Decreta Lanfranci: The Monastic Constitutions of Lanfranc*, 1st edn, NMT, Edinburgh, 1951; 2nd edn, in *Corpus Consuetudinum Monasticarum*, III, ed. K. Hallinger, Siegburg, 1967

1955, *The Historian and Character* [Inaugural Lecture], Cambridge, 1955

1960, *Lord Macaulay, 1800–1859*, Cambridge, 1960

1961, *The English Mystical Tradition*, London, 1961 [see 1927]

1962a/1988, *The Evolution of Medieval Thought*, 1st edn, London, 1962, 2nd edn, ed. D.E. Luscombe and C.N.L. Brooke, London, 1988

1962b, 'Academic history', *History*, 47 (1962), 223–32

1966, *From Pachomius to Ignatius: A Study in the Constitutional History of the Religious Orders* (The Sarum Lectures, 1964–5), Oxford, 1966

1967, *What is Mysticism*, London, 1967

1969a, *Christian Monasticism*, London, 1969

1969b, 'Denifle and Ehrle', *History*, 54 (1969), 1–12

1970a, *Thomas Becket*, London, 1970

1970b, 'St Augustine', in *The Diversity of History. Essays in Honour of Sir Herbert Butterfield*, ed. J.H. Elliott and H.G. Koenigsberger, London, 1970, pp. 19–33

1976, *Bare Ruined Choirs: The Dissolution of the English Monasteries*, Cambridge, 1976 [an abbreviated version of Knowles, *RO* III]

GHE: Great Historical Enterprises: Problems in Monastic History, London, 1963

HC: The Historian and Character and Other Essays, Cambridge, 1963 [reprinted papers, ed. C.N.L. Brooke and G. Constable]

MO: The Monastic Order in England: A History of its Development from the Times of St Dunstan to the Fourth Lateran Council, 940 [943 in 1st edn]*–1216*, 1st edn, Cambridge, 1940; 2nd edn [pagination unaltered, but with additional pages], Cambridge, 1963

RO, The Religious Orders in England, 3 vols., Cambridge, 1948–59

Knowles, M.D., A.J. Duggan and C.N.L. Brooke, 1972, 'Henry II's supplement to the Constitutions of Clarendon', *English Historical Review*, 87 (1972), 757–71

Knowles, M.D., and R.N. Hadcock, 1953, 1971, *Medieval Religious Houses, England and Wales*, 1st edn, London, 1953, 2nd edn, 1971

Knowles, M.D., and D. Obolensky, 1969, *The Christian Centuries*, II, *The Middle Ages*, London, 1969

Knowles, M.D., and J.K.S. St Joseph, 1952, *Monastic Sites from the Air*, Cambridge, 1952

Luscombe, D.E., 1969, *The School of Peter Abelard*, Cambridge Studies in Medieval Life and Thought, New Series, 14, Cambridge, 1969

McKitterick, D., 1984, *Four Hundred Years of University Printing and Publishing in Cambridge 1584–1984; Catalogue of the Exhibition in the University Library, Cambridge*, Cambridge, 1984

Mahn, J.-B., 1951, *L'Ordre cistercien et son gouvernement*, 2nd edn, Paris, 1951

Mayr-Harting, H., 1988, 'The foundation of Peterhouse, Cambridge (1284), and the Rule of St Benedict', *English Historical Review*, 103 (1988), 318–38

Mellows, W.T., P.I. King and C.N.L. Brooke, eds., 1954, *The Book of William Morton, Almoner of Peterborough Monastery, 1448–1467*, Northamptonshire Record Society, 1954

Moorman, J.R.H., 1952, *The Grey Friars in Cambridge*, Cambridge, 1952

Morey, A., 1938, *Bartholomew of Exeter, Bishop and Canonist*, Cambridge, 1938

1979, *David Knowles, a Memoir*, London, 1979

Morey, A., and C.N.L. Brooke, 1965, *Gilbert Foliot and his Letters*, Cambridge Studies in Medieval Life and Thought, New Series, 11, Cambridge 1965

Morey, A., and C.N.L. Brooke, eds., 1967, *The Letters and Charters of Gilbert Foliot*, Cambridge, 1967

NMT: Nelson's Medieval Texts (formerly Classics)

Norton, C., and D. Park eds., 1986, *Cistercian Art and Architecture in the British Isles*, Cambridge, 1986

OMT: Oxford Medieval Texts

Pantin, W.A., ed., 1931–7, *Documents Illustrating the Activities of the General and Provincial Chapters of the English Black Monks, 1215–1540*, 3 vols., Camden Third Series, 45, 47, 54, London, 1931–7

Parsons, D., ed., 1975, *Tenth Century Studies*, London, 1975

PL: *Patrologiae Cursus Completus, series Latina*, ed. J.-P. Migne, 221 vols., Paris, 1844–64

Postan, M.M., 1937, 'The chronology of labour services', *Transactions of the Royal Historical Society*, Fourth Series, 20 (1937), 169–93

1949–50, 'Some economic evidence of declining population in the later Middle Ages', *Economic History Review*, Second Series, 2 (1949–50), 221–46

Power, E., 1922, *Medieval English Nunneries*, Cambridge, 1922

Powicke, F.M., 1922, 'Ailred of Rievaulx and his biographer Walter Daniel', *Bulletin of the John Rylands Library*, 6 (1921–2), 310–51, 452–521; repr. separately (1922)

Powicke, F.M., ed. and trans., 1950, *Vita Ailredi Abbatis Rievall': The Life of Ailred of Rievaulx by Walter Daniel*, NMT, Edinburgh, 1950 [repr. OMT, Oxford, 1978]

Robinson, J. Armitage, 1919, *St Oswald and the Church of Worcester*, British Academy Supplemental Papers, 5, London, [1919]
  1921, *Somerset Historical Essays*, London, 1921
  1923, *The Times of St Dunstan*, Oxford, 1923
Salter, H.E., 1922, ed., *Chapters of the Augustinian Canons*, Canterbury and York Society, 29, 1922
Smith, R.A.L., 1943, *Canterbury Cathedral Priory*, Cambridge, 1943
  1947, *Collected Papers*, London, 1947
Stacpoole, A., 1975, 1976, 'The making of a monastic historian, I, II and III', *Ampleforth Journal*, 80 (1975), I, 71–91, II, 19–38, III: 'A bibliography of his writings, from 1963 (retirement) to 1974 (death)', 48–55; 81 (1976), 40
Symons, T., 1941, 'Sources of the *Regularis Concordia*', *Downside Review*, 40 (1941), 14–36, 143–70, 264–89
  1962, 'The *Regularis Concordia* and the Council of Winchester', *Downside Review*, 80 (1962), 140–56
  1975, '*Regularis Concordia*: History and Derivation', in Parsons 1975, pp. 37–59, 214–17
Symons, T., ed. and trans., 1953, *Regularis Concordia: The Monastic Agreement of the Monks and Nuns of the English Nation*, NMT, Edinburgh, 1953
Thompson, S., 1991, *Women Religious: The Founding of English Nunneries after the Norman Conquest*, Oxford, 1991
Tugwell, S., 1982, ed. and trans., *Jordan of Saxony: On the beginnings of the Order of Preachers*, Oak Park Il., 1982
Vaughan, R., 1958, *Matthew Paris*, Cambridge Studies in Medieval Life and Thought, New Series, 6, Cambridge, 1958
VCH Middlesex: Victoria History of the County of Middlesex
Vellacott, P.C., 1924, 'The struggle of James the Second with the University of Cambridge', in *In Memoriam: Adolphus William Ward, Master of Peterhouse (1900–1924)*, Cambridge, 1924, pp. 81–101
  1926, 'The diary of a country gentleman in 1688', *Cambridge Historical Journal*, 2 (1926), 48–62
Wallace-Hadrill, J.M., 1988, *Bede's Ecclesiastical History of the English People: A Historical Commentary*, OMT, Oxford, 1988
Wilmart, A., 1932, *Auteurs spirituels et textes dévots du moyen âge latin*, Paris, 1932
Youings, J., 1971, *The Dissolution of the Monasteries*, London, 1971

INDEX

Persons before 1300 are indexed under their Christian names, with a few exceptions, such as Abelard.

166

Index

Boleyn, Queen Anne, 115
Bollandists, 79
Boswell's *Life of Johnson*, 52–3
Bradley, A. C., 53
Bradwardine, Thomas, Archbishop of Canterbury, 76
Bridgettine nuns, 63
Brighton Technical College, 98
Bristol, Community of Good Shepherd nuns, and their Superior, 33; University of, 22
British Academy, 22, *and see* Raleigh Lecture
Brogan, Sir Denis, Fellow of Peterhouse and Professor of Political Science, 99, 110, 114
Bromsgrove, 3
Brooke, C. N. L., 23, 76–7, 124, 129, 138, 158; and *Heads*, 18–19, 55
Brooke, R. B. (née Clark), 21, 68n., 123–4, 129, 131–2, 157
Brooke, Z. N., 3, 18–19, 84; his death, 90
Brooks, Dom Alban, 37
Browning, Robert, 113
Bruges, 122
Bruton, Abbot of, 73–4
Burkill, C., Fellow, later Master of Peterhouse, 83
Butler, Dom Christopher, Abbot of Downside, later Bishop, 17–18
Butler, Dom Cuthbert, Abbot of Downside, 4–8, 31, 50–1, 54, 63, 128; his funeral, 38; DK's memoir, 78; his works: *Benedictine Monachism*, 36; *Lausiac History of Palladius*, 6; *Western Mysticism*, 31, 43
Butterfield, Sir Herbert, Fellow, then Master of Peterhouse, Professor of Modern History, 93, 99, 110; and DK's election to Peterhouse, 19, 82–4, 87; their friendship, 100–3; letters of DK to, 96, 106; election as Master, 117; as Vice-Chancellor, 100; his works: *Christianity and History*, 102; *Christianity in European History*, 101; *Whig Interpretation of History*, 110; his Festschrift (*The Diversity of History*), 103
Butterfield, Pamela, Lady Butterfield, 100
Byland Abbey, 3

Cam, Helen, 131
Camaldoli, Order of, Camaldolese, 145
Cambridge, 25; Benet House, 8, 52; Catholic Chaplaincy (Fisher House), 134; Church of Our Lady and the English Martyrs, 116, 135; Coe Fen, 94; Grantchester Meadows, 25; Hills Rd, 135; King's Parade, 135; St Bonaventure's friary (in Trumpington St), 134;

Colleges: Peterhouse, 67; foundation, 92; Catholic tradition in, 193; and Commemoration of Benefactors, 92–4; and study of history, 83, 110; Dean of, 91; Fellows, 95–6, *and see* Brogan, Burkill, Butterfield, Knowles, Lovatt, Lubbock, Wormald; DK's fellowship, 82–5 *and see* Knowles; professorial fellowship, 90–1; honorary fellowship, 22; Gisborne Court (DK's rooms), 21, 94, 110, 116; Governing Body, 82, 85, 87–9, 90, 95–6, 110; Masters, *see* Burkill, Butterfield, Cosin, Temperley, Vellacott, Ward, Wren
Other Colleges: Christ's and DK, 8–9, 11, 22, 91, 128; classics at, 128; and Downside, 91; Girton, 131; King's, 83, 124, 134; Trinity, 98
University, and DK, 18–23; and Catholics, 51; DK's friends, 107; Classics in, 8–9; History Faculty and Tripos, 46, 57, 96, 123; Faculty Board, 18, 101; Lectures, 156; Special Subjects, 123–9, 131, 135; 156; Specified (Intellectual History of Western Europe), 130, 135; Research Students, 157–8; Honorary Degrees, 22
University Press, 23, 62, 121; Printing House, 134
Cambridge Historical Society, 84
canon law, 48
canons regular, 57, 62–3, 66, 105 *and see* Gilbert, St
Canterbury, x; archbishops of, *see* Bradwardine, Hubert, Thomas
Canterbury and York Society, 22
Carmelite nuns, 43; *and see* Teresa, St
Carthusians, Carthusian Order, 25, 30, 43, 121–2, 145
Cassian, John, 28
cathedral schools, 130
Catherine of Siena, St, 39
Caussade, J. P. de, 36
Chalet, the, of F. F. Urquhart, 10, 25
Channel, the, 142
Chapman, Dom John, Abbot of Downside, 16, 33–8
Chaucer, Geoffrey, 69; his Franklin, 70; his Monk, 69
Chertsey Abbey, 48
Churchill, Winston, 21
Cicero, 29, 60
Cîteaux, Abbot of, *see* Robert, Stephen; Cistercian Order, 63–5, 76, 81, 105; its origins, Special Subject on, 126–8; and *Carta Caritatis*, 64, 136, 147; constitution, 136–7; General Chapter,

167

Index

Index

108; *Lanfranc's Monastic Constitutions*, 80, 108; *MO*, 1, 7, 10, 15, 40, 46, 47–65, 79, 103–7, 124, 138; reception of, 84; relation to articles, 75; relation to *RO*, 66–7, 73, 97; and Ailred's Rievaulx, 58–62; *Medieval Religious Houses* (and *Religious Houses*) (with R. N. Hadcock), 48, 55, 80, 124; *Monastic Sites from the Air* (with J. K. S. St Joseph), 78, 80; *RO*, 46, 63, 104, 124; *RO I*, 66–9, 91–2, 97, 104, 125; *RO II*, 69, 97; *RO III*, 44, 49, 65, 69–74, 92, 97, 103, 119; *Thomas Becket*, 77; *What is Mysticism*, 32, 45–6 and classics, 8–9; and cricket, 25; and ecumenism, 24; and English literature, 9, 11–12, 75; on mysticism, 10, 31–3, 130; love of nature, xi, 119; on obedience, 41–2; and railways, 25, 132; his style, use of English, 20, 57, 62, 69–74; visit to Sweden, 30n.
Knox, Mgr Ronald, 99
Kornerup, Dr Elizabeth, 16–17, 19, 23–4, 30n., 38–41, 46, 109–10, 114–15, 131; her family, 9; her spiritual life, 45; and DK's ration book, 88n., 89–90

Labour Government of 1945, 116
Langland, William, 69
Laski, Harold, 116
Latin literature, 9, 11–12
Lavenham, Father, 123
Lawrence, C. H., 135
Layton, R., 73–4
Leclercq, Dom Jean, 64, 80n.
Lee, Robert E., 13–14
Leff, G., 132–3, 157
Legh, T., 73–4
Leicester, Abbot of, *see* Clown; University of, 22
Leo XIII, Pope, 30n.
Liebermann, F., 52
Linch (Sussex), ix–x, 23–5, 110, 118, 133
Lincoln, Bishops of, *see* Alexander, Hugh, Robert
liturgy, 53, *and see* Bishop
London, St Gilbert in, 150; DK in, *see* Knowles, *and see* Ealing, Gloucester St., Warwick Sq. below; The Albany, 129; The Charterhouse, 73n., 105; monks of, 121–2; prior of, *see* Houghton; Crosby Hall, 135; Ealing, Priory later Abbey, 17, 33, 38–41, 92, 104, 106–7, 109; Gloucester St., 39–40; London Library, 40; Newgate, 122; Pimlico, Warwick Sq., 19, 92, 110, 133; University of, 22; Wimbledon, 23, 110

London, Vera, 18, 55
Lovatt, M., letter to, 121
Lovatt, R. W., 158; letter to, 121–2
Lubbock, R., Fellow of Peterhouse, 83
Lunn, D. M. C. J., 158
Luscombe, D. E., 76, 158

Mabillon, Dom Jean, 1, 7, 11, 14, 50–1, 54, 78–9, 81, 135; his *De re diplomatica*, 79, 135
Macaulay, T. B. (Lord), 20, 53, 57, 79, 137–8; his *Essays* and *History*, 12; his *Life*, 12, 53
Macbeth, 18
McFarlane, K. B., 108
McKisack, M., 130
Maitland, F. W., 47, 69, 100, 108
Malachy, St, Archbishop of Armagh, 145
Malton, Old, priory, 148, 150; prior, *see* Roger
Manning, H. E. Manning, Cardinal, 51
Mare, Thomas de la, Abbot of St Albans, 69, 105
Mass, 110; Latin, 24–5
Matthew, St, 97
Matthew Paris, 68
Maurists, Congregation of Saint-Maur, 1, 51–2, 54, 79, 135; Maurist tradition and Downside, 6–7
Mayne, R. J., 157
Melrose, 3
Mendips, 10
Mercati, Angelo and Giovanni (Cardinal), 52
Migne, J. P., *Patrologia Latina*, 99
Military (religious) Orders, 66
Miller, E., 125
Milton Abbey (Dorset), 34
Ministry of Food, 88n., 89
Missal, Roman, 56
Monte Cassino, 136
Monumenta Germaniae Historica, 79
Moorman, John, Bishop of Ripon, 15, 67n.
Moorman, Mary, and her *William Wordsworth*, 57–8
More, Sir Thomas, St, 2, 71–2; his daughter Margaret Roper, 72; his adopted daughter, *see* Clement
More, William, Prior of Worcester, 70–1
Morey, Dom Adrian, 39, 54; his *David Knowles*, ix, 35, 40, 54
Morrison, H. P., and Nelson's, 23, 75
Moscow, 12
Mount St Bernard, Cistercian Abbey, 30
Munich, 27, 34, 37
Mynors, R. A. B., Sir Roger, 10, 80n.
mystical theology, 31–3, 149; mystics, 130